Fever Reading

Becoming Modern
New Nineteenth-Century Studies

SERIES EDITORS

Sarah Way Sherman
  Department of English
  University of New Hampshire
Janet Aikins Yount
  Department of English
  University of New Hampshire
Rohan McWilliam
  Anglia Ruskin University
  Cambridge, England
Janet Polasky
  Department of History
  University of New Hampshire

This book series maps the complexity of historical change and assesses the formation of ideas, movements, and institutions crucial to our own time by publishing books that examine the emergence of modernity in North America and Europe. Set primarily but not exclusively in the nineteenth century, the series shifts attention from modernity's twentieth-century forms to its earlier moments of uncertain and often disputed construction. Seeking books of interest to scholars on both sides of the Atlantic, it thereby encourages the expansion of nineteenth-century studies and the exploration of more global patterns of development.

For a complete list of books available in this series, see www.upne.com

Beth L. Lueck, Brigitte Bailey, and Lucinda L. Damon-Bach, editors, *Transatlantic Women: Essays on Nineteenth-Century American Women Writers and Great Britain*

Michael Millner, *Fever Reading: Affect and Reading Badly in the Early American Public Sphere*

Nancy Siegel, editor, *The Cultured Canvas: New Perspectives on American Landscape Painting*

Ilya Parkins and Elizabeth M. Sheehan, editors, *Cultures of Femininity in Modern Fashion*

Brian Joseph Martin, *Napoleonic Friendship: Military Fraternity, Intimacy, and Sexuality in Nineteenth-Century France*

Andrew Taylor, *Thinking America: New England Intellectuals and the Varieties of American Identity*

Michael Millner

Fever Reading

*Affect and Reading Badly
in the Early American Public
Sphere*

UNIVERSITY OF NEW HAMPSHIRE PRESS

DURHAM, NEW HAMPSHIRE

KH

UNIVERSITY OF NEW HAMPSHIRE PRESS
An imprint of University Press of New England
www.upne.com
© 2012 University of New Hampshire
All rights reserved

Manufactured in the United States of America
Designed by Eric M. Brooks
Typeset in Monticello by Passumpsic Publishing

University Press of New England is a member of the
Green Press Initiative. The paper used in this book meets
their minimum requirement for recycled paper.

Library of Congress Cataloging-in-Publication Data
Millner, Michael.
Fever reading: affect and reading badly in the early
American public sphere / Michael Millner.
    pages cm. — (Becoming modern)
Includes bibliographical references and index.
ISBN 978-1-61168-242-7 (cloth: alk. paper) —
ISBN 978-1-61168-243-4 (pbk.: alk. paper) —
ISBN 978-1-61168-244-1 (ebook)
1. Books and reading — United States — History. I. Title.
Z1003.2.M55   2012
028.9 — dc23   2012003858

5 4 3 2 1

6/25/13

Contents

Acknowledgments

One's personal intellectual genealogy is difficult to trace because it entails so many blindingly intense transferences as well as unconsciously influential reaction formations—often with people you know only through their books. However, one thing I do know for sure is that this book would not have been written without the flesh-and-blood help of a number of people. I owe more than I can say to two of my graduate-school teachers. Eric Lott mixes a street-level knowledge of antebellum America with the flow of his twenty-first century engagements. He is my favorite Bowery B'hoy. The late and greatly missed Richard Rorty, I suspect, would question and disagree with much in this book. But he always taught us to hold disagreement and questioning among our highest values. I still hear his voice in my head.

I was also fortunate to work during the earliest stages of this project under the guidance of Franny Nudelman and Steve Cushman. I could not have asked for two more patient and perceptive advisors. In addition, Don Pease has been as tireless in his support of me as he has been of so many young scholars across the field of American Studies. The two readers of the book's manuscript for the University Press of New England—Russ Castronovo and Dana Nelson—did their reading with extraordinary care and intelligence; they are models of intellectual generosity, and I am deeply indebted to them for making this a better book. I would also like to thank Phyllis Deutsch at UPNE for her careful direction and enthusiasm for *Fever Reading*. It has been a great pleasure to work with Phyllis and everyone at the press.

Over the years many people responded to parts of this book at conferences and in other forums but, alas, I can't remember everyone, even when the comments caused me to rethink parts of the argument. I do however owe particular gratitude to David Anthony, Katherine Biers, Bill Brown, Christopher Castiglia, Elizabeth Maddock Dillon, Greg Jackson, Meredith McGill, Don Pease, Jordan Stein, Chip Tucker, and Jennifer Wicke for their comments on various presentations and essays.

The University of Massachusetts Lowell has offered me an astonishing amount of both freedom and support to pursue this project. That difficult balance of freedom and support is made possible by a wonderful group scholar-administrators who have always looked out for me in their various leadership positions: Ahmed Abdelal, Julie Chen, Nina Coppens, Charlotte Mandell, Paul Marion, Marty Meehan, Marlowe Miller, Melissa Pennell, Don Pierson, Nancy Selleck, Tony Szczesiul, and John Wooding. Tony Szczesiul has been a kind of mentor during my time at UMass Lowell. Tony as well as my Lowell colleagues Abby Chandler, John Christ, Bill Kaizen, Sheila Kirschbaum, Keith Mitchell, Sarah Moser, and Jonathan Silverman all read chapters of this book (in some cases, multiple chapters) and made important comments that shaped the project. No fruitful intellectual community is possible without a combination of straight-up hard work and downright fun, and the members of the UMass Lowell English Department have always provided both: Diana Archibald, Todd Avery, Laura Barefield, Shelley Barish, Dina Bozicas, Katherine Conlon, Maggie Dietz, Andre Dubus III, Paula Haines, Tom Hersey, Jeannie Judge, Susan Kirtley, Mary Kramer, Sandra Lim, Bridget Marshall, Marlowe Miller, Keith Mitchell, Julie Nash, Melissa Pennell, Bill Roberts, Nancy Selleck, Jonathan Silverman, Rita Sullivan, Tony Szczesiul, and Joe Zaitchik. At UMass Lowell I have also been sustained by the American Studies IDEA workshop (made possible in large part by Meg Bond) as well as a number of intellectual fellow travelers from across many disciplines: Christopher Carlsmith, Shehong Chen, Mignon Duffy, Bob Forrant, Marie Frank, Aart Holtslag, Andy Hostetler, Chad Montrie, Deirdra Murphy, Michael Pierson, Cheryl Najarian Souza, Christoph Strobel, Ardeth Thawnghmung, and Patrick Young.

I would also like to thank the wonderful editors of *ESQ: A Journal of the American Renaissance* (57:3) for permission to reprint parts of chapter 3.

Some of the best times in my life took place over the countless dinners in graduate school and since with Bill Albertini, Ben Lee, Daryl Levinson, Ana Mitrić, Derek Nystrom, Ken Parille, Lisi Schoenbach, and Danny Siegel. I shameless steal from those discussions, and others over the years with Katherine Biers, Paul Erickson, Heather Love, Mark Rifkin, Bryan Wagner, and many other friends both inside and outside the academy.

Fever Reading would not exist without extraordinary librarians and libraries. I owe special thanks to the librarians and everyone behind the scenes at the American Antiquarian Society, Harvard University, the Kinsey Institute (especially Catherine Johnson-Roehr), the University of Chicago, the University of Massachusetts Lowell, and the University of Virginia.

I am particularly thankful to B, Tina, Chris, and Toni Millner, as well as Dave Forney, Liz Coxe, Jackson, Colby, Fisher, Clio, and Beckett (and everyone else in the extended Millner and Forney families) for not asking too often when this book was going to be done (or even what it was about). It did take too long to write, and I wish my mother were alive to read it. I dedicate it to her memory and to two other people who have taught me how to flourish: my father and Jill Forney.

Introduction

Perhaps it is fitting to begin by addressing the reader. After all, this is a book in large part about how books and other forms of print culture attempt to govern their readers' relationships with books and print culture. It seems appropriate, then, to make an effort at such governance and control by telling the reader what this book is about.

Fever Reading seeks to understand the meanings of reading badly. Here "reading badly" does not mean deficiencies in decoding words on the page nor does it simply reference the reading of books that are considered bad in terms of content. Chiefly, reading badly means reading that causes you to lose a sense of self or free will, reading that is addictive, reading that makes you chronically distracted or, alternatively, reading that completely absorbs you, to name a few different possibilities. During the time period of this study — roughly the late eighteenth to the mid-nineteenth century — there was intense worry over the effects of such reading. These anxieties remain with us today with respect to, say, televisual and hypertextual "reading," but their real moment of mass emergence was the time period covered in *Fever Reading*. These abject forms of reading — forms that are often associated, for instance, with pornography, stories of scandal, certain religious texts, as well as the Internet — have frequently been dismissed as without much public meaning. They are seen as delinquent and even pathological because they dissolve critical distance and undercut the possibility of reflection — elements thought essential to a proper public sphere and good citizenship. However, the hypothesis of *Fever Reading* is just the opposite: it argues that such bad forms of reading are critical, reflective, and essential to modern democracy and the public sphere.

It will take time to unfold this argument, and it will require the weaving together of several different kinds of argument from various academic fields. *Fever Reading* is, among other things, part historical argument, part critique of certain influential ideas in political theory, part normative political theory, and part methodological experiment in understanding the consumption of texts. Because emotion is such a central concern in the discourses about reading badly, *Fever Reading* develops a theory of affective reading. One of the project's central methodological interventions is to use recent work in cognitive science on affect to re-think the way literary and cultural historians think about reading that touches us emotionally. Hopefully these parts will make a whole. The remainder of this introduction attempts to sketch that whole in somewhat better detail.

Arguments and Archives

One account diagnoses a future of "mental dissipation and imbecility." In the view of other experts, the effects range from nausea to gonorrhea. The problem for yet another observer is not physical or mental but a "depravity" of morals. Of whatever category, the disease spreads quickly: "the poison soon circulates with the juices of the system and speedily penetrates too far to be overtaken." It operates like alcohol or opium; once experienced, it's required, "as the drunkard does his potion." It "enervates" and "enslaves"; it's "deranging and debilitating." Madness and suicide and murder may well follow. It causes a "fever of the brain," a "feverish passion," and the "symptom of a fever."

These are descriptions of the hazards of reading the wrong things in the wrong way—of reading badly—from the first seventy-five years of the United States.[1] They are only a few of the cautionary tales about feverish reading that circulated in the late eighteenth and early nineteenth centuries. The expansion of literacy and reading is one of the great, salutary stories told of modernity, but during the period of expansion itself the fears of a public reading badly were portrayed and particularized with far more energy than were the benefits of reading. As reading became necessary and common to American life during the early years of the nation, readers were insistently reminded of its dangers. The risk to women stirred considerable panic, as has long been recognized by scholars; however, the hazards to men, youth, and other new reading publics interfused almost all discussions of reading. Famously perilous was the new genre of the novel, but equally worrisome was the easy access to pornographic reading, the mindless enthusiasms of religious reading, and the seductive excitements of reading about scandal and celebrity. According to the accounts of bad reading, the danger was located in the method of reading encouraged by such genres as much as it was a result of the content of the genres. The menace was in reading anything addictively, desultorily, too bodily, too inwardly, too voraciously, with utter absorption, with a loss of distance, with a loss of self, or in a fever.

For instance, in 1789, the well-known reformer and statesman Benjamin Rush feared that "the frequent and rapid transition of the mind" common in the desultory and unfocused reading encouraged by the popular press could well result in "madness" and "derange[ment]" (37). The paroxysms about bad reading were a way of standardizing a kind of good, critical reading which valued distance from the text, power over the text, reason over emotion, the productivity of reading, the public conversation enabled by reading, and a number of other elements. The fears of reading badly were rampant at least into the late nineteenth century (the end point of this study), when other modes of mass information uptake pushed reading to the side as a primary object of anxiety (although anxieties about reading badly lived on, for example, in worries about comic-book reading in the 1950s and hypertext reading at the end of the twentieth century).

From one perspective, such hysterics seem to be an absurd obsession of unsophisticated readers, not unlike the reactions of early moviegoers who, perhaps apocryphally, dove from their seats to avoid speeding locomotives. But from a different angle, the discourse reflects the central issues and anxieties of modernity and modern society. Reading improperly is associated with questions of agency and choice (when reading is addictive and involuntary), the loss of objectivity and reliable knowledge (when it is utterly absorptive), the collapse of the line between public and private (when the private practice becomes a matter of public health), the confusion of proper relations between mind and body (when it is excessively affective), and a host of other perceived problems. The early American discussions of reading were ways of representing and regulating these conflicts. They were ways of imaging and enforcing the proper values of the period's new mass sociality and mass public sphere—that is, what would count as knowledge, communication, the self, and agency in that public sphere and society.

But *Fever Reading* is not only a story about disciplining readers out of their bad reading. It is also about the meaning and value of reading badly—of reading too emotionally, too physically, too absorptively, too inwardly, unproductively, masturbatorily, in a fever. How do such forms of reading have meaning? What are their uses? How do they too allow for knowledge, communication, notions of the self, and agency in the public sphere? In the early United States, such modes of reading were seen as dangerous, but *Fever Reading* suggests that these forms of bad reading produce powerful kinds of knowledge that are critical, reflective, and essential to the workings of the modern public sphere and society. Reading badly enabled a relationship different from "good," critical reading to questions of agency and choice, objective and subjective knowledge, publicity and privacy, mind and body, and other issues of modernity and modern society. It was also everywhere in the early nation; the norm was bad reading, it seems, not good. Recovering the meanings of reading badly is important if for no other reason than its overwhelming prevalence, both in the first several decades of the United States and in our own time.

I make this set of arguments by examining four main archives. The first is the discussion of pathological reading as it developed between the late eighteenth and late nineteenth centuries in an array of American popular print culture. The other three archives are nineteenth-century pornography, antebellum scandal papers, and religious fictions from the first part of the nineteenth century. This second set of archives allows an investigation of the practices of fever reading because each—through its material form, forms of address, stylistics, scenes of reading, modes of circulation, themes and subject matter, and other aspects of composition—attempts to structure the relationship among reader, texts, and the public sphere. Such archives are not merely of antiquarian interest, for they are on a continuum with the present day. Indeed, the antiquarian archives of pornography, religious enthusiasm, and sensational scandal at the center of this study constitute the beginning of the twentieth- and twenty-first centuries' public sensorium.

Origins

If you have read this far into this introduction you probably haven't been reading in ways that make you sick or addicted or corrupt. Indeed, you've probably been reading like most good academics—muttering out loud your skepticism, constructing arguments for and against the ideas presented here, connecting those ideas to other texts you've read, re-reading certain sentences with an especially critical eye, writing approving little checks in the margin, or scrawling disapproving exclamation points. In other words, you've been reading critically. You may not always read in such ways—there are surely infinite manners of reading—but the genre of this text and the text's mode of address do suggest an ideal kind of relationship between reader and text that might be called critical reading. One of the central arguments of *Fever Reading* is that this ideal of critical reading has a history, one that is closely connected to the development and dissemination of an ideal of democratic discourse and the public sphere in the eighteenth and nineteenth centuries. As a critical reader, you may be unconvinced that the kind of affective, addictive, and absorptive reading that *Fever Reading* explores can function in ways similar to your critical reading. How I understand affective reading as critical reading will take a good number of pages of this book to explain and will lead the discussion into recent scholarship in cognitive science, reader-response theories, and other areas. But here, in this short introduction, I can begin to make clear why such a project seems important.

Fever Reading is born of dissatisfaction with several aspects of the current state of research. The first is the simple fact of our limited understanding of the emotions of reading. This may initially seem like a strange, inaccurate claim after the considerable amount of scholarship on emotion-charged genres like eighteenth-century sensibility and nineteenth-century sentimentalism, genres that involve the "moral" sentiments—along with others like the sublime, empathy, and compassion. But the list of the moral emotions leaves aside a vast array of moods and feelings that are not instrumental or productive in the ways sensibility or sentimentalism are often understood. How is one to consider the ethical and political dimensions of, for instance, nausea, satiety, boredom, anxiety, delirium, trepidation, or a glow? These emotions are far different from the moral sentiments, although they are certainly common to the reading experience, and especially the kind of mass cultural reading that began to emerge in the late eighteenth and early nineteenth centuries in the United States. They are among the responses elicited by the genres investigated here—pornographic, sensationalistic, and religious. But as prevalent as such emotions have been in the public sensorium since the late eighteenth century, there is still little understanding of their workings, especially as they relate to reading.

Any better understanding of emotion and reading will have to look beyond the humanities' conventional models for understanding emotions. Cognitive science, economics, anthropology, and other scientific and social-scientific fields have developed models of emotions which are significantly different from those usually used in the humanities. In general, instead of following the humanistic models of emotion as "symptomatic" or "instrumental," these fields have understood emotion as "diagnostic" and "evaluative." The scientific and social-scientific models are ultimately important because they present a way of understanding emotion as critical, as in some respects even reflective. The point is not to definitively replace one model of emotion with another but to add to our repertoire for understanding the complex category known as "emotion" and its cognates (like affect, feeling, and mood). Humanistic study has been shy about incorporating the non-humanistic models, but such incorporation seems essential to understanding the role of emotion-charged reading in the public sphere.

Considering emotional responses to texts, especially when using the new models for determining what emotion is and does, could change the way reading and readers are understood. The act of reading is usually imagined as an interpretative process, as a kind of decoding. A variety of critical camps, from New Criticism to deconstruction to New Historicism, have developed sophisticated methods of decoding. The critics practicing such interpretation realize that everyday readers don't read texts in such ways, but the decoding-interpretation model nevertheless often rules the way texts are understood by those critics. Theoretical work on reading practices also presumes that readers interpret texts: influential conceptualizations of reading include Wolfgang Iser's emphasis on "gaps" (285) and the way readers fill them with their own interpretations and Stanley Fish's concept of "interpretative communities" (465). Even certain practitioners of cultural studies and the history of reading (as well as its close cousin, the history of the book) who focus on the "uses" of texts place significant weight on the interpretation of texts as one of their primary uses. But is the reading of texts always the interpretation of texts? Might the meaning of texts also be located elsewhere? There is a long (if disjointed) history of such questions, ranging from Nietzsche's demand that readers of his texts practice a new kind of hermeneutics that is akin to the ways cows eat (23), to Susan Sontag's call for an "erotics of art" (*Against* 14) in the place of a hermeneutics, to Eve Sedgwick's suggestions of a style of "reparative reading" (*Touching* 123), to the neo-phenomenology of Steven Connor and Rita Felski, which tries to break down the interpretive model. These non-interpretative reading techniques are often left fairly vague, but the new work on emotion in the sciences and social sciences is suggestive in that it provides a way of understanding interactions with texts that do not rely on typical understandings of interpretation.

The current problems surrounding thinking about reading, interpretation, and emotion drew me back to the late eighteenth and early nineteenth centuries, when many of the long-lived suppositions about reading, interpretation, and emotion were put in place. During this period of the burgeoning of mass reading, the rules of good, critical reading were broadly inculcated against an image of bad, absorptive, affective reading. The period offers a view of what was at stake in the disputes over these forms of reading and in the forms themselves. At stake were questions about democracy, the self, autonomy, and the public sphere, among other issues. Indeed, these questions surrounding emotion and reading are still important today for understanding our own public sensorium.

An Overview

Fever Reading's five chapters are divided into two parts. The first part (chapters 1 and 2) provides a history of the discussions of good and bad reading and explains how this history is also a history of the public sphere. The second part (chapters 3, 4, and 5) uses the context provided by the first part to investigate the use and meaning of bad, pathological forms of reading.

The first chapter begins with an example of the discourse of good and bad reading, taken from William Hill Brown's novel *The Power of Sympathy* (1789), which was well known at the time. The novel helps outline the characteristics of reading deemed proper and those deemed pathological. The goal at this point in *Fever Reading* is not to provide a historical perspective on this discourse but to introduce what was at issue in discussions about reading as it became ever more central to everyday life. Brown's novel shows how important debates about reading were to the shaping of the public sphere. The chapter explains the often forgotten role of reading in the public sphere, as well as the controversial role of emotion, by looking at public-sphere theory from Jürgen Habermas to Michael Warner. To consider the public sensorium (rather than the public sphere), a clear understanding of emotion, affect, and embodiment is required. The chapter briefly reviews some of the work on affect in recent literary and cultural studies (by Sedgwick, Brian Massumi, and others) before turning more fully to a model of emotion which grows out of the experimental sciences and which is substantially different from that used in the humanities. Using the sciences' model, William Reddy has developed a theory of emotional expression — what he calls "emotives" — which will help explain the reflective and critical work of emotional reading. The chapter also answers preliminary questions that readers might have about methodology, periodization, geographical focus, the role that the categories of gender, race, and class will play in the succeeding chapters, and about the project's relation to scholarship in the history of the book and reading.

Where the first chapter establishes the book's theoretical and methodological foundation, the second chapter provides its historical context. It first indicates the breadth of discussions of fever reading from the early republic through the antebellum period. It then looks backward to reading in seventeenth- and early-eighteenth-century New England (with the help of scholars of the period) as a point of contrast with reading in the late eighteenth and early nineteenth centuries. Such a broad perspective brings the later period's transformations in models of reading into relief. The remainder of the chapter outlines in detail the characteristics of proper and pathological reading in this later period, emphasizing the way these characteristics changed. In brief, these changes were entwined with a shift from republican to more liberal ideas of the public sphere. Chapter 2 outlines this historical trajectory by examining discussions of reading in long-forgotten popular print productions but also in canonical writings by Olandah Equiano (and other African diasporans), Charles Brockden Brown, Edgar Allan Poe, Nathaniel Hawthorne, Nat Turner, Frederick Douglass, and others.

Part 2 of *Fever Reading* turns from the discourse of good and bad reading to the three archives of bad reading. The first archive, antebellum obscene reading, is the focus of chapter 3. The genre's emergence, regulation, and basic characteristics are outlined using extant texts, bibliographic records, and obscenity arrests reported in newspapers. The chapter then focuses on the structure of obscene reading as those structures are put forward by two subgenres: the sporting press and obscene books (including novelettes by George Thompson, "Charles Paul de Kock," and other, anonymous authors). The final part of the chapter considers the way the obscene constructs its reader as a body that bypasses conventional readerly emotions. This avoidance of emotion indicates a resistance to both rational-critical discourse and certain conventional emotional discourses as the foundation for the public sphere. If any emotions can justly be attributed to antebellum pornography, they are an ambivalent combination of excitement and boredom set in motion by endless stimulation and repetition. This excitement-boredom response is an "emotive" (borrowing Reddy's idea) that reflects on sentimentalism, privacy, agency, and the understanding of emotion itself. This chapter suggests that pornography—apparently the most irrational and uncritical of modern genres—is central to an embodied but still critical public sphere.

Chapter 4 examines a collection of mini-genres—intrigues, scandal chronicles, and novelettes about notorious characters—that became popular in the mid-nineteenth century in the United States. The texts include the anonymously authored *The Eventful Lives of Helen and Charlotte Lenoxa*; George Thompson's *The Countess: or, Memoirs of Women of Leisure*; and Poe's "The Murder of Marie Roget." The various genres share an interest in the liminal space between novel and news, fiction and fact, as well as an interest in revealing the machinations, sexual and otherwise, of the powerful. After outlining the emergence and conventional characteristics of these genres, it is possible to see how they cause their readers to ritually cycle through feelings of trust and distrust. This emotional cycling was a mode of reflection focused on the growing complexity of bureaucratic systems and new questions of agency in antebellum America. To participate in this emotion-based public sphere was to participate in an evaluation of, reflection on, and judgment of such systems.

Central to the birth of mass media in the United States were not only obscene literature and scandal publications but also religious reading. This third kind of reading is often thought to be dramatically different from the first two, but it shares certain characteristics with them. In an early essay, Susan Sontag captures one similarity between pornographic reading and religious reading when she notes that pornographic books aim "to 'excite' in the same way that books which render an extreme form of religious experience aim to 'convert'" (*Styles* 48). Both operate, in other words, through affect rather than ideas, through the body rather than the mind. The Second Great Awakening saw an explosion of "extreme forms of religious experience," some of which involved religious reading. Tract societies and other religious institutions tried to clearly define proper religious reading during this period, attempting to make sure it didn't become fever reading. This chapter begins with this story of regulation, which is also a story about religion's and religious reading's place in the public sphere during the early and mid-nineteenth century. As religious reading became mass reading, it had to be disciplined so as to properly contribute to the dominant values of the public sphere. From this perspective, one couldn't be lost in religious revelation and also be self-reflective and critical. But religious reading was difficult to discipline, especially in the form of religious novels. This chapter's second half looks at the way these popular religious novels constructed their readers. Instead of dismissing such novels as constructing their religious readers as outside the public sphere, *Fever Reading* sees them as attempting to imagine a different kind of public-sphere interaction, one based on fervor and conversion rather than rational-critical debate and argument.

In *Fever Reading*, I provide a kind of genealogy of good and bad reading, showing how such valuations are linked to the construction of the public sphere. I've tried to parochialize our notions of good, critical reading by showing how there is nothing natural or universal about that reading. In doing so, I have also tried to open up our thinking about pathological reading, suggesting that it was often a way of participating in a public sphere with values and protocols different from those of the dominant public sphere. The epilogue of *Fever Reading* takes up one final line of inquiry: why might such questions about reading, emotion, and the public sphere be of interest and importance now? The age of *Fever Reading* is, in many respects, our age too.

Part One

Chapter One

The Senses of Reading

Reading Well and Reading Badly: An Example

A specific instance from the reading archive will help bring into focus many of the primary concerns of *Fever Reading*. William Hill Brown's early American novel *The Power of Sympathy* (1789) raises the question of what form reading should take in a public sphere that aspires to produce "judgment," "knowledge," and "reflection"—all key terms for Brown (22, 25, 27, and elsewhere). With so much at stake, reading is an important and, if not done properly, even dangerous endeavor in Brown's novel. The significance he places on reading is in no way exceptional in the canon of late eighteenth-century U.S. fiction. As Cathy Davidson has noted, all of the period's novels, without exception, didactically comment on right and wrong kinds of reading (66). Indeed, the novels themselves—with their narratives of young women and men led astray by their reading—are in large part about the dangers of print media, not just the novel genre. They serve as guidebooks to a new media environment that was coming into being in the late eighteenth century. Brown's *The Power of Sympathy* provides a particularly elaborate example, and one that focuses specifically on the relation of reading to the public sphere, which makes it a good place to begin.

Brown suggests some of the dangers of reading by having one of his characters share an "Allegory" (22) of reading badly. Mr. Holmes describes the "human mind as an extensive plain and knowledge as the river that should water it." "[I]f books, which are the sources that feed this river, rush into it from every quarter it will over flow [*sic*] its banks,

{ 3

and the plain will become inundated," and eventually "stagnant" (22). Mr. Holmes is clear about what sorts of reading practices lead to such inundation and stagnation: they are characterized as "immoderate" (26) and "desultory" (23), and associated with "repeatedly reading the same thing" (21). The mind that reads in such ways swims about aimlessly and may well be flooded, drowned, and washed away.

This description of dangerous reading is interesting in several respects. Brown, through the character of Mr. Holmes, indicates his fear of the general onslaught of print media and unregulated information that was just beginning in the United States in the last decades of the eighteenth century. It is important to note that Brown is less fearful of particular bad books or particular genres of books (even the much demonized novel, which he is of course writing himself) than he is of improper reading practices which will provide, in his view, little ballast in this flood of print information. "Immoderate," "desultory," and repetitive reading is the problem, as is being "insensibly attached" (26) to one's reading and the ideas garnered from it. To be insensibly attached is to be attached without Sensibility (the eighteenth century's highly theorized idea of the interconnection of the senses and rationality). It is to read with the senses but without sensibility. This bad form of attachment leads to an excessive privacy characterized by the "hoard[ing]" of knowledge. "By *immoderate reading*," says Mr. Holmes, "we hoard up opinions and become insensibly attached to them" (26). These problem practices — immoderation, repetition, insensible attachment, inundation, desultoriness, and knowledge hoarding — lead to a number of larger problems, such as desiring too much, feeling too intensely, being undisciplined and irrational, being too close to ideas, and having no clearly delineated self with respect to one's reading.

In Brown's view, bad reading practices limit one's ability to be "reflective," to come to "judgment," or to determine value ("form an estimate of the various topicks [*sic*] discussed" [22]). These apparently cognitive and self-conscious actions require, it seems, the kind of detachment and control that is the opposite of inundation or insensible attachment. Against the above allegory of bad reading, Brown develops a picture of proper reading that emphasizes detachment and control as integral to positive and constructive reading. What "make[s] reading really useful" (26), Brown suggests, are two things. First, proper relations between book and reader. Instead of inundation and insensible attachment, the best practice of reading is "penetrating" (22), "channel[ing]" (22), and "methodical" (22). These adjectives suggest a clear divide and distance between reader and text. Proper reading requires avoidance of excessive attachment. To penetrate, channel, or methodically address texts is to clearly divide the text from the self. Moreover, the reader in such cases acts upon the text, asserting agency, rather than being acted upon, or "washed away" in the flood. The reader may "penetrate" the book and expose its interior, but the reader does so while remaining importantly whole and distinct. Such reading emphasizes the power of the reader over the book, not the book over the reader. The metaphorics of penetration and channeling suggest a reader in a relation of opposition to the text.[1]

If *The Power of Sympathy*'s first strategy for "making reading useful" is establishing proper object relations with texts, the second entails submitting reading to what Brown calls "conversation," as "*conversation only can remedy this dangerous evil* [of immoderate reading], *strengthen the judgment, and make reading really useful*" (italics in original; 26). Proper reading is not at all a private, isolated practice of reader and text. Recall that immoderate reading is characterized by Brown as "hoard[ing] up," which suggests a problematic privacy. Good reading practices understand books as "friends" (23), "company" (20, 21, 22), and a form of "conversation" (20, 26). Brown pictures reading at its best as interaction and communication with others. "They [books and conversation] mutually depend upon, and assist each other" (26). Out of the conversations one has with books—and with others about books—develops Brown's notion of "reflection" and "judgment." Conversation about books and with books "strengthen[s] the judgment" (26). Judgment here does not correspond to something internal to either the self or the book, but instead is realized intersubjectively, through "[o]ur ordinary intercourse with the world," which is made possible through reading books and conversing about reading books.

In other words, proper reading, according to Brown, is a public practice in that it enables discussion of ideas "with the world." Good reading, therefore, is closely associated with what can accurately be called "the public sphere," even though a more technical definition of the concept will need to be developed later in this chapter. Brown's idea of reading in the service of "conversation" oriented toward the "world," and which will precipitate "reflection," "judgment," and "value," is a pretty good initial definition of the public sphere as classic public-sphere theorists like Jürgen Habermas have described it. But what Brown helps reveal is something about reading that most public-sphere theorists haven't considered in much detail. It is not just any sort of reading that contributes to this public sphere of reflection and judgment. Reading in the service of the development and support of the public sphere (call it public-sphere reading) must be aligned with conversation and it must also exhibit proper object relations. The kind of public sphere that Brown and Habermas imagine requires a practice of reading that keeps the contents of the text objective, extractable, transposable, replicable, circulatable, and discussable. Texts which are too close to the reader—texts to which readers become "insensibly attached"—are more difficult and perhaps impossible to bring into public conversation. The kind of public sphere Brown envisions involves a notion of books and texts as penetrable, to recall his own language. In fact, this public-sphere idea requires a whole epistemology—a set of views about what knowledge is: something separate from the subject, something which can be transferred, something which the subject has power over. The reader's practice supports this epistemology of the critical public sphere. There are, of course, models of reading—say, religious reading or pornographic reading—which work in very different and nearly opposite ways, valuing the complete erasure of the lines between subject and object, reader and text. The goal of much pornographic reading and some religious reading is to make you forget that these are words on the page and that this is a book in your hand.

From the perspective of Brown and many others of his day, such reading is pathological. It leads to fevers of the body and mind, of the body politic and the social psyche. The next chapter will look closely at this discourse of the eighteenth and nineteenth centuries, which distinguishes between good reading and pathological reading. Then, the following three chapters will examine the practices of reading badly. How might reading practices that are about immersion, inundation, attachment, embodiment, repetition, and emotion (rather than detachment, rationality, and penetration) contribute to a public sphere? But before turning to such questions, it is necessary to define more fully two key concepts. First, the public sphere. Then, the more difficult area to conceptualize: the experience of inundation, immersion, and overattachment. The latter, I believe, can be developed through some recent work on emotion, affect, and feeling. In the end, these two conceptual areas—the public sphere and emotion—can be brought together in hopes of better understanding reading in the eighteenth and nineteenth centuries, and also in hopes of better understanding our own public sensorium.

Reading, the Public Sphere,
and the Public Sensorium

One of the complexities of the public sphere as a concept is that it is both commonsensical and highly specialized, both easy and difficult to summarize. The term is used in everyday conversation but also has a long, intricate history of theoretical debate. The purpose here is not to summarize these debates so much as outline some basic aspects of the public-sphere idea and then explain the complexities pertinent to questions of reading and emotion.

It is helpful to begin with Habermas. The kind of public sphere he understood as coming into being during the long eighteenth century is very different from older kinds of public spheres extending back to antiquity. In one sense, there have always been public spheres: the sovereign sent messengers to read edicts to a public sphere of his people; the aristocrat circulated poetry in manuscript in the public sphere of the court; Shakespeare put on plays in front of a public from a wide range of classes; and the minister spoke to a public of congregants. Indeed, a public sphere might well develop around anything at all that circulates — a book, a speech, a gesture, a fashion accessory. But the kind of public sphere pertinent to *Fever Reading* — and the kind that Habermas outlines beginning with *The Structural Transformation of the Public Sphere* (first published in 1962; translated into English in 1989) — is of a different, special sort. Habermas understands the new public sphere as a new form of power in the long eighteenth century. In this new public sphere, power is located *in* a public rather than exercised *before* a public (10 and elsewhere). The new power came from discussion and deliberation by the individuals making up that public sphere whereas, in the older public sphere, aristocrats, ecclesiastics, and others of status exerted their authority over a public, sometimes by simply appearing before that public. Habermas called this older form "representative publicness" (5 and elsewhere) in order to capture the way power came through representation of status and authority before a public rather than through discussion and argument in public. The new public sphere was a collection of anonymous, abstract strangers who argued and discussed rather than individuals who exerted power through status and rank (especially 54–55). The development of a wide-reaching periodical culture allowed these anonymous, abstract individuals to argue and debate. In the pages of the *Tatler*, the *Spectator*, and the *Guardian*, pseudonymous authors argued about current events and culture (40–43).

Importantly, the individual's self-abstraction in public underwrote the public sphere's power. It works like this: argument and discussion among the general, abstract public (which anyone and everyone is able to enter without restriction along lines of status, lineage, or otherwise) precipitate fair conclusions which, because of their disinterested derivation, have authority over interested institutions like the aristocracy, the state, and the church (especially 54). The word "public" began to develop its modern sense, which remains in common usage today: a public is not a group or a crowd who might easily know each other, but a collection of people indefinite in number, space, and identity. A public is an assortment of strangers, anonymous and abstract to each other. Their power and agency is located in their critical discussion, which itself garners power because it is critical discussion among anonymous, unbiased discussants.

In some sense, what Habermas suggests about the new, modern public sphere is utterly commonsensical and taken for granted in Western democracies. That is, open and free public discussion precipitate ideas which should guide, govern, and regulate society. As straightforward as this may seem, *The Structural Transformation*'s significant contribution is to show just how complex the idea and its history are. A great deal had to be in place in order for even the idea of the public sphere to become a possibility. Habermas documents the social, political, and intellectual transformations that enable the emergence of the new public sphere—from the explosion of periodical publication, the rise of the bourgeoisie, and the emergence of liberal political philosophy to transformations in transportation, new organizations of the state, the rise of reading clubs and coffee houses, and new forms of architecture. One can also begin to see the relationship between Habermas's understanding of the public sphere and a very specific practice of reading. Habermas doesn't have much explicitly to say about reading practices per se, but the public sphere he is describing does require a particular kind of relation to text and textual uptake. Like William Hill Brown, Habermas emphasizes the values of critical distance, autonomy, and public communication with respect to cultural texts as being essential to development of the modern public sphere. The rise of public concerts, salon culture, public museums, and periodical culture "institutionalized the lay judgment of art," and "art became an object of free choice" (40). The judgment and coinciding sense of autonomy were developed by private citizens' "verbaliz[ation] and rational communication with one another" about a cultural product so as to "determine its meaning on their own" (37).

The importance of critical distance and autonomy in the uptake practices of the public sphere becomes especially clear when Habermas discusses the bad relations with texts encouraged by the technologies of
mass culture. As he spends the second half of *The Structural Transformation* criticizing twentieth-century mass culture for its destruction of a
critical public sphere, he worries that contemporary mass media encourages too much attachment to and immersion in their texts. "Radio, film,
and television," Habermas says, "reduce to a minimum the distance that
a reader is forced to maintain toward the printed letter—a distance that
. . . made possible the publicity of rational-critical exchange about what
had been read" (170). Here Habermas sounds something like Brown in
The Power of Sympathy when the latter fears that the flood of media in
the late eighteenth century will inundate readers, prohibiting the detachment and distance required for judgment and evaluation. As Habermas
puts it, distance makes possible the "rational-critical exchange about
what has been read" (170); it is essential to what it means to be critical,
to exert judgment and evaluation.

This distance underwrites several requirements of the public sphere.
First, the reader maintains power over the text and avoids absorption.
His or her autonomy is thus underwritten by the act of reading. Furthermore, such anti-absorption makes possible not only the critical perspective, but the "publicity" of the critical. In other words, it allows for the
externalization of what is read, which in turns allows it to be replicated
and transmitted between participants in the public sphere. Here again
Habermas converges with William Hill Brown's thinking about reading.
In both authors' views, judgment issues not from the individual but from
"[o]ur ordinary intercourse with the world."[2]

The Brown-Habermasian mode of reading may be summarized by the
following points:

~ critical distance (rather than the immersion and attachment
  characteristic of, say, popular forms of religious reading or
  pornographic reading)
~ an opposition between text and reader
~ the reader's consciousness of a text as a mediating object
~ the reader's consciousness of a text's circulation among other
  anonymous readers
~ the extraction of the reader from the commands of direct textual
  address

~ an outward orientation—that is, the understanding of reading as a form of conversation and a generator of conversation.

It is certain that the long eighteenth century did not invent this mode of reading from whole cloth, but it did become the norm during this period (its normalization is the primary subject of the next chapter). Today it self-evidently seems like the proper way of reading intelligently, but this was not always the case. In the seventeenth and early eighteenth centuries, at least in the northeastern colonies, a very different mode of religious-oriented reading dominated the vernacular practice of reading (discussed in the next chapter). But with the emerging idea of the public sphere at the end of the eighteenth century, a practice of reading that was distanced, oppositional, self-conscious, and outwardly oriented became the norm. It might accurately be called public-sphere reading.

To say that this style of reading becomes the norm does not mean that everyone reads in this way, much less reads in this way all the time; instead, it is to say that this style of reading became the measure for value, the metric for good and proper reading. The same is true for Habermas' idea of the public sphere. Some have criticized the Habermasian version of the public sphere as idealist fantasy, as never having been a reality in the eighteenth century or any other.[3] In this view, no such sphere of rational-critical debate existed, nor did any sphere open to indefinite, abstract others disconnected from status markers. For his part, Habermas has generally responded by emphasizing that his argument understands the public sphere emerging as an *idea*, if not a reality, in the long eighteenth century.[4] It became conceptually available for use as an ideal or aspirational norm to which one might orient one's understanding and actions. This is true (as the next chapter shows) of the eighteenth-century United States: what came into existence then was the hegemonic ideal of the public sphere rather than an actually existing public sphere as Habermas (or Brown) imagined it.

The more damning critique leveled against Habermas is that, even as an aspirational ideal, the public sphere is deeply limiting in that it makes hegemonic a collection of values and self-understandings while all the while masquerading as something more general and democratic—a forever-open sphere, or even a spirit.[5] Those hegemonic values include the public sphere's foundational ideals of abstract subjectivity, unbiased debate, and reason itself. From this perspective, joining the public sphere—even making oneself intelligible in the public sphere—means changing the self, not the public sphere. The experience is familiar: workers or a racial minority or a sexual underclass gain entrance to the mainstream public sphere, but then their interests appear as "private interests," not a collective interest which might transform the very foundations of the public sphere. For instance, the U.S. military's notorious policy of "don't ask, don't tell" opened a part of the public sphere to non-heterosexual service members but also excluded significant aspects of their experience and prevented that experience from having much effect on the dominant values of the public sphere. The world that some gays, lesbians, and queers might imagine — one of, say, embodied rather than abstract sociability or one where ethics and morality are not derived from rational-critical debate but physical responsiveness — has no public meaning or relevance. Such a world appears to have nothing to do with public deliberation.

Of critics who make this kind of argument against Habermas, Michael Warner has developed it most helpfully because he emphasizes reading practices where bodily, affective response plays a crucial role. Warner asks what a public sphere would look and feel like where a participant "throws shade, prances, disses, acts up, carries on, longs, fantasizes, throws fits, mourns, 'reads'" (*Publics* 124), rather than observes the more authorized communication practices of arguing, opining, reasoning, making a case, debating, and reading critically. What if a public sphere prized "curling up, mumbling, fantasizing, gesticulating, ventriloquizing, writing marginalia, etc." (*Publics* 123), instead of distanced, disciplined argument — that "may scrutinize, ask, reject, opine, decide, judge, and so on" (*Publics* 123)? For Warner it is at this level of reading and other uptake and response practices that the values and ethics of a dominant, rational-critical public sphere are both inculcated and contested. In his view a public sphere founded on embodied, attached reading might offer a different phenomenology of what it means to be public. Warner is ultimately suggesting here that such practices entail values; they have an ethical-political dimension. A public sphere based on the pleasures, pains, and desires of the body might well carry a different set of values than the bourgeois, liberal, Habermasian public sphere, which takes as its model the rational-critical debate of, say, the *Spectator* or the *Economist* and the abstract exchanges of Wall Street and the "free" market. Such a public sphere as Warner imagines might well make the experiences of the laboring body or the queer body meaningful — in fact, the norm for determining what is meaningful. In such a case, these practices and the ethics they inculcate would not be understood as having been relegated to the private sphere but as having public significance. He hopes that such alternative communication practices which foreground the body might contribute to the formation of a public sphere with the aspiration "of transforming not just policy but the space of public life itself" (*Publics* 124).

Warner's work is extremely helpful and promising to the project of rethinking the public-sphere concept. He offers some starting points for investigating the workings of a public sensorium rather than an abstract public sphere. But there is also a great deal left unexplained. First, the kind of affective public sphere that Warner values isn't exactly counter to a dominant rational-critical public sphere. The characteristics of purportedly counterpublic interactivity that he points to—throwing shade, prancing, dissing, carrying on—have a queer resonance, but it is easy to imagine a similar set of practices for many aspects of mainstream popular culture. This fact does not diminish the insights of Warner; instead, it suggests that the questions he asks about the power of non–rational-critical practices are important across the mass public sphere, not just among counterpublics. It is also important to recognize that the affectual public sphere does not necessarily or automatically run counter to the rational-critical public sphere. Habermas in *The Structural Transformation* emphasizes an emotional component of the public sphere as it developed in the eighteenth century: the culture of sensibility and sentimentality (experienced primarily through the eighteenth-century novel) produced a sense of shared feeling and common humanity, that in turn underwrote an unbiased discussion (48–51). All discussants shared a pure humanity which then became the ground for argument. Habermas's more recent work has continued to find emotional constellations like empathy important to discourse ethics (*Justification* 194–95). But sentimentalism and empathy cover only a very small range of the affects that seem central to the modern public sphere. What role does the sensational play, or the ecstatic, or for that matter, the boring or the disgusting? Alternatively, Warner encourages an examination of the public sphere that considers the most abject yet prevalent emotions.

But a key question arises that Warner doesn't address: how does embodied, emotion-based reading provide public-sphere participants with the means of critical reflection, evaluation, and judgment? Warner himself suggests the question but doesn't linger over it when he asks, "what if it isn't true, as we suppose, that critical reading is the only way to suture textual practice with reflection, reason, and a normative discipline of subjectivity" ("Uncritical" 16)? In other words, what if it's true that *uncritical* reading—reading that is embodied, affect-generating, emotion-ridden—can suture textual practice with reflection, reason, and criticality? One can clearly see how emotion and immersion might subvert reason, reflection, and detachment, but how do the former operate as reflection and criticism? There might be good reason to want to reject the specific normative forms for public-sphere interactivity that Habermas puts forward—namely, the abstract, universalized participant practicing a distanced reading and discussion that he sees as essential. However, it might well be wise to hold onto Habermas's vision of the public sphere's power as a space for critical discussion and reflection.[6] How does an erotics of reading—a form of reading founded on affective, feeling, embodied attachments—do this? Reading too erotically, too affectively, with too much attachment to the texts, isn't usually understood as developing a critical public opinion. A necessary step for thinking about the critical and reflective possibilities of an embodied reading is an inquiry into how the body can be understood as a critical, reflective apparatus. One way of doing this is by turning to recent scholarship on emotion.

Critical Affects: How Emotions Think

Since the 1970s, significant transformations have occurred in the understanding of emotion across a number of fields—cognitive psychology, neural science, anthropology, philosophy, economics—although these transformations have yet to be absorbed across the humanities or the social sciences. The long-held views of emotions as private, irrational, involuntary, or unconscious are now suspect. No longer is emotion thought of as located in the body rather than culture, or in culture rather than the body. Nor are emotions still understood as counterposed to cognition or rationality. Such dichotomies—emotion/cognition, body/mind, nature/nurture, individual/society, internal/external—have been deeply complicated as conceptual frameworks for thinking about emotion. Instead, cognitive scientists suggest thinking in terms of "cogmotion" (Barnett and Ratner 303), and neural scientists have discovered that damage to parts of the brain that affect emotion also affect decision-making (Damasio, especially 216–17). Philosophers have articulated a "cognitive/evaluative view" of emotion (Nussbaum 5) that revalues the work of the Stoics and the Scottish Enlightenment, among others. Anthropologists have carefully avoided arguing that emotion is a purely cultural construction, while they have also detailed how it should not be understood as trans-cultural either: emotions have very different constructions in different cultures (Levy; Lutz).[7]

The research on emotion is extraordinarily rich and complex, and there are many issues lacking consensus. But most of the work in the experimental sciences does agree on one general point: emotions are ways of interacting with and evaluating the surrounding environment. In her review of the literature on emotion, Lynn Smith-Lovin observes that the term's technical definition across the experimental sciences is "any evaluative (positive or negative) orientation toward an object" (135–36). Jenefer Robinson, in her detailed overview of emotion as an object of study in philosophy, cognitive psychology, and neurophysiol-ogy, repeatedly returns to the core idea that emotions are appraisals of the surrounding environment. They are "*evaluative* judgments" (12), they are used to "appraise or evaluate" (43), and their function "is to draw attention automatically and insistently by bodily means to what-ever in the environment is of vital importance to me and mine" (97). Researchers in these fields have very different views concerning what constitutes an "evaluation." For some it is simple positive or negative appraisal, a response in the form of either anticipated pleasure or pain (the kind of evaluation of the surrounding ecology shared by both hu-mans and animals).[8] For other researchers, the appraisals are more com-plex. Antonio Damasio's experiments have demonstrated the necessity of emotional response to complex assessments in mathematical games and judgments about future situations, and Daniel Kahneman and others working in the area of behavioral economics have concentrated on the role of emotions in economic decision-making and the appraisal of risk. Researchers also often have very different definitions of what they mean by the "environment." Some have focused on environment as the natu-ral, non-human surroundings that the organism must negotiate in order to survive. Others understand evaluations as constructed in relationship to the surrounding social, rather than natural, environment, where the point is not survival but the achievement of goals, wishes, and norms es-tablished by the individual and society more generally. The latter group is distinguished from the former in an additional way: to see emotion as an appraisal of socially constructed norms and goals is to see it as learned rather than innate.[9] This view doesn't claim that emotion is therefore a social construction, but rather that complex, evaluative emotions are learned in relationship to innate reflexive reactions, which are themselves complex and involve both physiological and reasoning portions of the nervous system (even in frogs), interacting in intricate processes and feedback loops. Ultimately, however, no matter their views on the definitions of evaluation, environment, and learning associated with emotion, almost all the science scholarship agrees on the basic model that emotional response is an appraisal of the environment.

This model differs substantially from those frameworks commonly used to understand emotion in literary and cultural studies, and the evaluation model of emotions may well be able to open up new areas of inquiry in these humanities fields and especially in the area of reading. Two broad models of emotion usually dominate in literary and cultural studies. The first might be loosely called "symptomatic" because it sees emotion as a symptom of something else, and the second is fairly accurately characterized as "strategic" because it understands emotion as having a deliberate, tactical importance. The "symptomatic" framework calls for looking beneath the anxiety generated by, say, a gothic text for what is generating that anxiety — perhaps a socially destabilizing homoeroticism or an unsettlingly powerful imagination, as a number of critics have suggested. As in Freud and early psychoanalysis, the emotional sign is understood to represent or be produced by something implicit or unconscious, and often this unconscious content is political or ideological in nature. The emotion might be taken to be a reaction formation with respect to this content or an escape from it or some other manifestation of it.[10] Alternatively, the "strategic" framework sees emotion as deployed, sometimes in a hegemonic war of position and sometimes as the foundations for a counter-community.[11] There is crossover in both of these models, and they are both closely related to the common approach of seeing text-generated emotion as a site for the ideological interpellation of subjects. Any particular ideology is most powerful when it is felt as a constellation of emotions rather than understood as a constellation of ideas. The symptomatic model of critique looks for the ideology beneath the emotion and the strategic model of critique looks for how the emotions are harnessed to the ideology.[12] However, the evaluation model from the experimental sciences suggests a third framework, one that sees text-generated emotions as allowing for the evaluation of, or a critical relationship with, the surrounding environment. This third model doesn't rule out the first two models. Ideology, the political unconscious, and more concrete forces like governments and institutions still shape emotion, but the evaluation model does suggest a different perspective on what emotions do and why they matter. Under this model, they can no longer be understood as simply the products of ideology or the reactions to it. Instead they are a form of perception, even a form of critical thinking. Understanding texts and emotions in this way has the potential to develop new understandings of emotions in the public sphere.

The development of this model will require a fuller explanation of what is meant by emotion in the experimental and cognitive sciences. The humanistic scholars of print culture have been shy about turning to recent work in the sciences, instead relying primarily on various critical frameworks developed out of several different traditions, ranging from Aristotle on the passions in the *Rhetoric*, to Spinoza and William James on affect and cognition (further developed by Gilles Deleuze and Félix Guattari), to the 1970s psychologist Silvan Tomkins.[13] One of the reasons for this reluctance is the lack of a sophisticated scientific understanding of the verbal mediation of emotion, an area of particular importance to historians and literary scholars. What happens to the subject and to the emotion when an emotion is put into words? Or, to take another step, what happens when a verbalized emotion is read or recited? Does it change emotion in some way to speak it or write it or read it? There is often a taken-for-grantedness about emotional utterances that sees them as simply expressing an internal state of the speaker; the analysis ends there. But this explanation isn't very satisfactory. It doesn't explain, for instance, the common experience of expressing an emotional state only to have the expression itself amplify the emotion. Of course, the opposite also happens: the statement of the emotion can ease to some degree its intensity. Sometimes uttering an emotion gives the speaker more control over it, sometimes less. If reading is understood as an activity involving the verbalization or uttering of emotion, then these experiences become pertinent.

One of the few researchers to take up the issue of verbalized emotions is William M. Reddy. His work over the last decade provides a very sophisticated definition of emotion grounded in experimental cognitive science. His definition adheres to the evaluation model that is common across cognitive science, and he concurs with much else in that field (emotion is physical and cognitive; emotional appraisal is a process; it involves a great deal of feedback between systems; and it is required for complex decision-making as well as primitive, survival reflexes). But, in addition, he also provides a theory of verbalized emotions, which he calls "emotives" (63–111). He doesn't specifically discuss reading but does offer a conceptual framework that will be useful for historians of reading. Reddy himself is trained as an historian, but one deeply influenced by anthropology's focus in cultural forms. As such, one of the primary goals of his work is to develop the findings of cognitive science into useful tools for better understanding the repeated, formulized emotional practices of past cultures. Such practices are not very distant from the highly formulized and highly emotionalized print genres of pornography, scandal, and religious enthusiasm. Lauren Berlant has developed a helpful definition of genre as "an aesthetic structure of affective expectation" (4), and such a definition certainly holds for the genres discussed here.

Following the recent work in cognitive science on emotion, Reddy understands emotion as the multipart processing of a complex array of stimuli. Emotion is the interaction of conventional sensory stimulus (seeing, hearing, smelling, etc.), proprioceptive sensation (the body's perception of itself, say, in space), interoceptive sensation (the body's perception of its internal organs), the consciousness of ideas, and memory (ranging from that which allows specific movement and basic skills—"muscle memory" in lay parlance—to the kind of involuntary memory that enables, for instance, speech, to unconscious and more conscious memory of past experience); this stimulus is processed by various neurological and physiological systems. The details of this definition of emotion hold less importance for our purposes than the ways Reddy makes them useful to the study of culture and history.[14] In this respect, the key emphasis is on *translation*: what we typically call an emotion is in his view a translation between many different mediums and systems. The concept of translation is important for Reddy because no translation (especially across mediums) can ever be complete. This idea is well accepted in the humanities; in any translation, there is always a remainder, an excess, a gap, a supplement. At all the multifold moments of translation from one system to another, some emotional information is activated and some remains un-activated. The verbalization of an emotion is yet another point of translation. Reddy develops the idea of emotives by borrowing from J. L. Austin's well-known idea of performative speech.[15] In brief, as Reddy explains it, the evaluative capability of the emotive works in this way: the expression of emotion is a limited, gap-filled translation of all the thought material which floods the system, and as such, the expression of emotion calls attention to and even appraises its relationship to the gaps and overflows. The emotive is, in other words, a way of "navi-gating" (one of Reddy's key terms for what emotives, like performa-tives, do) through an array of stimulus information processed by various systems.[16] To say "I love you" is to express an emotion and to fulfill a convention but also to evaluate the emotion (to see how the feeling feels, one might say). The emotive "I love you" could lead to a number of rec-ognitions about an array of stimuli. In a similar fashion, one might smile as part of a formalized performance only to discover that one is happier, or sadder.[17] Reddy thus makes the point that emotives have the ability to explore and perhaps, under certain conditions, alter one's relation-ship with thought material, especially thought material that has been lost in translation. Emotives are both "self-exploratory" and "self-altering" (101), as he says. Any emotional expression can be diagnostic: it con-firms or disconfirms. Any emotional expression also can be altering: it intensifies or attenuates the emotions claimed. Reddy speaks of emo-tives as navigatory, and navigation not only suggests that emotions are direction-finding, but also that they have the ability to lead to changes of direction.

Reddy is centrally interested in evaluative, navigatory emotives as they function in common cultural forms and customs, ranging from practices traditionally understood to be ritualistic, like mourning rites, to other conventions of daily life, such as the expression of an expected sentiment in response to a familiar encounter. The focus on such broad emotional *habitus* allows him to move from particular instances in the historical archive to more general claims about a culture or period. In his view, anthropologists and historians have had difficulty deciphering the meaning and work of such ritualistic emotional expression. The two disciplines tend to see these rites and customs as either a clear repre-sentation of internal states or, alternatively, as a way of manipulating, of ideologically shaping, emotional response. He notes that "[s]uch [ritual] performances have raised many methodological difficulties; experts dis-agree about how to approach them. Is such formalized emotional ex-pression insincere? Or do such forms aim at creating emotion? These questions have remained difficult to answer because researchers have too often neglected [an additional] feature of first-person emotional claims [that is, the navigatory or exploratory effects of emotives]" (101). As an illustration of the different perspective that the emotive concept might open up, Reddy offers the example of the way young, female Awlad 'Ali Bedouins in Egypt recite from memory stylized and emotionally charged folk poetry in order to express sentiments to husbands and male elders. Anthropologists like Lila Abu-Lughod have generally understood the poetry as a form of self-fashioning and self-mastery but along cultural norms that maintain male power (in the end the poetry emphasizes obedience and the value of female suffering). But Reddy argues that it is plausible to understand this formalized emotional expression as having "exploratory effects" that enable "the navigation of difficult seas" (135). Sometimes the young women act on the deviant emotions expressed in the poems, despite the anthropologist's view that their recitations are intended to discipline.

Another near-synonym for this sort of navigation—a synonym that brings our discussion back to concerns with the public sphere—is reflection. In Habermas's view, reflection on laws, morals, norms, and systems is made possible by rational-critical debate in the public sphere. Such reflection would precipitate agency and power over those laws, morals, norms, and systems. But, if emotives offer a kind of reflection, the public sphere might be understood in new ways—as a public sensorium rather than an abstract sphere. What I'm suggesting here about the critical, evaluative dimension of emotions has been suggested by other humanist scholars who study the eighteenth and nineteenth centuries, albeit without an emphasis on what might be learned from cognitive science. Lauren Berlant, who is a kind of distant muse for *Fever Reading*, has written extensively on the critical, reflective agency made possible through the emotions generated by American popular culture, beginning with *Uncle Tom's Cabin* (1851). She says,

> This very general sense of confidence in the critical intelligence of affect, emotion, and good intention produces an orientation toward agency that is focused on ongoing adaptation, adjustment, improvisation, and developing wiles for surviving, thriving, and transcending the world as it presents itself. (2)

The vocabulary of the evolutionary sciences infuses Berlant's description of what critical affects facilitate—"adaption" and "adjustment," survival and thriving—although she doesn't explicitly turn to the kind of science research I've presented here.[18] But a turn to cognitive science makes Berlant's "general sense of confidence" in the critical emotions somewhat more exact and definite. The cognitive science perspective also opens up further potentials. Berlant holds onto a tactical or strategic perspective on emotions: they enable the ongoing development of what she calls the "intimate public" (viii) of "women's culture" (ix). No doubt this is the case for the constellation of emotions traveling under the name "sentimentalism"—the primary topic of Berlant's work. But what of the emotions that lack this sort of strategic or tactical agency, that don't contribute to collectivities or even (perhaps loosely held) identities? What of emotions like boredom or distrust? A turn to cognitive science and an understanding of these emotions as evaluative or navigatory—but not necessarily tactical or strategic—can be very helpful. Chapters 3, 4, and 5 investigate three highly formalized sets of non-strategic emotives which navigate various systems and established schema. But there are other central methodological issues that need to be addressed before going much further. Reddy's account of emotives does not specifically discuss reading, and it is necessary to show in greater detail how the concept of emotives helps analyze certain kinds of reading.

On Reading Reading

Readers are capricious. They don't read in the ways that texts tell them to read, or according to the rules that they are told to read by, or in alignment with a particular aesthetic theory. Readers use texts in ways never imagined by the author, the text, or the culture. Nor can readers themselves tell us everything about their capricious reading. Their own accounts of reading are imbricated in the unstated, implicit rules of reading which govern their particular moment and situation in frequently unrecognized ways. When readers speak of their experiences of reading, they are only articulating partial truths. This is especially the case with an affective response to reading, if such response is understood as being a complex process.

Reddy doesn't discuss reading in any specific way when he develops his theory of emotives. He is most interested in first-person expressions of emotion—the kinds of utterances made face to face or in personal letters—perhaps because he does not want to take up the thorny, complex questions surrounding the relations between reader and text. But at points he does suggest that private, silent reading can be understood as a kind of emotive experience. It is not necessary in his view that emotives actually be spoken; readers might well "rehearse them in our speech center" (321). Texts which are "sensory-rich participatory performances"—this category includes "literature, art, music, iconography, architecture, dress"—"can be viewed as emotive in character" (331). Indeed, he notes that "[t]he subject matter of virtually all the disciplines of the humanities and social sciences can fruitfully be analyzed from this perspective [of emotives]" (331), and Reddy does turn to the eighteenth-century novels of sensibility to make his argument about French sentimentalism. But he doesn't discuss how this analysis of what could be called the third-person emotives of texts might work. He tacitly deploys a mirroring model of reading, where the reader is understood as reflecting an emotion signified in the text. But this is an oversimplified model. The emotion signified in the text may well be very different from the emotion experienced by the reader. Readers may be bored by a sentimentalism that attempts to inspire them; an ecstatic text may bring melancholy; a grossly dull text may amaze in certain respects. Sianne Ngai has coined a term, "stuplimity," (248) for the fairly common modern experience of reading a text (consider some works by Gertrude Stein) which produce a kind of sublimity through their stupefying repetitions. It is clear that the mirroring model of reading deserves to be met with some degree of suspicion.

However, Reddy in other respects does imply, without making it precisely evident, an extraordinarily complex and productive notion of the relation among texts, readers, and world. Texts and the emotives they generate function like experiments at linking readers to the world. They represent some part of that world or environment back to the reader so that the reader can evaluate it. This isn't to suggest a special position for the text-generated emotive outside the environment, in the way a long history of literary theorists (for example, Matthew Arnold or Lionel Trilling) have understood literature as occupying a special position allowing reflection on culture. Instead it is to suggest the kind of positive feedback system that evolutionary theory has used to explain the interactions among humans, culture, and the environment. In this view, experiments in the manipulation of the environment through tool use took advantage of anatomical changes in the hand, while anatomical changes in the hand facilitated experiments in tool use. Following this logic, the prehensile thumb is not the result of a change in the environment, the body, or the culture alone, but a result of the positive feedback system involving all three.[19] To return to our immediate concerns, the emotive may also be best understood as mutually constituted by text, reader, and cultural environment. Such circularity makes for a great deal of complexity for the analyst.

To summarize, Reddy's idea of emotives begins to open up the ways readers are understood as approaching texts. Literary studies has variously imagined readers as — here naming only four of many possibilities — identifying (and sometimes dis-identifying) with texts or parts of texts, decoding or diagnosing texts as if they were symptoms of deeper ideological structures or diseases, being hailed or interpellated by ideology through texts, and being alienated (sometimes negatively from oneself and one's labor and sometimes productively from interpellating ideology) by texts. Cultural studies (if a distinction can be made at this late date between literary and cultural studies) has focused on the way reading plays a role in the ongoing war of position for hegemony among various groups. But, understanding reading through Reddy's lens of emotives offers a different view, one that see the uses of reading differently than the above approaches without completely rejecting them. Reading reading through the emotive lens allows us to think about how reading is diagnostic, testing, operational, and navigating of the environment it represents and participates in.

This approach, as mentioned earlier, presents a number of complexities. Although all the complexities involved in such reading analysis can never be resolved completely, there is no secret to how to begin to address them. There is only the intricate work of reconstructing the reading experience using the tools at hand. The different approaches are well known: from the "implied reader" of the German reception theorists of the 1970s to the "informed reader" of Stanley Fish's "interpretative communities" to James Machor's "historical hermeneutics"; from Roger Chartier's notion of reading as a dialectic of "appropriation and imposition" to the concept of "articulation" outlined within (primarily British) cultural studies; from work on readers done in the sociology of literature or using Robert Darnton's concept of the "information circuit" to that done under the auspices of the experimental psychology of perception; and, most recently, from an old phenomenology of reading to a neophenomenology.[20] These methodologies have their advantages and disadvantages, as well as their compatibilities and incompatibilities. A bricolage approach is possible, but it does deserve a clear presentation. The chapters that follow pay close attention to the ways texts project readers. In the same way that Michael Fried and other art historians have analyzed the ways visual works of art always consider their beholders — indeed, constructing the very characteristics of "beholding" (96) — texts project characteristics of their reading. Sometimes they do this very explicitly, by providing a clearly articulated theory of reading (which the work may or may not hold to); other times they model the practice of reading through scenes of reading within the texts themselves. The texts' formal attributes—their plot structures, characterology, vocabularies, syntactic rhythms, topics of attention, generic expectations—also play a significant role in projecting reading's characteristics. Such formal elements have the ability to suggest reading which is variously embodied, absorptive, immediate, abstract, distant. The experience and practice of reading is also shaped by texts' material forms, paratactic elements, and modes of circulation. These ways of constructing the reading experience are intricately entwined with (that is, producing and produced by) the contexts of their receptions, which are cultural, political, and social, as well as individual.

Another approach to solving these problems of reader experience involves a particular orientation towards evidence, which is well described by Franco Morretti's term "distant reading" (57) as opposed to "close reading." Close reading is a "theological exercise" (57) in Moretti's view that necessarily depends on an extremely small canon. Alternatively, "[Distant reading] allows you to focus on units that are much smaller or much larger than the text: devices, themes, tropes—or genres and systems" (57). The benefit of reading from a distance is "understand[ing] the system in its entirety" (57)—not possible when focused on a small number of texts. There is an additional benefit for reader analysis gained from this focus on repeated and ritualized devices, themes, tropes, genres, and systems, and that is the identification of feedback loops between authors, publishers, and readers. When the same devices, themes, genres and other characteristics are frequently repeated by producers, it is possible to make an assumption, with some degree of accuracy, that readers are reacting in some way or another. That is, readers return again and again to certain elements, and these elements thus structure readers' experiences in significant ways. The following chapters focus on recognizing patterns across generic archives—the archives of discussion of good and bad reading and the archives of pornography, scandal, and religious fervor. In this way, *Fever Reading* isn't about idiosyncratically exceptional texts but everyday genres. Such genres provide the basis for some of the central emotional rituals of nineteenth-century America. The broadness of the evidentiary archives—or, put another way, the broadness of the data—means that the project can be statistically significant with respect to the claims it is making about reading and culture more generally.

This methodological approach can be presented more clearly with an example. The third chapter's discussion of "obscene literature" (the term "pornography" didn't exist at the time) examines the narrative structures, content and themes, material forms, modes of circulation, and general theory of reading that are ritualized across the genre. This archive also offers examples of scenes of reading and a recurring compositional strategy that encourages readers to project themselves into texts in certain ways. In turn, this genre- and text-focused analysis can be situated in the historical context of the discussion about good and bad reading (the subject of the next chapter) as well as discussions about the reading of other genres (like the sentimental, with which the pornographic exhibits similarities but also emphatic differences). Because "obscene readers" of this period rarely left any kind of explicit record (other than condemnation and arrest reports), no standard sociology of reader reception is possible. But it is possible by using the above methods to piece together the ways in which the genre frequently projects the relationship among readers, texts, and an idea of a public sphere. All readers might not have read in these ways (as unpredictable as individual readers are), but it is clear that the texts and contexts encouraged them to do so. "All works of art," notes the aesthetic theorist Nicolas Bourriaud, "produce a model of sociality" (104); he might also have said that they all produce a model of readers and a public sphere. That model is what the following chapters hope to recover.

An Addendum: Unanswered Questions

These introductory remarks situate this project in the recent theory and research on the public sphere, emotions, and reading, and outline some of the methodological questions and approaches that arise in examining their intertwined histories. These are the primary concerns of *Fever Reading*, but a number of other issues and questions have shaped the project.

First, the source material is limited, for the most part, to American archives. In many ways this has been difficult, but it was nevertheless necessary to accomplishing some of the project's central goals. The issues here span (at least) the Western world and Western modernity. With regard to reading, the United States was in no way exceptional, and the archives of good and bad reading in Germany, France, and England are extraordinarily rich. But while these contemporaneous but also distinct developments across the Atlantic have been enlisted as backdrop, the concentration on America allows for a deep focus on its shifts in political philosophy, economy, and notions of selfhood.

Second, the analysis focuses on texts of the early national through the antebellum period. The specifics of this timetable are easier to justify than the geographical restrictions. It was during this time that reading became, as the historian William Gilmore puts it, "a necessity of life" (21) and simultaneously a major cultural anxiety. The last decades of the eighteenth and the early decades of the nineteenth centuries witnessed the mass implementation of the ideology of the critical public sphere. These years—and especially the Jacksonian and antebellum years—also saw the rise of a mass-cultural book industry which encouraged an array of kinds of reading far different from the critical sort. The period of study ends in the second half of the nineteenth century, when reading was no less a necessity of life, but was significantly transformed by an explosion of what was "read"—especially in terms of visual and audio material. The new media landscape didn't mark a complete and utter break from the old media—and the idea of a critical public sphere continued—but the expansion of reading is significant enough and novel enough to serve as an end to this study.

A third issue involves the incompatibilities of social-constructionist humanistic studies and predict-and-control scientific studies. Multidisciplinary approaches are commonplace in the humanities, especially in cultural history, cultural studies, literary studies, American studies, and political theory. Interdisciplinarity is *de rigueur* in such disciplines, and *Fever Reading* takes as one of its main objectives the cross-pollination of these fields. But frequently interdisciplinarity does not take into account the profound incompatibility of some disciplines on certain points. Cognitive scientists and neural biologists, for instance, do not easily cotton to the idea that their findings are historically embedded social constructions, although scholarship in the humanities and social sciences has often suggested that emotion be understood as such. *Fever Reading* approaches such conflicts by abstracting a general structure of emotion from cognitive science and other sciences, one that is understood as universal across time and space. Emotion is evaluative, a complex process, and learned. These universal characteristics are then understood as encountering, shaping, limiting, and amplifying an array of historically contingent forces from ideologies to social reconfigurations to transformations in the book as a material object. Such an approach is not particularly complex or intellectually difficult, but it does produce an unusual kind of cultural history because it identifies a foundation, a constant thread, that is in some sense beyond history and serves as a force in history. *Fever Reading* is far from suggesting a biological or physiological determinism—I don't believe that biology (or any other foundation) is so strong as to determine everything else—but it does take biology and physiology seriously. One of the effects of this perspective is that past and present are joined more closely, and what they share makes the past that much more useful for the present.

Fourth, it is crucial to acknowledge that identity groups—informed by gender, race, ethnicity, and class—play important roles in determining the meaning of reading. Women in the eighteenth and nineteenth century, for example, were often thought to read differently than men. Reading held a dramatically different significance for slaves like Frederick Douglass than for whites like Douglass's masters. A book market specifically directed at working-class men—and which encouraged them to read in ways different from those of the middle classes—seems to have developed in northeastern urban centers in the mid-nineteenth century. Indigenous peoples in America have often used texts in ways distinct from Euro-Americans. The past three decades have produced considerable scholarship on the construction and meaning of these differences.[21] A recognition of them and of how they were constructed is woven through what follows, but gender, race, ethnicity, and class do not serve either as primary categories or lenses for analysis. For instance, religious tracts are not understood in chapter 5 through the lens of women readers; similarly, obscene reading is not investigated in chapter 3 using the category of working-class men to structure the analysis. I will not be making arguments that suggest readers formed "imagined communities" or "counterpublics" centrally based on gender, race, or class. These analytic categories can certainly be revealing with respect to these genres of reading, yet they can also be limiting, and not simply because the readers of these forms of print culture were not restricted to women or the working class, respectively. In what follows I attempt to capture and analyze the ways pornography, scandal papers, and religious tracts hailed their readers not as particular groups but as a mass, and how readers became aware of themselves—through reading—as participating in a mass public.

Ultimately, *Fever Reading* addresses a large subject in a relative short number of pages. The primary aim is not to provide an all-inclusive history of bad forms of reading, critical reading, pornography, scandal, and religious reading. It is, instead, an attempt to link certain parts of the history of reading with certain ideas about the public sphere which have been developed in political theory. It is an argument about how emotion and the public sphere might be better understood. It is also an example of how the experimental sciences might be usefully conjoined with the rhetorical sciences and the social sciences. But these lofty goals of inter-mixing disciplines and revaluing emotion in the public sphere should not obscure the fact that *Fever Reading* is deeply engrossed in the archive. Indeed, the title makes a distant reference to Jacques Derrida's *Archive Fever*, which had the French title, fittingly enough, *Mal l'Archive*—the bad archive, a trove of feverish reading which exceeds the conceptual frameworks buried in our epistemic methods, habits, biases, and com-mon sense, thus serving as a sign of that framework's inadequacy, its unwellness or disease. But the fever itself also suggests a response that might well lead to a cure.

Chapter Two

Good and Bad Reading in the Early United States

Reading Becomes a Problem

Although the indictments of reading badly are often accompanied by the breathless claim that we face a new cultural pathology (a "new kind of bacillus," as one commentator warns), there is nothing new about an anxiety associated with reading.[1] From Don Quixote's romance-induced insanity to the suicide-inducing *Wertherfiebre* in Goethe's Leipzig, from nineteenth-century reform tracts linking reading with masturbation to present-day fears that hypertextual reading might be making us all, as one author in the genteel *Atlantic* puts it, "stupid" (Carr 56), certain kinds (and ways) of reading have often inspired unease, fear, and even panic. Within this long history, the late eighteenth and early nineteenth centuries call for special attention, marking as they do a ferocious escalation in debates, theorizations, and conceptualizations around bad reading. In Germany the addiction to reading was given special names — *lesewut, lese-sucht, leseseuche,* and *schwärmer* — while in the English-speaking world a manic reader was dubbed a *helluo librorum,* a reading worm. Hundreds of articles appeared in U.S. newspapers and journals attempting to shape the way people read and what they read. These polemics went by titles like "On the Art of Reading," "On Novel Reading," "Novel-Reading a Cause of Female Depravity," "Reading and Information," "On the Ill Effects of Reading without Digesting," "On Reading to Excess," "Sewing and Novel Reading," "Reading Room Loafers," "The Injurious Influence of Fictitious Reading," "Daniel Webster's Reading Habits," and "Fatal

Effects of Reading Bad Books," to name only a few. The discourse about reading also took other forms, perhaps most famously in the commentaries within novels themselves about novel reading. But the worry over reading appears as well in conduct books, statistical accounts of modern life, obscenity laws, anti-masturbation screeds, and religious sermons and tracts. Reading improperly is associated with delusion, passivity, inattention, sexual depravity, social isolation, ruined wills, and ruined women, not to mention commodity fetishism, the eradication of agency, the loss of objectivity, the confusion of proper relations between mind and body, and a host of other problems. But it is also worth noting that these negative accounts of reading always implicitly (and often explicitly) picture good forms of reading. These debates over reading classify and hierarchize reading practices, outlining the proper and improper, providing a whole etiology and ethics of reading.

This chapter reads discourses of good and bad reading from the late eighteenth and early nineteenth centuries as ultimately about the developing idea of the public sphere in the early United States. It recovers the primary tenets of normative reading to better understand how they contributed to the development of that public sphere. Sometimes the issue of reading in these discussions is explicitly about the public sphere, but most often the discussions outline the normative structures for the self, the passions, and reason that make a particular kind of public sphere imaginable and possible. The good/bad reading discourse addresses questions like what sort of relation should one have with information, what kinds of understanding of the self should flourish, and what is the proper relation between reason and feeling—all questions with consequences for understanding the public sphere. All these relations changed over time, and this chapter shows how their changes are connected to changes in the understanding of the public sphere. The chapter has one additional goal: it seeks to identify where the norms of reading and the public sphere began to fracture and break apart. Even as it changed, the good/bad reading discourse remained essentially conservative and hegemonic. Whether it describes the dangers or the benefits of a relation between reader and text, its purpose is to interpellate readers. But in so explicitly outlining fears of bad reading, the discourse also indicates what doesn't fit into the norm; it suggests where normative ideas about the public sphere begin to break down. This is one reason the good/bad reading discourse of the newspapers and journals is so rich and helpful; unlike readers' accounts of their own reading and educators' accounts of reading pedagogies, both of which are often relatively unconflicted, the good/bad discourse offers a window into what troubles proper reading and why.

Before Public-Sphere Reading: Reading in Seventeenth- and Early Eighteenth-century New England

To understand why reading became viewed as a particularly pervasive problem in the late eighteenth century, it is necessary to see what earlier structures the new reading replaced. At that time, the normative structures of reading shifted in relation to the emergence of the idea of the public sphere. This is not to suggest that the older structures disappeared; they lived on in powerful ways, albeit transformed and with a different relevance and meaning. Defining normative structures of reading in America before the last third of the eighteenth century is difficult, because the period encompasses a large geographic and chronological swath. Even in the seventeenth century, when book circulation was limited, there were various types of reading, materials for reading, and genres of reading: Bibles, of course, and related religious material (psalters, devotional manuals, catechisms), but also business contracts, historical treatises, scientific discussions, almanacs, confession pamphlets, captivity narratives, obscene ballads and broadsides, and romances. A number of institutions of reading had developed, from the church to the university to the tavern to the frontier. It bears mention that books and other objects of print culture were not simply read in the standard sense. The Bible could be like a flag atop a pole in battle, a device of divination and decision-making, a totem to ward off Satan, a talisman to heal the sick (Cressy 94–95). The printed page provided housing insulation, kindling, pie-pan liner, and toilet paper. But even amid these diverse uses, forms, and structures of reading in seventeenth-century New England, an overarching ideal or ideology prevailed about its practice. Philosophically, the practice was grounded in reformist Protestantism's relation to the Bible—the idea that one achieved direct access to the Spirit through the biblical Word—but, as David D. Hall observes, this kind of textual relation with the Bible was a model for reading other kinds of texts, from histories to poetry to legal documents. Hall summarizes the idealized exercise: "To read or hear [read or recited] the Bible was to come directly into contact with the Holy Spirit. Scripture had no history, its pages knew no taint of time. Its message was as new, its power as immediate, as when Christ had preached at Galilee" (*Wonders* 24). Such a notion of unmediated contact with the spirit through the word encouraged what Matthew P. Brown has called "heart piety" (24): the idea that through reading the spirit is imprinted on the heart or the self. Or, as the *New-England Primer* would put it at the end of the seventeenth century and throughout the eighteenth, "My Book and Heart / Must never part," lines accompanied by a woodcut of book or Bible encircled by a heart (n.p.). The epigram and image dramatized the hope that such a reading practice would eliminate the distance between text and self. This mode of religious reading constituted a "vernacular" practice, to use Hall's word, not the elaborately theorized hermeneutical or higher criticism developed during the Middle Ages. All might participate (all capable of a certain level of literacy, of course, but literacy in New England was by all accounts very high).

The ideology of heart-piety reading is theorized and exemplified at many moments in seventeenth-century discussions of reading. In a state of meditation the minister Thomas Shepard experiences the holy book as "set before my eyes," and there finds that God's "spirit should not teach but by the word, [and] that his word could not teach but by the spirit" (166). During the witch crisis, the reading of the Bible before the possessed sometimes exorcised the spirit possessing the witch. The minister Deodat Lawson recounts visiting the bedside of Thomas Putnam's wife, who in her possession seems to argue with an "apparition" about the existence of a biblical passage, and when Lawson finally reads the passage (the third chapter of Revelations), Satan is repelled and the woman returns to this world. Mary Rowlandson, in her well-known narrative of her capture in 1676 by the Narragansett and Wampanoag tribes during King Philip's War, repeatedly describes herself and her predicament as addressed directly by her Bible. More precisely, she believes herself to be addressed through her Bible by God:

> I cannot but take notice of the wonderful mercy of God to me in those afflictions, in sending me a bible. . . . I took the Bible, and in that melancholy time, it came into my mind to read first the 28th Chapter of Deuteronomy ["if thou harken unto the voice of the Lord thou will be blessed; if not thou will be cursed"], which I did, and when I had read it, my dark heart wrought on this manner, That there was no mercy for me that the blessings were gone, and the curses come in their

room, and that I had lost my opportunity. But the Lord helped me still to go on reading till I came to Chapter 30 the seven first verses, where I found, there was mercy promised again, if we would return to him by repentance; and though we were scattered from one end of the earth to the other, yet the Lord would gather us together, and turn all those curses upon our enemies. I do not desire to live to forget this scripture, and what comfort it was to me. (25–26)

Rowlandson practices a form of reading that she understands as actually guided by God's hand. She praises him for "sending me a bible," and he brings her to specific passages—"it came into my mind to read first the 28th Chapter of Deuteronomy" and "the Lord helped me still to go on reading till I came to Chapter 30"—which in turn provide guidance in her situation. Not only does God directly guide her to and through the text, but the text directly addresses her captivity: Deuteronomy 28 declares those disobedient toward God will lose their cities, suffer in captivity, and wander the earth with their enemies. The analogy is horrifyingly clear to Rowlandson, who has no need to explain the passage to her readers (she knows that they know it). A few pages later in her account, God's hand again seems to be on hers as she turns the pages of her book: "before this doleful time ended with me [where God seems to provide no guidance], I was turning the leaves of my Bible, and the Lord brought to me some scriptures" (60–61). When guided in this manner, there is hardly any need for exegetical method or other forms of mediation to explain the text. Indeed, it's not a "text" at all but the voice and hand of the divine. In fact, if the spirit was the word, and the word was the spirit, there might not be any need to read at all. Reading itself might be an avoidable mediating practice, and the book itself might be all that is necessary. Thus in seventeenth-century New England, Bibles could become totems and talismans, carried like flags into battle and randomly opened with a faith that providence would guide the hand to the right passage.

David Hall notes that this vernacular reading practice applied to print culture beyond the Bible and other sacred texts. Common in seventeenth-century New England writings was the trope of the book-as-a-life. Anne Bradstreet's testament of her spiritual life (addressed to her children to be read after her death) begins with a poem expressing the text's living quality: In "This Book," she tells those readers left behind by her death, "you may find / What was your living mother's mind" (quoted in Hall,

Worlds 28–29). Michael Warner similarly observes that *The Book of the General Lawes and Libertyes* (1620) is prefaced by a command to the reader to overcome the mediation of the law's printed quality: "When Laws may be read in men's lives, they appear more beautiful than in the fairest Print, and promise a longer duration, then engraven [*sic*] in Marble" (quoted in *Letters* 19). Even current events and the natural world could be read as the Bible was read, as the Puritan tradition of typology suggests. Puritan history was a repetition of biblical history (the original type within the structure of typology). From epidemics to conflicts with natives, from storms to earthquakes, the history of everyday New England was understood as a repetition of Old Testament events and thus a kind of direct communication with God. Typological reading of this sort was a kind of public form of Rowlandson's private reading practice. In both instances the text is addressed directly to the reader.

Even while New England's radical Protestants practiced a form of reading that emphasized immediacy and lack of mediation, it was of course a practice that depended on considerable mediation and interpretation, as present-day commentators like Hall, Warner, and Brown fully understand. Reading in the way Rowlandson reads may have seemed like a self-evident activity to many seventeenth-century readers, but it required an immense amount of education (the knowledge of scripture), the cultivation of a particular relation with the scripture, and an obfuscation of the ways texts were mediated by markets, gift economies, and their own materiality. For instance, direct-access reading required one to forget that one's reading was structured by decisions over what was financially feasible to print, by the obligations associated with the gift of a book from the church or clergy (a frequent occurrence), or by what the state would allow to be printed at the presses in Cambridge and Boston, or imported from London. Michael Warner sees such a highly controlled and structured reading practice as indicative of the ways reading was a "technology of the self," and he remarks while discussing Cotton Mather that "[t]he ideal that Mather articulates here [about reading] contains a norm for subjectivity: reading, ideally, is a way of internalizing that is simultaneously a feature of literacy and a feature of the sacred order" (*Letters* 19). Following a similar line of thought, Hall comments that "[l]earning how to read and becoming 'religious' were perceived as one and the same thing" in seventeenth-century New England (*Worlds* 18). Normative, religious subjects were taught to see themselves simultaneously as autonomous — free of the clerisy, free of the market — and as under the power and authority of the word. The text's authoritative address of the reader is often represented spatially in the accounts of reading, so that Shepard says the holy book in his vision was "set before my eyes," as both a gift from God and a command to read, and Lawson says even Satan "*cannot stand before that text!*" because of its overwhelming authority (157–58). The freedom attained through reading the Bible and the subjectivication required in reading it correctly were in this sense one and the same in the discipline of seventeenth-century Protestant reading in New England. In fact, because these reading practices allowed readers like Rowlandson so much autonomy and freedom—removing any liturgical interference or apparatus—they had to be carefully pedagogicalized and even policed. John Winthrop reports in his journal that the governor of Hartford's wife "was fallen into a sad infirmity, the loss of her understanding and reason, which had been growing upon her divers years, by occasion of her giving herself wholly to reading and writing." Like the women involved in the antinomian and witchcraft crises, it seems that the governor's wife had begun to unsettle the unspoken structures, embedded in Puritan understandings of reading practices, that mystified the relations between autonomy, supplication, and the social order. In the end, her condition was severe, and "no help could be had" (April 13, 1645). There was a thin line between proper and pathological ways of melding text and self, especially for women. Such moments call attention to the way that the Protestant Reformation contributed to the spread of a hermeneutics of the text, where the possibility of multiple interpretations was recognized. Talmudic and Christian hermeneutical interpretative practices had long recognized such a possibility, but the Protestant focus on the individual's relation with the word couldn't help but propagate the idea beyond a professional class of readers. In this respect, the vernacular style of heart-piety reading sowed the seeds of its own destruction.

Matthew Brown calls attention to the difficulties that seventeenth-century New England's book market posed to the development of public-sphere or civic reading. The small size of the market combined with state governance over the presses in both New England and England restricted the range of competing ideas expressed in the public sphere. Books were certainly understood to have public significance—houses were inspected to make sure they had Bibles, and bad reading practices were disciplined because they were a perceived threat to social structures—but, as Brown says, "[a]ny notion that books acquaint readers with a range of ideas and

opinions and thus promote critical thinking would be especially quali-
fied in the print marketplace of early New England" (24). Warner notes
that the seventeenth-century ideology of reading as heart piety also made
a critical public sphere impossible. "Sacred internalization," Warner
writes, "renders the nature of print in such a way that the publication of
broadsides or newspapers could only be seen as inferior uses accidental
to the godly effort to 'print' the divinely ordained laws 'in our hearts.'
In this case we do not see individuals emancipated by print; instead, it
is the individual who is printed from an authoritative stamp" (*Letters*
19–20). Warner suggests here that reading in the name of heart piety did
not cultivate the kind of critical distance and sense of self-determination
that is needed to imagine a modern, critical public sphere.

The seventeenth century's ideologies of reading continued long into
the eighteenth century. Hall and Elizabeth Carroll Reilly indicate that
"[t]he most pervasive framework of meaning in eighteenth-century
America was not new but old, the nexus between reading and the inner
self that Protestants had taken over from the middle ages and refash-
ioned in the sixteenth and seventeenth centuries" (*Colonial Book* 405).
Indeed, the kind of heart-piety reading Brown describes only becomes
more intense. Around the Great Awakening, the spiritual autobiography
commonly described a kind of apostolic reading, where the flame or light
of God enters the body and transforms the self. The most famous example is provided by Jonathan Edwards, who describes in his "Personal
Narrative" (1739) an experience that at first seems to resemble Rowlandson's and others of the seventeenth century: the Scripture addresses him
directly, and it gives him direct access to God beyond interpretation. But
this reading experience is different in that it demands non-negotiable
submission, going so far as to destroy the old so as to build the new:

> As I read the words [1 Timothy 1:17], there came into my soul, and
> was as it were diffused through it, a sense of the glory of the Divine
> Being; a new sense, quite different from anything I ever experienced
> before. Never any words of Scripture seemed to me as these words
> did. I thought with myself, how excellent a Being that was; and how
> happy I should be, if I might enjoy that God, be wrapped up to God
> in heaven, and be as it were swallowed up in him. I kept saying, and
> as it were singing over these words of Scripture to myself; and went to
> prayer, to pray to God that I might enjoy him; and prayed in a manner
> quite different from what I used to do. (284)

This is a near mystical experience where, through reading, one is incorporated into the godhead—"wrapped up," "swallowed up." The relation between subject and object disappears. The meaning or interpretation of the actual passage read doesn't matter; instead, it turns into a primarily aesthetic, ritualistic, and affective experience: Edwards sings the words repeatedly to himself. This is different from the reading of Rowlandson and Shepard, for whom the passages are still important in terms of content and often provide insight and guidance relevant to a specific situation. It is essential that Rowlandson be guided to Deuteronomy 28 and 30. But for Edwards, cognition of the actual words seems much less important. What little distance there was between text and reader in much seventeenth-century reading has now vanished. This form of reading is frequently repeated in the eighteenth century, even among a much less learned class of readers and writers. The Connecticut farmer Nathan Cole writes in his spiritual autobiography,

> I was filled with a pineing [sic] desire to see Christs [sic] own words in the Bible, and I got up off my bed being alone; and by the help of Chairs I got along to the window where my bible was and I opened it and the first place I saw was 15th Chap.: John—on Christ's own words and they spake to my heart and every doubt and scruple that rose in my heart about the truth of God's word was took right off; and I saw the whole train of Scriptures all in a Connection, and I believed I felt just as the Apostles felt and truth when they writ it, every leaf line and letter smiled in my face: I got the bible up under my Chin and hugged it; it was sweet and lovely; the word was nigh me in my hand, then I began to pray and to praise God. (quoted in *Colonial Book* 406; original 96)

Again, the actual meaning of the words on the page disappears; the print doesn't become song in this instance but art and affect: "every leaf line and letter smiled in my face." The Bible doesn't swallow Cole up, as it does Edwards, but he does embrace it like a dear relative or friend. Such intense and affective experiences sometimes border on the terrors of the sublime, as they do in Abigail Hutchinson's reading in the 1740s (as told to Jonathan Edwards) where "there was a sudden alteration, by a great increase of her concern, in an extraordinary sense of her own sinfulness, particularly the sinfulness of her nature, and wickedness of her heart, which came upon her (as she expressed it) as a flash of lightning, and struck her into an exceeding terror" (Edwards, *Revivals*, 88).

The intensification of these extreme forms of piety reading was surely in part generated by a sense of embattlement caused by the emergence of a print culture more vast and more competitive than the one that existed in the seventeenth century. Edwards and other Great Awakening ministers were both participants in and objects of commentary in an inter-colonial collection of newspapers, magazines, and pamphlets. This new public sphere did not encourage an ideology of reading as pious internalization of the word/spirit but of reading as part of a debate. In a kind of antinomian response, Edwards and others developed a form of apostolic reading, yet this was really the last gasp of heart-piety reading as a majority vernacular form. Universities and other educational institutions, newspaper and periodical culture, reading societies, social and circulating libraries, and the careful delineation and hierarchizing of genres (especially the new genre of the novel) all determined the ways texts were received and interpreted, and these ways greatly differed from the former religious ways. It would be impossible here to discuss each of these reading cultures, but I do want to suggest that they shared some basic tenets, and that these arose in league with ideas about the public sphere.

A signal moment in the development of this new public sphere occurred in 1719 when a second newspaper commenced publication in Boston: the *Boston Gazette*. The first Boston paper was the *Boston News-Letter*. Established in 1704, it was the first continuously printed paper in British America and, for the first fifteen years of its existence, mainly published (or, more accurately, republished) outdated news reports from London. The *News-Letter* wasn't governed by the senses of nowness, topical debate, or locality that are usually associated with the news; generically, it was akin to reading a history. But the *Gazette*, as well as a third Boston paper, the *New-England Courant* (established in 1721), printed letters from readers which discussed local issues and encouraged debate. James Franklin, associated with both the later papers, organized the *Courant* along the model of Addison and Steele's *Tatler* and *Spectator* in London. Presiding over Franklin's *Courant* was Mr. Spectator's equivalent, "old Janus," "who is a Man of such remarkable *Opticks*, as to look two ways at once." The cultural historian David S. Shields suggests that the guiding presence of Janus might well be understood as "print itself" (266) personified. Or, perhaps more accurately, Janus is a metaphor for a particular relation with print. Janus is a reader of the paper as much as he is its producer (after all, the paper was in large part composed of readers' letters). The *Courant* outlines this relation in a passage that begins as an observation about diversity of opinion but becomes a meditation on reading and interpretation under the new conditions of news publication, which emphasized competition of opinions:

> There is nothing in which Mankind reproach themselves more than in their Diversity of Opinion. Every Man sets himself above another in his own Opinion, and there are not two Men in the world whose Sentiments are alike in every thing. Hence it comes to pass, that the same Passage in the Holy Scriptures or the Works of the Learned, are wrested to the meaning of two opposite Parties, of contrary Opinions, as if the Passages they recite were like our Master *Janus*, looking *two ways at once*, or like Lawyers, who with Equal Force of Argument, can plead either for the *Plaintiff* or *Defendant*.[2]

At the beginning of this passage, a style of reading that could look "*two ways at once*" is understood as a natural sentiment but, by the end, it is associated directly with Janus's newspaper production. Such a relation to texts might be understood as underwriting the reader's freedom, choice, and autonomy, as it would later in the eighteenth century but, for the Boston authorities of the 1720s, it was a threat. In 1723 James Franklin served a stint in jail for libel and was eventually forced out of the paper and out of Massachusetts.

James's brother Benjamin met a somewhat better fate. Although Benjamin Franklin, it is sometimes surprising to remember, was a contemporary of Jonathan Edwards, his *Autobiography* (begun in 1771) provides a picture of reading very different from Edwards's "Personal Narrative." Franklin discusses reading dozens of books that "[i]nfluence" him, as he says of Cotton Mather's *Bonifacius* (9), but they surely don't transform him by obliterating his old self and opening him up to God. Instead, he transforms the books, using them as models for what he might write or examples of what he might print and sell. Indeed, Mather's book "influenced" Franklin by providing the target of a spoof he wrote under an early pseudonym "Silence Dogood." Franklin thinks of books not as sacred objects but as information-delivery technology, as exemplars whose styles might be copied (as he does with a volume of the *Spectator*), and as commodities. *Pilgrim's Progress* is one of his favorite books, but after reading it as a boy, Franklin sells his volume in order to buy new books. Later, on his way by boat to Philadelphia, he pulls a drowning man from Raritan Bay and finds in his pocket a copy of *Pilgrim's Progress*, a discovery that is much more interesting to Franklin than his own life-saving heroics. He comments on the book as a beautiful commodity, not an allegory. Franklin frequently relates books to other books (the style of *Pilgrim's Progress*, he tells his reader, influenced the style of Defoe and Richardson), and he often speaks of books and reading as forming the foundation of interaction with others and community life. He trades poems and writing with friends in a kind of ongoing writing contest; he borrows books from friends to solidify his relationships with them.

The kind of reading that Franklin describes is central to a modern, critical public sphere of the sort that Jürgen Habermas discusses emerging in Europe and that Michael Warner has charted arising in the American colonies and the early republic in *The Letters of the Republic*. The kind of reading that Rowlandson, Lawson, Edwards, and others describe is also part of a public sphere, but theirs differs substantially from the one in which Franklin understands himself to be a participant. In Franklin's public sphere, reading is extensive instead of intensive; it is about community interaction rather than individual transformation; books are commodities and information, not totems or sacred relics; reading is detached and self-directed rather than consuming and involuntary.

Franklin does not explicitly theorize public-sphere power, but theorizations of this power do appear in eighteenth-century colonial publications with such clarity that it is worth pausing over one account. In 1753, William Livingston celebrated the fact that "[t]he wide Influence of the Press is so dangerous to arbitrary Government, that in some of them it is shut up, and in other greatly restrained," and that

> [t]hro' the Press, Writers of every Character and Genius, may promulge [*sic*] their Opinions; and all conspire to rear and support the Republic of Letters. The Patriot can by this Means, diffuse his salutary Principles thro' the Breasts of his Countrymen, interpose his friendly Advice unasked, warn them against approaching Danger, united them against the Arm of despotic Power, and perhaps, at the Expense of but a few Sheets of Paper, save the State from impending Destruction.[3]

In Livingston's view it is essential that this "Republic of Letters" be made up of many individuals, in large part regardless of status ("of every character and genius"). With the "Art of Printing," he says, "The Public has the Advantage of the Sentiments of all its Individuals." That public is a collection of many, and its members cannot be known with any sort of specificity. In fact, Livingston notes that this abstraction of the individual is one of printing's benefits. He calls it "secrecy," since "by Means of this Art [of secrecy] he [the author] may write undiscovered, as it is impossible to detect him by the Types of the Press." Critical discussion among such abstract individuals can lead to the regulation of "arbitrary Government" and "the Arm of despotic Power."

Livingston was writing in 1753. In 1790, James Madison thought of public opinion in similar terms — as developed by a collection of disinterested and educated citizens: "Those philosophical and patriotic citizens who cultivate their reason" (500–501, quoted in Wood, *Empire* 309).[4] Madison, like Hamilton and a large proportion of Hamiltonian Federalists, and even like some aristocratically inclined (almost always Southern) Republicans, thought of public opinion in semi-Habermasian terms. In this view, an unbiased elite would argue issues among themselves and from that discussion would emerge truth that could be acted upon. The free discussion grounded the agency of the truth. But at almost the same moment that Madison and others were putting forth this view, a different, more democratic idea of public opinion was vying for dominance, one that spoke of "an aggregation of individual sentiments" from any number of participants from any and all walks of life that would lead to "the ultimate triumph of truth." In this view, public opinion was derived from a multitude of sources and even the rabble itself. It depended as much on "sentiments" as on cultivated "reason" (Wortman 118–19, quoted in Wood, *Empire* 311). For Thomas Jefferson it didn't matter if those opinions were "false, scandalous, and malicious" for, as Jefferson theorized, they could "stand undisturbed as monuments of the safety with which error of opinion may be tolerated where reason is left free to combat it" (493, quoted in Wood, *Empire* 310). Jefferson is here arguing for understanding public opinion as a free market of ideas, one open to all, and truth as a kind of wisdom of the crowds, in our contemporary parlance. The idea that falsehoods and scandal might mingle freely with truth and reason in the public sphere infuriated Federalists of the 1790s. But the Federalists were on the wrong side of the great social transformations put in motion by the American Revolution. The voice of the emerging "middling sort" began to enter the public sphere, especially through the rise the republican press in the 1790s. The Sedition Act of 1798 was an attempt to control this new kind of public sphere, to bring it back to the Federalist's genteel ideal. The act criminalized the writing, printing, voicing, or publishing of anything "false, scandalous, and malicious" about the federal government, the president, or members of the House and Senate. But the dye was cast. In place was the idea of a democratic public sphere located in the public press (rather then the personal letters of the genteel) that could produce knowledge and truth. It would serve as an ideal going forward.

Livingston, Jefferson, and Madison don't have much to say about reading in this prescient outline of a modern public-sphere ideal, but little more than a decade and half after Madison and Jefferson's remarks, reading would begin to become a central topic of conversation in the newspapers and journals of the new republic. Before that, there is almost no mention of reading as a topic to be theorized or worried about in American magazines or newspapers, or in the broader culture. Seventeenth- and early eighteenth-century colonial writers read in specific ways, as I've indicated, but rarely were those reading practices pored over and scrutinized at the time. They are seldom self-consciously brought into view as practices and are never understood in the popular press as one among many possible practices. There are some panics over bad reading in early eighteenth-century New England—namely, the obscenity controversies in Northampton, Massachusetts, and New London, Connecticut—but these didn't lead to an extensive theorization of reading practices. All of this, however, changed in the last third of the eighteenth century.

Public-Sphere Reading: Good
and Bad Reading, 1780s–1850s

The sense of threat arose partially from a fear of the public's growing access to texts and of an emerging mass audience. The control of reading practices was a way of controlling readers' relations with this new media environment. At the beginning of the nineteenth century, editorials repeatedly mention that there is just too much printed matter, requiring too much reading. "Too much reading is injurious," counsels a journal in 1802, and another echoes it in 1804: "we should be content with few books, and study them perfectly."[5] As the first decades of the century unfold, the rhetoric about the onslaught of print becomes more hyperbolic. In 1808 one writer complains about "that heterogeneous mass [of books] which is daily accumulating from every quarter of the literary world," and another writer, several years later, laments that "the world is deluged with books, reviews, pamphlets, and newspapers, it is no easy task for common readers to direct their attentions so wisely, that much of their time shall not be lost, and worse than lost, by an injudicious choice of matter."[6] By mid-century the flood—especially of cheap novels—has reached biblical proportions: "And thus a plague has come upon the land. We are overrun with novels. They come into our houses like the frogs of Egypt, filling even our kneading troughs. Go where we may— into railroad cars, or into the cabins of ships or steamboats, we find chairs, sofas, and tables, spread with this yellow-covered Literature."[7] Even if the increase in print media in the late eighteenth and early nineteenth centuries does not in retrospect look like an explosion compared to what occurred just a few decades later (with the advent of new printing technologies in the 1830s), it was nevertheless perceived in this way by many. The structuring of reading as a problem and the accompanying rules about proper reading are easy to understand as a way of coming to terms with this new media environment.

Another explanation for the period's anxious focus on reading is the fact that, by definition, a republic founded on a written constitution foregrounds questions of reading and textual interpretation. Alexander Hamilton clearly and repeatedly expresses the fear that the everyday reader of the Constitution will be a bad one. The first five paragraphs of his introduction to the *Federalist Papers* are preoccupied with the ways that reading and reason can go wrong under the sway of "ambition," "avarice," "personal animosity," "jealousy," "violent love," "enthusiasms of liberty," and "illiberal distrust." Such "views, passions, and prejudices," Hamilton reiterates to his reader, are "little favorable to the discovery of truth."

Commentators in the early republic reacted to these anxieties by creating elaborate discourses about proper and improper reading. In what follows I turn to the ubiquitous topics of these discussions—the sociality of reading, the proper methodologies of reading, and the problems with novel reading—to explain how they encouraged a particular understanding of the public sphere. These discourses on proper reading go hand in hand with those on the dangers of reading and, in turn, the dangers identified point toward tensions in the version of the public sphere imagined by those proper practices.

THE SOCIALITY OF READING

Reading was not to be a private act, according to the discourse about good and bad reading in the early United States. It was to be outwardly oriented, toward a collection of friends, a group of conversationalists and, in some instances, a more general, abstract public. Reading is often presented in the late eighteenth century as both a form of conversation (with authors who are themselves friends and citizens) and as a topic of conversation (with friends and other individuals). Typical is this comparison of good reading to good conversation, from 1793: "Some books are to be read once and some always to be read, just as we find some persons in the world whose company we never wish to be in a second time, and others whom we wish to be with often, and always, if it were possible."[8] The same author notes that reading should be like "the most instructive conversation"; another author, writing in 1797, suggests that the conversation one experiences when reading is superior to ordinary, face-to-face conversation because it connects us with an abstract public beyond our immediate group of friends and acquaintances: "By reading of books we may learn something from all parts of man-kind; whereas by observation we learn all from ourselves, and only what come within our own direct cognizance; by conversation we can only enjoy the assistance of very few persons, viz. those who are near us, and live in the same time as we do, that is our neighbors and contemporaries."[9] Reading was conceived as a "silent conversation"[10] and a way of "conversing with men of sense and genius."[11] Like conversation with one's friends and associates, reading shaped character, for "[t]he character of a man is as much indicated by the books and papers which he reads as by the company with which he associates," as *Scientific American* reported.[12] Even novels could make decent companions. Although the novel has long elicited some of the fiercest paroxysms about bad reading, novels did garner support from some, who argued that such books forced readers outward into a conversation with the world. For instance, a commentator in 1826 writes, in a tentative defense, that "[n]ovel reading is in some measure a substitute for company. . . . Novel reading is not company, but it gives us some notion of the manner in which other people live."[13]

But books were seen not only as a means for having conversations, they also were meant to be topics of conversation. In the early 1790s a "member of the Belles-Letters Society at Dickinson College" indicates the importance of being in conversation with others about one's reading. Parents and friends should recommend those books that were "most proper and profitable" so that young people "would experience the most satisfaction in the company of persons of understanding."[14] In a similar fashion, a journal contributor calling herself Mrs. Chapman suggests to young women that, from their reading of history, they recount "interesting passages to a friend, either by letter or conversation."[15] Mrs. Chapman goes on to explain that "[b]y such conversation . . . you will learn to select those characters and facts which are best worth preserving."[16] There is certainly a disciplinary function at work here: reading—especially reading by the young—needs oversight. But there is also the idea that conversation about reading precipitates judgment, taste, and discrimination. "By this means," the belles-lettres society member says, "judgments ripen and strengthen." Such a rationale wasn't prevalent only in belletristic societies; a contributor to the *Lowell Offering* (the paper of the "factory girls" in the United States' first planned industrial city) offers similar logic. "But by what test shall we decide the merit of books?" she asks. "[L]et us gather around us a choice circle [of books]," she responds to her own question, "from the good and wise of all ages and commune with them until we can appreciate and delight in the truths which they teach . . . that we may unpresumptuously style them 'our own familiar friends.'" Only then will the paper's readers know how to "discriminate" among them.[17] Discussion of the kinds of reading that contribute to publicly derived judgment is often repeated in connection with early lending libraries, which were indeed like parliaments or national conventions in the sense that they featured individuals engaged in "disputation." A correspondent in 1798 reports back to the young United States about "reading shops" in Paris "which may deserve imitation in other countries." Such institutions have "done more to form the public mind of the Parisians than the disputation of the National Convention." One Paris shop calls itself "the Cradle of Opinion" and another "the Coffin of Prejudice." The reading of newspapers is also frequently conceived of as a new form of community. The world without such newspaper reading looks primitive and provincial, and individuals in it are deprived of a certain kind of power: "Before newspapers were in use, local knowledge was so circumscribed, that few gentlemen knew more of politics, or contemporary affairs, than what government pleaded to discover."[18] These frequent depictions of reading as a kind of communal conversation are obviously very different from the seventeenth-century New Englanders' conception of reading as a mode of communication with God, not others. Such depictions also differ significantly from those of the Great Awakening's spiritual autobiographies, in which individual self-transformation was at stake. Instead, reading has become a model of sociality. This later period prizes outwardly oriented reading as another form of public interactivity. As one newspaper sums up the situation, "It is with books as with society."[19]

There were dangers, however, to this community-oriented reading. First, discriminating among texts was not always an easy task, especially with so many possibilities. If books were friends, they could also be foes. With a playful double entendre, one journal jokes, "Truly, intercourse with bad books is often more dangerous than intercourse with bad men."[20] Second, good reading—that is, reading oriented toward conversation and public discussion—could be mirrored by bad reading, characterized in the periodicals as selfish and absorbing. A commentator in the *Virginia Evangelical and Literary Magazine* condemns an "excessive spirit of reading as a very selfish propensity" and declares such readers as possessing "the hateful characteristic of absorption."[21] Although there were dangers perceived in spending too much time in the general activity of reading, the most dangerously absorptive kind of reading was acknowledged to be novel reading. The reading of novels (and their close relatives, romances) is sometimes compared to being irrationally absorbed in one activity—often a physical activity with addictive potential like eating, drinking, or even opium smoking.[22] Reading novels is also closely connected to another solitary, absorptive pastime: masturbation.

The historian Thomas Laqueur has thoroughly documented the ways in which masturbation and certain kinds of reading were linked as problems in the long eighteenth century in Europe. Laqueur points out that both activities were thought dangerous because they encouraged an absorption into privacy and the imagination that threatened proper socialization into capitalist, rationalist modern structures (302–17 and 320–58). In the United States, the same connections and arguments were increasingly made during the first part of the nineteenth century. Translations of long, dense anti-masturbation tracts, like those of Samuel-Auguste Tissot, began to be published in New York and other East Coast cities in the early 1830s. Tissot often warned of the dangers of reading too sensually and suggested avoiding books that encouraged such reading (110, 112). In the 1840s, such treatises were transformed into short, accessible pocket books, produced by American reformers and directed at a mass audience. In these texts, a preoccupation with the connection between reading and masturbation became even more intense. Reading in bed is warned against, for there the "mind becomes fascinated with the morbid gratification of exciting and libidinous reading and imaginings" (Bell 51). One commentator notes that "numerous causes tend to deprave the feelings, and pollute the imagination"; as it turns out, most of those causes are closely connected to the culture industry: "books, pictures, the light reading that covers the land, in the form of novels, magazines, papers, filled with stories, tales, verses, and all spiced with love or grosser sentiments, to adapt them to popular tastes" (Cutter 44). The over-investment of self and the senses that such books required did not fulfill proper models of sociality.

METHODS OF READING

One antidote to absorption into the text was distantiation from the text, and distancing and detachment could be achieved through specific methods of abstracting and extracting. In a significant departure from the seventeenth- and eighteenth-century discourse of vernacular religious reading, the popular discourse around reading at the end of the eighteenth century often encouraged readers to read like lab technicians, dismantling and reconstructing texts. One writer suggests that readers transform poetry into prose so as to "divest both [the poetry and the prose] from their outward ornament."[23] A newspaper suggests that to avoid getting lost in a book, one should read it aloud.[24] Both of these techniques of reading as transposition (poetry to prose, written to spoken) are meant to fend off a dangerous absorption in form. In addition, they help the reader achieve power over texts, rather than vice versa. The reading techniques also assist in clearly objectifying and extracting the content of the text without the confusion of subjective responses to ornaments. Furthermore, a reader reading in this way is encouraged to understand content as always mediated—in this case by form (poetry or prose) and even by textuality (as in the second example).

Many of these ends—a power over the text, a resistance to absorption, a sense of mediation—also could be developed through a common reading technique involving note-taking and annotation. Customary in the popular press of the period is the admonition that one read with pencil in hand, so as to "underline" or "make an asterisk over the first line" of an interesting passage and "make a small abstract of memorable events (especially when reading history)."[25] The correspondent "Crito" suggests a kind of "encyclopedic reading" in which people read widely, then make abstracts of their reading for their own review.[26] The novelist Charles Brockden Brown, in his comments on reading in 1806, praises the reading of indexes, suggesting that the index is a pathway to gaining control over a text. "An index-reader," he writes, is "let into the secrets of an author."[27] Another work suggests the careful parsing of books, recommending that, at first, one read the preface, read in "a more general and cursory manner," and "survey the table of content" as overview.[28]

Much of this methodologized reading seems commonplace to us today, especially for university humanities professors, highly trained as we are in such routines of close reading (which paradoxically involve distance from the text rather than closeness). However, for readers like Rowlandson and Edwards, such techniques would seem very strange indeed. They had their own methods of reading, but those methods did not require this kind of abstracting and detachment, and their use often remained implicit. Such methodologies of reading were not an invention of the late eighteenth and early nineteenth centuries, but they do at that time become a topic of mass conversation and mass pedagogy, while previously they had been the domain of specialists. This was the case, perhaps most obviously, because such techniques helped readers sort out and organize an ever-increasing amount of print culture. But the distancing, abstracting, and transposing also helped readers turn their reading into objects that might be transmitted and shared. For the content of reading to travel, to be replicable, it has to be separate and at a distance from the self. The public sphere as Livingston and Habermas imagined it relied on this kind of reading and this kind of relation to texts.

The practice of transposing and abstracting was in part meant to reiterate the reader's command over the text, just as the practice of treating reading as a mode and object of conversation was intended to resist the reader's absorption in the text. Such practices of reading were ways of underlining and inculcating a sense of the reader's autonomy and agency. For one commentator, applying a strict method to reading did not abrogate the individual's power of choice but went hand in glove with it: "for reading without method, choice, or taste affords but little real improvement to the mind."[29] It took labor, but repaid that labor with autonomy. As one newspaper writer remarks, in a discussion of the way reading difficult texts can at first seem like hard work, "what began in labor or necessity, becomes the choice."[30] Indeed, one of the most common observations about proper reading is that it is labor—rewarding labor that allows readers to actualize themselves.

Understood in this way, reading can be construed as anti-authoritarian. The author "Arc-En-Ciel" notes that "[t]he knowledge acquired from pursuits [of reading] thus dictated by choice, makes, perhaps, more useful impressions, than all the learning of the schools."[31] The same author remarks that he has a "library rather considerable" but that "it is composed of books all chosen for my own use." Reading, learning, book buying, and library construction were ways of demonstrating the power of the individual to choose and also the power to "use" what is chosen. Yet, the connection between reading and choice should not be reflexively understood as liberating; it was no less a "technology of the self" than heart-piety reading. It inculcated readers into a particular social order that prized individual autonomy. While it could be anti-authoritarian with respect to some institutions, it also accustomed its practitioners to hard labor and strict method (which encouraged a detached, objective relation to information). Proper reading of this kind tends to mystify its own structures. Strict method was represented as freedom. As choice and autonomy became thematized attributes of proper relations with texts, they were also perceived as constantly threatened, thereby re-enforcing the norm. The sheer onslaught of print materials presents a problem, as the rising tide threatens to overwhelm one's own thoughts. As one writer notes in 1802, "Too much reading is injurious as the habit of receiving ideas from others prevents thinking."[32] The emphasis on choice and agency is mirrored by condemnations of submission and involuntary responses to print. Novels are a particular problem because they tell "that love is involuntary, and that attachments of the heart are decreed by fate."[33] Such novels teach of "personal attachment conceived at sight, and matured in a moment."[34]

But before I turn more fully to novel reading, a summation is in order. The primary point to make about these two discourses of proper reading—reading as sociality and reading as method—is that they helped put into place some essential ideas of the public sphere. Reading will be oriented toward others and the world; from the outward focus will precipitate knowledge and judgment. Reading will also reinforce the idea of the autonomous self who can make unbiased and objective evaluations; the knowledge and information developed through this reading will be akin to an object that is transferable between readers. In turn, these components of public-sphere reading are disciplined by the threat of bad, absorptive reading.

NOVEL READING

Scholars have long examined the illicitness of novel reading in the eighteenth and nineteenth centuries. Controversy over the possibly corrupting effects of Richardson's Lovelace, the *Wertherfiebre* sparked by Goethe, and the thematization of the ills of novel consumption in Madame Bovary are but the best known of hundreds of accounts preoccupied with the ill effects of novel reading. Michael Warner doesn't exaggerate when he says that Americans in the early republic wrote about their "fears [of fiction] in virtually every magazine and newspaper in the country; no figure of the period seems to have been exempt from the anxiety" (*Letters* 175). Novel reading seems to epitomize the disempowering absorption these writers feared. The apprehensions extended far beyond the early republic and appear repeatedly throughout the first six decades of the nineteenth century. The mass religious press that began to develop in the 1820s was particularly inimical to the novel and was often convinced of the form's depravity. By the 1840s and 1850s, as a belletristic novel culture became acceptable and professionalized, accounts of the evils of most types of novels began to abate. But American journals and newspapers during this period became increasingly concerned with a particular kind of novel—the cheap, sensational, yellow-covered novelettes rolling off the steam presses. The earlier discourse of bad reading was applied to this new form of print culture.

What is perhaps most interesting about this well-known fear of novel reading is that praise (or at least calm acceptance) of novel reading was as often expressed as condemnation. Indeed, acceptance and criticism could sit side by side in the same reader, as they did for Thomas Jefferson. In January of 1800, Jefferson, then serving as vice president of the United States, responded with praise to a first-time novelist's gift of his new book:

> Some of the most agreeable moments of my life have been spent in reading works of imagination, which have this advantage over history, that the incidents of the former may be dressed in the most interesting form, while those of the latter must be confined to fact. They cannot therefore possess virtue in the best and vice in the worst forms possible, as the former may.

The novelist is Charles Brockden Brown and the novel is *Wieland*. Brown's own letter to Jefferson, whom he did not know personally, is painfully respectful and anxiously hesitant. He fears that the novel—because it is fiction—will offend Jefferson. It doesn't contribute to the public sphere like other forms, such as "social and intellectual theories."[35] But Jefferson responds to Brown reassuringly, commenting that imaginative literature serves a pedagogical function: it teaches better than history about virtue and vice. But nearly twenty years later, in an 1818 letter to Nathaniel Burwell, Jefferson is less confident about the novel's ability to inculcate virtue and warn against vice:

> A great obstacle to good education is the inordinate passion prevalent for novels, and the time lost in that reading which should be instructively employed. When this poison infects the mind, it destroys its tone and revolts it against wholesome reading. Reason and fact, plain and unadorned, are rejected. Nothing can engage attention unless dressed in all the figments of fancy, and nothing so bedecked comes amiss. The result is a bloated imagination, sickly judgment, and disgust towards all the real businesses of life. This mass of trash, however, is not without some distinction; some few modeling their narratives, although fictitious, on the incidents of real life, have been able to make them interesting and useful vehicles of sound morality. Such, I think, are Marmontel's new moral tales, but not his old ones, which are really immoral. Such are the writings of Miss Edgeworth, and some of those of Madame Genlis. For a like reason, too, much poetry should not be indulged. Some is useful for forming style and taste. Pope, Dryden, Thompson, Shakespeare, and of the French, Molière, Racine, the Corneilles, may be read with pleasure and improvement.

Here Jefferson repeats what had, by 1818, become boilerplate condemnations of novels and other imaginative literature: for the most part they poison, waste time, derange the senses, and threaten moral reasoning. Yet, what is most interesting here is not the condemnation but the fact that some fictions and fiction-reading practices are acceptable and some not. He doesn't dismiss "pleasure," but pleasure must be useful; he doesn't reject the possibility of "interesting" fictional narratives, but they must be based in "real life." What Jefferson is praising here is just the right distance from the text and just the right level of absorption. One was to be infused with affect at the same time that one objectified the affect and understood it as part of moral and social practice.[36] Such sensible reading is a fragile practice. Jefferson himself doesn't seem quite able to define it—he can't explain why later Marmontel is more acceptable than earlier; he simply knows morality when he sees it. Such reading could easily result in its opposite. Portrayals of vice might well encourage vice rather than moral repulsion; portrayals of virtue might remain perfectly private—"pocket handkerchief sensibility," as one writer puts it. Reading with sensibility had to be carefully disciplined, or else the reader might well end up like young Werther or Emma Bovary.

If sensibility was so risky, why was it so central? Habermas suggests that the grand eighteenth-century novels of sensibility were actually essential to the development of the modern public sphere (*Structural*, 49–56). For him that public sphere was not simply grounded in reasoned debate but required the emotional component provided by sensibility. Sensibility allowed participants in the public sphere to see themselves as bonded with other participants through their shared humanity. In other words, sensibility for Habermas helped humanize and personalize the abstract, generalized subject that served as the foundation for the modern public sphere. It made the participants of the public sphere feel that they shared a status as common human beings. It also solidified the category of the "human" as a kind of foundational identity that was free, equal, and prior to ideology. Thinking of oneself as a human and thinking of oneself as a member of the public sphere become one and the same thing. In this way, a humanity-generating literature of sensibility authorized the public sphere.

The identification of the humanizing effects of sensibility with the abstract generality of the public sphere was (and is) extremely difficult to maintain, as Habermas well recognized. To begin with, women, servants, and other figures restricted from participation in the public sphere of political life were often some of the central participants in the public sphere of imaginative literature. It thus becomes difficult to sustain the assumption that sensibility's emotions are simply human and do not serve a particular class. Some emotions were seen as more proper than others. Thus the humanity-generating effects of sensibility had to be both promoted and strictly disciplined. People had to read (and thus feel) in the right ways, and we see examples of this in the debates over reading. Habermas allows us to see two things in such debates: first, that reading novels provided a central arena for developing the fragile connection between certain emotions and humanness; second, that there is not necessarily any conflict between emotion and reason, between the passions and the rational public sphere. Although this is a common argument, it should be made carefully; in the following chapters, I will address it with specific emphasis on the emotions of reading.

What we see established in these various discourses on reading is a particular idea, or even ideal, of the public sphere. There is little evidence that a public sphere of the sort projected by the forms of reading outlined here—that is, a public sphere founded on an abstract sociality of autonomous readers practicing a careful sensibility in relation to texts so as to produce objective knowledge—ever existed as an actuality. But it did exist as an idea, an ideal, and an ideology. This ideology of public-sphere reading was nurtured by a particularly American version of republican political theory, one that combined classical notions of republican virtue—which call for rising above private interests and define liberty as a share of the power of the state—with notions of a possessive individualism and a definition of liberty as personal freedom. This political philosophy supported the idea of a public sphere where private acts of reading are understood as part and parcel of participation in the public sphere, and meaning and judgment are constructed intersubjectively. The republican notions of individualism and private sacrifice did not always sit so easily with each other and, as the nineteenth century progressed, one side of the equation—the side that prized possessive individualism, a separation between private and public life, and personal freedom from the state—became more greatly valued. These are the values of liberalism but, while liberal modes of thinking replaced conflicted republicanism in many arenas (more on these liberal modes of reading in the next section), this wasn't precisely the case in the rhetoric surrounding reading and the public sphere or even surrounding the public sphere more generally. Throughout the nineteenth century, such rhetoric remained deeply republican. Even as it became increasingly difficult to see the republican public sphere as a reality, it remained a hegemonic ideal. We've seen how this was the case in the numerous evocations, in newspapers and journals, of reading as knowledge-generating conversation.

From Charles Brockden Brown to
Antebellum Reading: Liberalism and
the Hermeneutics of Reading

The historical trajectory outlined here—from heart-piety reading to public-sphere reading—is a trajectory roughly marked out by Jane Tompkins, albeit in somewhat different contexts and without an emphasis on the public sphere. In "The Reader in History: The Changing Shape of Literary Response" (1980), Tompkins takes the long view, beginning with Plato and concluding with deconstruction and reader-response criticism, to argue that the major shift in understanding of reader reception and theories of literature takes place in the second half of the eighteenth century. That turn was from understanding reading as, in

Tompkins' terms, "a force acting on the world" or "a form of power," to the understanding of reading as approaching a text "as a series of signs to be deciphered" (203). In other words, the late eighteenth century brought a new emphasis on interpretation, on the specification of meaning. From the classical period through the Renaissance and into the Augustan period, the focus had remained on what the text does, not what the text means—hence the emphasis on techniques of rhetorical power in the classical period, the entwining of stagecraft and statecraft in the Renaissance masque, and the pointed political satire of the seventeenth and eighteenth centuries. At the end of the eighteenth century, however, a shift is marked by the rise of a modern aesthetic theory that was more interested in how a text meant something than how it did something.[37]

Tompkins' argument is grounded in canonical reception theory, ranging from Plato and Longinus to Sidney, Pope, Lord Kames, Shelley, Wordsworth, Pater, I. A. Richardson, and W. K. Wimsatt and Monroe Beardsley; she focuses on what it means to read "literature," not popular narratives or the Bible. But her argument remains generally true for the course of popular reading I've been outlining here. The discourse of heart-piety reading understood the purpose of reading as not significantly different from classical, Renaissance, and Augustan readers' understanding of the aims of rhetoric, the masque, and satire: all were to incite reading that would exert power in a particular direction and produce results—results in the social world (in the case of rhetoric, the masque, and satire) or results in the world of the heart or soul (in the case of religious reading). In a similar fashion, the discourse of what I've been calling public-sphere reading that developed in the late eighteenth century shares a great deal with what Tompkins calls interpretative reading: both understand reading as entailing the "objectivify[ing]" (Tompkins 201) of the text, so that it can be penetrated and discussed in terms of its meaning.

Tompkins is particularly insightful on the issue of affectual reading and its connection to interpretation, and here again she parallels the argument made above about the disciplining of emotion in the discourse of sensibility. The theorists of literary appreciation from the Scottish Enlightenment to the New Critics sought to turn reader emotion into both an object of interpretation and a mechanism enhancing proper interpretation. Tompkins notes that eighteenth-century reader-response critics like Lord Kames, Edmund Burke, and Joshua Reynolds were more interested in examining the emotional response to texts as a way of understanding the mind than as a way of effecting action in the social world.

They transform Longinus from a theorist of the uses of the sublime to a scientist of emotion. Another philosophical thread in the discourse of sensibility attempted to see readers' emotional responses as potentially binding humans together in shared sympathies. But as Tompkins points out these sympathies were not so much meant to change the social world as they were to mediate one's experience of that world. So Wordsworth puts forth the idea that poetry's sentiments are powerful not in the sense that they affect the contingent, historical world of the moment, but in that they offer a higher, universal relation to that world. Wordsworth writes in the second edition of *Lyrical Ballads* (1800) that poetry has the ability to strengthen and purify the affections, which in turn counteracts the "gross and violent stimulants" (xviii) characteristic of modern urban life. Later in the nineteenth century Pater took up the subject of the purpose of emotional response to culture in this way:

> Not to teach lessons, or enforce rules, or even to stimulate us to noble ends; but to withdraw the thoughts for a little while from the mere machinery of life, to fix them with appropriate emotions, on the spectacle of those great facts in man's existence which no machinery affects. . . . To witness this spectacle with appropriate emotions is the aim of all culture. (quoted in Tompkins 219)

Culture-generated emotion is best, Pater suggests, when it serves as a kind of scientific instrument which readers use to "fix" or objectify their thoughts, separating them from "the mere machinery of life." In the 1920s, I. A. Richards further refined the normative relationship between emotion and reading as essential to proper interpretation of the world. In Richards' criticism, affective reading wasn't quite yet a "fallacy," as it would become for the high New Critics Wimsatt and Beardley, but it did need to be carefully managed, or "canalised," in Richards' peculiar phrasing. As Tompkins explains, Richards "defines the ideal human condition as one of equilibrium, a perfect adjustment and conciliation of conflicting impulses, a condition in which no single emotion predominates and 'interest is not canalised in any one direction'" (219). When one reads proper poetry properly, this state is induced. It was only a small step to the Kantian disinterestedness of the New Critics and the immense value placed by T. S. Eliot on the "escape from emotion" (43) — which was an "escape from personality" (43; quoted in Tompkins 220) — or on the "objective correlative" (48), which was a way of distancing and containing emotion by turning it into an object separate from the subject.[38]

Tompkins is less interested in the causes of these shifts in the understandings of reading than she is in outlining the shifts themselves. Such changes were surely the result of multiple forces, and I've been arguing here that they are entwined with the developing ideas of the public sphere. It became important in the eighteenth century to objectify texts and the emotions they produced, to penetrate texts, to maintain individual agency in relation to texts—all elements of the normative reading practices implicitly or explicitly indicated by the canonical aesthetic theorists that Tompkins examines, and all elements of the kind of reading usually thought necessary for the modern form of the public sphere. What is true of the canonical theorists is also true of popular newspapers, journals, and works of fiction, as this chapter has traced out: they argued for and inculcated a kind of interpretive reading very different from the transporting or force-oriented heart-piety reading of the seventeenth and early eighteenth centuries. But the popular discourse recounted in detail in this chapter also adds nuance to Tompkins' long view. Interpretive, public-sphere reading wasn't always the same kind of interpretive, public-sphere reading. Sometimes it was understood as outwardly directed and intersubjective, as in William Hill Brown's *The Power of Sympathy*; at other times, especially as the nineteenth century unfolded, interpretive reading became much more inward and privatized, purportedly the work of an individual genius reader. The outward-oriented, intersubjective public-sphere reading outlined above seems to me to have remained a general ideal, if never an actually reality, but the inward-focused, privatized reading continues to represent an extraordinarily powerful model, from the nineteenth century to our present moment. It is worth pausing over this latter structure because it too provides a context for the following chapters.

In 1806 Charles Brockden Brown published "Remarks on Reading," a work that offered a perspective very different from those expressed in his correspondence with Jefferson or in his novels themselves.[39] The essay appeared in several different papers, suggesting wide distribution. Brown contrasts two kinds of reader: one "will have enriched his own mind by a new accession of matter, and find a new train of thought awakened and in action. The other quits his author in a pleasing distraction, but of the pleasures of reading nothing remains but a tumultuous sensation." In other words, Brown begins by making a now familiar observation contrasting two categories of readers, the thoughtful and the feeling. The remainder of the article tries to explain this difference—

how emotional reading comes about and how to avoid it. In doing so, Brown repeats what had already become a central concern of the period, albeit in one of the most vivid and elaborate versions. Reading requires "discrimination," which involves the treatment of ideas as if they were "objects" that can be arranged: "It is only when these objects exist in the mind, and are there treasured and arranged as materials for reflection, that they become ideas." Brown offers an array of different mechanisms for accomplishing this form of reading. He applauds the "index-reader," who "is, indeed, more let into the secrets of an author, than the other who attends him with all the tedious forms of ceremony." He praises "the inventor of indices; and I know not to whom to yield the preference, either to Hippocrates, who was the first great anatomiser of the human body, or to that unknown labourer in literature, who first laid open the nerves and arteries of a book." Reading is also about establishing choice, although Brown is only partially confident that most readers will be able to accomplish this: "A reader is too often a prisoner chained to the triumphal car of an author of great celebrity, and when he ventures not to judge for himself, conceives, while he reads to obey works of great authors, that the languor which he experiences arises from his own defective tastes." Reading well additionally requires the exertion of the reader's own skill and imagination. It is not about passive acceptance of what is read, "for there is something which a reader himself must bring to the book. . . . There is something in composition like the game of shuttlecock, where, if the reader does not quickly rebound the feathered cork to the author, the game is destroyed."

But even as Brown repeats these systems of public-sphere reading he also suggests that they are not enough. In the end there remain "secrets in the art of reading" and "mysteries in the art of reading" that cannot quite be cracked. For Brown there is ultimately something concealed in the text. His essay ends with this enigmatic statement, which itself seems to be hiding something: "One ought not to see every thing distinctly, but only certain parts of it; the imagination properly supplies the intermediate links. Hence are derived what some consider the obscurities of genius, which indeed are only the *obvious parts* which it wishes to *conceal*." There is a double concealment suggested here. First, genius "wishes" to hide things to stimulate the imagination to act. Second, Brown seems to imply that there is something hidden even beyond these *"obvious parts"* that *"some"* readers understand as marking genius. In either case, Brown encourages an interaction with texts that looks for what is hidden. He has already suggested that reading based in taste, sensibility, and erudition is not sufficient.

There is surely a line connecting this kind of reading with the mode of public-sphere reading that has been developed in the balance of this chapter. Charles Brockden Brown's form of reading is suspicious of affect, is objectifying of the text, is posed against the text, and seeks to construct knowledge in ways similar to, say, William Hill Brown's form of reading in *The Power of Sympathy*. But Charles Brockden Brown's mode of reading is also significantly different from William Hill Brown's idea in its interest in the individual "genius" reader bent on discovering what is "hidden" in the text. This is a much more extreme form of opposition to the text than what we have seen before. It seeks to know something about the text that the text might not know about itself. We see here a movement from understanding reading as exegesis (a kind of in-depth literal reading) to an understanding of reading as hermeneutics (a kind of in-depth decipherment of hidden codes). The ideas of judgment and knowledge formation are also different in the two different kinds of reading. In the case of Brown's essay, judgment and knowledge are no longer located in others and conversation with others but in the genius of individual and private appreciation, in the ability to see what is hidden in texts. I suspect this hermeneutical relation with texts will seem like a familiar way of reading to many professional, academic readers of this chapter. It is the kind of reading that professional scholars and teachers often nurture in their students. It might be accurately understood as a thoroughly liberal structure in that it understands knowledge as generated by the individual in private, rather than by the public sphere itself, and then offered up to the public. If William Hill Brown valued a kind of reading that inculcated a form of subjectivity associated with republicanism—an outward orientation, a continuity between private and public—then Charles Brocken Brown in this essay suggests a kind of reading that shapes a subjectivity allied with liberalism—an inward orientation and clear line between private and public. Such a mode of reading fit well with the developing liberalism of the nineteenth century and has become a dominant way of reading in the thoroughgoing liberalism of the twentieth and twenty-first centuries.[40]

Liberal, hermeneutical reading is often dramatized in Brown's immediate gothicist successors—Hawthorne and Poe will serve as examples here—and it becomes an important point of reference for antebellum African-American writers like Frederick Douglass. *The Scarlet Letter*

(1851) rather obviously foregrounds hermeneutical, interpretative reading—what is the secret meaning of the letter A?—but what has been
less evident to critics is that the novel stages a drama of conflicting sorts
of reading.[41] It offers a memorable scene of reading in its introduction,
"The Custom-House," when the narrator discovers in the attic enclave
of the Salem Custom House a piece of cloth, "the capital letter A." He
treats it as a kind of text to be interpreted: there is "deep meaning in it,"
it is "most worthy of interpretation," he "cogitat[es]" upon it, develops
"hypothesizes," and historicizes it. As he asserts himself in these acts of
critical, interpretive reading, he forgets what he is doing and lifts the
letter to his breast, and it burns him.

> My eyes fastened themselves upon the old scarlet letter, and would not
> be turned aside. Certainly, there was some deep meaning in it, most
> worthy of interpretation, and which, as it were, streamed forth from
> the mystic symbol, subtly communicating, itself to my sensibilities,
> but evading the analysis of my mind.
>
> While thus perplexed,—and cogitating, among other hypotheses,
> whether the letter might not have been one those decorations which
> the white men used to contrive, in order to take the eyes of Indians,—I
> happened to place it on my breast. It seemed to me,—the reader may
> smile, but must not doubt my word,—it seemed to me, then, that I
> experienced a sensation not altogether physical, yet almost so, as of
> burning heat; and as if the letter were not of red, but red-hot iron. I
> shuddered, and involuntarily let it fall upon the floor. (25)

The scarlet "A" draws upon itself this mode of reading—"involuntary,"
"not altogether physical, yet almost so," a burning heat—but the rest of
the novel resists it. If Hawthorne's novel teaches anything about reading,
it is not to read in this way. The book's sophisticated irony encourages
us to keep our distance. Too much sympathetic reading is dangerous,
and Arthur Dimmesdale becomes the object lesson. His reading is dis-
eased: "We [the narrator and readers] impute it, therefore, solely to the
disease in his own eye and heart, that the minister, looking upward to
the zenith, behold there the appearance of an immense letter,—the letter A,—marked out in lines of dull red light" (107). Such reading leads
Dimmesdale to "the verge of lunacy" (114); he suffers continuously from
a "nervous sensibility" (48). It is Roger Chillingworth who is the ex-
pert reader, or at least the reader who reads most successfully. When
Hester refuses to reveal her lover, Chillingworth responds by saying

that he can find him by reading with a scientific, enlightenment kind of sympathy:

> Believe me, Hester, there are few things—whether in the outward world, or, to a certain depth, in the invisible sphere of thought—few things hidden from the man, who devotes himself earnestly and unreservedly to the solution of a mystery. Thou mayest cover up thy secret from the prying multitude. Thou mayest conceal it, too, from the ministers and magistrates, even as thou didst this day, when they sought to wrench the name out of thy heart, and give thee a partner on thy pedestal. But, as for me, I come to the inquest with other senses than they possess. I shall seek this man, as I have sought truth in books; as I have sought gold in alchemy. There is a sympathy that will make me conscious of him. I shall see him tremble. I shall feel myself shudder, sudden and unawares. (53–54)

Knowledge here comes from specialized interpretative powers: Chillingworth "come[s] to the inquest with other senses than they [the village inhabitants] possess." These senses become a scientific instrument or distinctive faculty that allows Chillingworth to read what is concealed by others in the same way he seeks truth in books. Chillingworth seems to say that he senses, and then he objectifies and observes what has been sensed. Hawthorne seems less convinced than I. A. Richards that such a style of scientific reading is essential to civilization, but there is a connecting thread.

Scenes of reading are ubiquitous in Poe's stories: the proper and improper ways of reading purloined letters, romance novels, and newspapers serve among the central subject matter of his narratives. In the detective Auguste Dupin, Poe creates a kind of genius, hermeneutical reader not unlike Chillingworth; in "The Mystery of Marie Roget" (1842), Dupin uncovers the secret by reading the "public papers" (509). But even stories that seem to be about subjects other than reading, such as "The Fall of the House of Usher" (1839), can be without much difficulty understood as meditations on reading. Its unnamed narrator is, after all, drawn to the Usher mansion by the peculiar experience of reading a letter from his boyhood companion, Roderick Usher:

> The MS. [of the letter] gave evidence of nervous agitation. The writer spoke of acute bodily illness—of a pitiable mental idiosyncrasy which oppressed him—and of an earnest desire to see me, as his best, and

indeed, his only personal friend, with a view of attempting, by the cheerfulness of my society, some alleviation of his malady. It was the manner in which all this, and much, was said—it was the apparent *heart* that went with his request—which allowed me no room for hesitation—and I accordingly obeyed, what I still considered a very singular summons, forthwith. (318)

The remainder of the narrative might well be considered a dramatization of the struggle with various textual summons to "obey" with "no room for hesitation." Roderick Usher suffers from "a morbid acuteness of the senses" (322) which, among other things, makes him unusually sensitive to tastes, touch, sights, sounds, and stories read aloud. The narrator often reads to Usher, and Usher responds intensely—or "harkens" to the words, as the narrator says—at one point with a "wild, overstrained air of vivacity" (332). Indeed, so vivid are the tales read within the tale itself that they verge on becoming one and the same tale. Usher believes that his own experience and the story of Sir Launcelot (which the narrator reads to him) are one and the same, and the narrator too almost believes it, before "concluding that my excited fancy had deceived me" (332). The collapsing of reality and fiction that so many nineteenth-century commentators on the dangers of novel reading fear actually becomes the case in "The Fall of the House of Usher." In the end, the narrator resists becoming a bad, feverish reader like his friend and potential double Roderick, escaping the miasma of the house before it sinks into the tarn. In the story's final sentence, the house becomes a quotation-marked, italicized object: "and the deep and dank tarn at my feet closed sullenly and silently over the fragments of the '*House of Usher*'" (336). The house no longer has any human characteristics or agency as it did at the narrative's beginning with its "sickening of the heart" (317) and "eye-like windows" (317, 318). It is now distanced and objectified—an italicized book or story to be safely contemplated.

If in Brown, Hawthorne, and Poe books and texts are rendered as objects upon which agency is exerted through interpretative reading, in the late eighteenth- and early nineteenth-century narratives of free North American blacks and diasporan Africans, the book has considerable agency: it seems to talk. Henry Louis Gates calls "[t]he trope of the Talking Book . . . the ur-trope of the Anglo-African tradition" (131). Ukawsaw Gronniosaw (1772), John Marrant (1785), Quobna Ottobah Cugoano (1787), Olaudah Equiano (1794), and John Jea (ca. 1811) all play off the trope of a book, usually the Bible, which seems to the naïve and illiterate observer to be in conversation with a reader. The example from Equiano's narrative is perhaps best known:

> I had often seen my master and Dick employed in reading; and I had a great curiosity to talk to the books, as I thought they did; and so to learn how all things had a beginning: for that purpose I have often taken up a book, and have talked to it, and then put my ears to it, when alone, in hopes it would answer me; and I have been very much concerned when I found it remained silent. (68)

Sometimes it is the literate African encountering illiterate natives, as in the example offered by the black missionary John Marrant among the Cherokee (27); in other instances, such as John Jea's (33–38; quoted in Gates 160–63), the otherwise illiterate African is "spoken" to by a Bible (he's taught to read by an angel in fifteen minutes) but can make sense of no other text. As Gates notes, the fact that the Talking Book appears repeatedly across these narratives suggests the way it represents a calculated trope, one that self-consciously signifies cultural difference and the power of print and reading. Importantly, even as the trope often pokes fun at the naïve and illiterate younger self of the narrator, it also simultaneously indicates the ability of that black narrator to take up the power of the book and overcome the cultural divide: after all, the narrator is now writing the very book that is "talking" to the reader (Gates 155). Such a trope may well have served to disarm white readers with its ingenuous pose, while making a point about African ability and agency. For our current purpose it is most important to note that this is a very particular vision of reading, one that emphasizes reading as conversation, not unlike *The Power of Sympathy* and other accounts of proper reading in the journals and magazines of the period. Literacy may be a kind of secret kept from the younger selves of these narrators, but reading itself is understood as part of a public-sphere dialogue.

After Jea's narrative of approximately 1811, the Talking Book does not reappear in Anglo-African literature. Henry Louis Gates wonders what happened (166–67). Although Gates doesn't consider it, one possibility for the Talking Book's disappearance is that it was no longer conceivable as a disarming image of reading and public-sphere agency. The significance of Anglo-African reading changed dramatically, at least in the United States, in the twenty years following Jea's publication. Those years saw an escalation in fear over the relationship between reading and slave insurrections. Denmark Vesey—executed in Charleston, South Carolina, in 1822 for conspiracy to rebel against the white establishment—was reportedly well versed in abolitionist writings, histories of the Haitian revolution, and the Bible (Howe 161). Seven years later, in 1829, David Walker published one of the most daring political pamphlets of the nineteenth century. Like Vesey, Walker had been a congregant at Charleston's African Methodist Episcopal Church. By the time his *Appeal* was published, he was working on the Boston waterfront. Walker emphasized the power of reading and print, calling "all coloured men, women and children of every nation, language and tongue under heaven" to "try to procure a copy of this Appeal and read it, or get some one to read it to them, for it is designed more particularly for them" (2). He goes on to recommend reading history as well as accounts of the revolution in Haiti, all in the name of overthrowing the "cruel oppressors and murders" (2). Walker used his waterfront contacts in Charleston and other southern ports to circulate the *Appeal*. In reaction, slave states quickly passed additional ordinances against the distribution of seditious literature and strengthened "negro seamen laws," which detained free black sailors while in port so as to prevent contact with slaves (Eaton 323–34 and Hinks 25–40 and 127–31, cited by Howe 424–25).

The Talking Book's dramatization—and the *Appeal*'s theorization—of a republican, abolitionist form of reading was replaced by 1830 with an image of bad African-American reading. One of the most startling reports of feverish reading in the first half of the nineteenth century is recounted in *The Confessions of Nat Turner* (1831), the jailhouse statement given by the leader of the foremost slave rebellion in U.S. history, which led to the deaths of over fifty whites and many more blacks in Southampton, Virginia, not far from the major port at Norfolk. Turner purportedly tells his untrustworthy amanuensis—the local, white, slave-owning lawyer Thomas R. Gray—that his acquisition of literacy was sui generis and required no special training or regulation: "The manner in which I learned to read and write, not only had great influence on my own mind, as I acquired it with the most perfect ease, so much so, that I have no recollection whatever of learning the alphabet—but to the astonishment of the family, one day, when a book was shown me to keep me from crying, I began spelling the names of different objects" (6). Such proficiency in a young slave was surely one of white Southampton's most alarming nightmares. Especially when the slave reads like this: "I discovered drops of blood on the corn, as though it were dew from heaven—and I communicated it to many, both white and black, in the neighborhood—and then found on the leaves in the woods hieroglyphic characters, and numbers, with the forms of men in different attitudes, portrayed in blood, and representing the figures I had seen before in the heavens" (9). Turner's reading is revelatory, without distance, and far from any idea of public-sphere conversation. From the perspective of Thomas R. Gray and the anticipated white audience for the *Confessions*, such reading may well have seemed horrific, an essential example of feverish, bad reading. We have seen how such reading practices were associated with young women and men as a disciplining mechanism; in the case of Turner's *Confessions*, bad reading is racialized. From the perspective of possible African-American readers, however, this millennial, hallucinogenic mode of reading may have been understood as completely outside the practices of any conventional public sphere—republican or liberal in orientation. In this sense, it could be seen as an attempt to establish a kind of counterpublic practice.

This style of reading is very different, of course, from one of the most famous accounts of reading and literacy in antebellum African-American writing. In his 1845 *Narrative*, Frederick Douglass describes teaching himself to read, first with the help of his master's wife and then, after being banned by his master from learning more, with the help of poor white boys on the streets of Baltimore with whom he trades bread for the meanings of written words. Douglass explains that reading was an extraordinary power because it connected him to a world he would otherwise have never known, because it made him aware of an abolitionist movement, and because it was precisely what his master and other whites wanted to keep from him. Reading also brings him an initial consciousness of self and the ability to recognize his own thinking; reading, Douglass says, "enabled me to utter my thoughts" which heretofore "had frequently flashed through my mind, and died away for want of utterance" (84). Because reading for Douglass is the first step toward self-consciousness and freedom, these passages have become standard components of the U.S. high school curriculum. Douglass's narrative of reading acquisition provides in some ways a classic story of liberal self-making: against all odds an individual achieves a sense of autonomy and his or her own agency through the acquisition of literacy. This self-making through reading is in accordance with what Elizabeth Maddock Dillon has called "the temporality of liberalism" (19–25), where "the *narrative* of liberal subjectivity begins in privacy and moves forward into public agency" (19). Such a narrative in Dillon's view often tends to problematically fix a line between public and private—which is essential to liberal theory and practice, but often serves to maintain white patriarchy.

To some degree Douglass does support an understanding of reading as essential to liberal subject formation. He is particularly cautious to construct his *Narrative* of 1845 so as to avoid encouraging reading like Nat Turner's. The *Narrative* tends to assert an emotional distance between the text and its reader. Douglass can seem more like an ethnographer than a memoirist as he describes Maryland's plantation culture and economy. He also refuses to narrate the bloodthirsty whipping of Aunt Hester, surely because it is a personally traumatic primal scene of his life as a slave, but also because he wants readers to maintain, with respect to the text, a cool, rational distance that he associates with agency. This self-consciousness and distance from sensational reading is a characteristic of much antebellum African-American writing. For example, in *Incidents in the Life of a Slave Girl* (1861), Harriet Jacobs skirts sensationalism with references to her sexual activities and apologizes for coming so close: "Pity me and pardon me, O virtuous reader! You never knew what it is to be a slave" (55). Reading, for Jacobs, is a site for making virtuous selves and, therefore, a site for potential corruption.

From a different perspective, both Douglass and Jacobs question liberal notions of the power of reading. Jacobs risks corruption of the reader in order to circulate bitter truths about sexuality and slavery in the mainstream public sphere, while Douglass finds reading to be both blessing and curse: "freedom now appeared," he writes, and this awareness "opened my eyes to the horrible pit, but to no ladder upon which to get out" (84). He often finds that his new reading proficiency leaves him "regretting [his] own existence, and wishing [himself] dead" (85), and proclaims that reading "had given me a view of my wretched condition, without the remedy" (84). Reading, in this sense, has only taught Douglass how to curse. To achieve any real sense of freedom, he must assert himself violently against the overseer Covey—it is that struggle which inspires him with "a determination to be free" (113)—and eventually escape to the north.

These two authors' ambivalent relationship with what I have been calling liberal forms of reading might best be understood as their navigation of complex and highly racialized cultural and political terrain. The endorsement of republican forms of reading by African-Americans was increasingly understood as dangerous to the white establishment, so African-Americans writing for an abolitionist audience were often compelled to privilege liberal forms of reading. This dynamic hints at the extent to which a fear of African-American reading produced texts that encourage what I've referred to as liberal reading practices.

Counter to the development of liberal forms of reading in the nineteenth century emerges another possible relation to texts, one that is linked to the values of republican reading in the late eighteenth century but is also considerably different. The emergence occurs in the 1830s. The idea of a "reading revolution" has become rather suspect for many scholars, because the word "revolution" suggests too grand and holistic a transformation for what was in fact more piecemeal and uneven. Nevertheless, there were dramatic changes in the meaning of reading—and, by extension, changes in the public sphere—during the late eighteenth century and the Jacksonian/antebellum period, even if they cannot be understood as constituting a complete break with the past. Here we might consider the public sphere and reading at two different points of transformation: in the late eighteenth century, when a new idea of "the public" became available and popular, and around 1830, when ideas about the public and reading shifted again, in part due to the emergence of the massification of print culture. Although the late eighteenth century has long been recognized as an important time of transformation in reading, several dramatic changes begin in the Jacksonian period. First, as the sociologist Paul Starr and the historian Daniel Walker Howe have outlined, the 1830s saw the beginnings of the most substantial communications revolution in American history. By 1830, the major new technologies of printing were in place: stereotype plates replaced traditional type, steam-powered cylinder presses replaced hand presses not tremendously different from Gutenberg's, and machine papermaking had cut the price of paper by more than half. Additionally, certain segments of the book publishing industry, especially Bible and religious tract publishing, were beginning to employ practices often associated with twentieth-century mass media: targeted audiences, highly organized distribution chains, and differential pricing (where books are sold at different prices depending on the buyer). For instance, in 1829 the American Tract Society developed a plan it called "Systematic Monthly Distribution," which aimed to put the same religious tract in the hands of every inhabitant of New York City (Nord 85). The speed at which print material could be circulated had been increased by railroads, and with the invention of the telegraph in the late 1840s, the speed of information was literally approaching the speed of light. Meredith L. McGill in her work on the antebellum period's systematic "culture of reprinting"—before modern copyright law—has shown how circulation of literary works was understood in very different terms than it would be in the twentieth century (but also perhaps in terms similar to today's culture of "reposting" on the Web).

How did these developments in publishing and circulation transform reading and the public sphere? On July 11, 1856, when many of these transformations had become the norm, Henry Conrad Brokmeyer, a self-professed mechanic as a youth who became a politician and cofounder of the St. Louis Philosophical Society, wrote in his diary a long entry about reading. He begins by describing his devotion to Hegel's *Logic* (1811–16): "I have recommended my annual course in Hegel's 'Logic' [to friends and imaginary readers of his diary]. It is a strange book and attractive to me, on account of its noiselessness. Whenever the world within or without commences to brawl so loudly that I cannot hear my own voice, I take a journey into the realm of this primeval solitude" (55). Then Brokmeyer imagines how Hegel might have written his book differently if he himself could have experienced the brawl of modernity—and even written for a reader caught up in that brawl. Brokmeyer wants Hegel to be "useful," even a "popular entertainment," but this would require a very different mode of address.

I sometimes think it is a great pity that the man did not live today, or at least at a time when the railroad facilities were far enough developed to show him what a book ought to be for a man when he travels by steam. As it is, I don't know a single chapter, page, or paragraph that can be read and understood in passing by it at the moderate rate of speed of, say, forty miles an hour, no matter how large the letters might be made, or how long the fence to give room to the display. Yet, even in his day, it was known that a book should be written in such a manner "that he who runs may read" [Habakkuk 2:2], and the circumstance that we do our study, not while running, but while rushing along, leaves us necessarily in a condition the more seriously to regret that he did not comply with the canons of his art, as calculated for his own day and generation. Had he done so, there can be no doubt, when the superior sagacity of ourselves is duly considered, that the increased speed, the haste at which we have arrived, would not have been a detriment to the general usefulness of the book. As it is, I fear it never will be much value as a source of popular entertainment. (55)

Yes, it is doubtful that Hegel's *Logic* will ever be considered a popular entertainment. That the thought is conceivable is testament to Brokmeyer's faith in reading and logical argument as useful practices for the masses. But what is most interesting about this passage is the way Brokmeyer describes reading in relation with the steam railroad and speed. It was not uncommon in the Jacksonian and antebellum periods to associate the new reach and speed of print with the power of the locomotive, but Brokmeyer here imagines a kind of locomotive reading and writing. The space-and-time-dissolving locomotive, in fact, seems to demand a new way of reading. That new way seems to be unavoidably public — like words painted on a fence (or a modern billboard) — rather than in the private realm of "primeval solitude." This mode of reading also seems to be fast and immediate — the kind of reading that happens before one even knows it is happening, that occurs with the many words that one reads automatically, without volition or intent, especially when they appear on billboards (or even in newspapers). Even more striking is Brokmeyer's matter-of-fact recognition that reading changes with the times and that technology and the general environs change reading. He recognizes, in other words, that reading is always a form of mediation and that that mediation is historically contingent.

Charles Brockden Brown's hermeneutical reading and Henry Conrad Brokmeyer's locomotive reading provide as much context for the next three chapters as does the idea of public-sphere reading that this chapter outlined in detail. The notion of public-sphere reading arrives at the end of the eighteenth century and operates as a norm that must be kept in mind as we discuss pornographic reading, scandal reading, and religious reading. These kinds of reading in the Jacksonian and antebellum periods follow, in some respects, the republican ideal of a reading that contributes to the public sphere, even as they begin to take on the characteristics of Brokmeyer's locomotive reading. The liberally inflected hermeneutical reading that Brown theorizes furnishes a different kind of context, one that we should be wary of because it is our own. To see all reading through that lens colors and distorts our understanding of the uses of reading in the past.

Part Two

Chapter Three

Obscene Reading

The Senses of Reading Badly

This chapter counterintuitively argues that obscene reading—a form of reading which first became both popular and a problem in the United States during the antebellum period—is a kind of critical practice focused on the public sphere itself. The chapter is the first of three that attempt to outline the critical agency of what has in previous chapters been called "bad" reading—reading which is often tarred as too absorptive, too affective, and too addictive. Pornography is frequently understood as encouraging this kind of reading, even if in actuality the experience is much more complex. Reading or viewing pornography is often an experience of extreme contrasts. Privacy collides with publicity, the personal with the impersonal. Bodies are presented in palpable detail and distinction but remain interchangeable. Readers and viewers are rendered as abstract, disembodied voyeurs even as they are encouraged to participate in the most embodied ways. The genre's characters lack any interiority but the genre itself charges fantasy life. Pornography is about intensifying sensory response while also being vacant of what is usually called feeling. It's about identification and alienation. It is exciting yet boring.

The delineation of these contradictory experiences will require more detail, but if such experience is one of the main subjects and aims of the pornographic, then what sense of it might we make? What is the meaning behind the genre's production of cycles of excitement and boredom, identification and alienation, disembodiment and embodiment in its consumers? I suspect there are a number of helpful ways to approach this question—psychoanalytic, physiological, gender-focused, to name several useful frameworks—but here I am interested in the double experience in the context of the public sphere.

The previous chapter offered a view of the ideas of proper reading practices that developed in the early era of mass reading and connected reading to a specific ideology of the public sphere. Pornographic reading might well be understood as the most egregious sin that one could commit against that orthodoxy. What could be more antithetical to distanced, discussion-oriented, autonomy-creating, and reflective public-sphere reading than absorptive, addictive, and secretive pornographic reading? This was the view commonly repeated in a multitude of anti-masturbation tracts, medical treatises on reading-induced insanity, and textual (as well as visual) representation of both masturbators and pornographic readers during the mid-nineteenth century. One of the central problems with pornographic reading, these sources suggest, is that it focused readers inward, into their imaginations, fantasies, and bodies, and not outward towards society, labor, and the public sphere. In arguing just the opposite, this chapter suggests that pornography often reflects some central antinomies of the modern public-sphere idea and experience. And, more ambitiously, it argues that pornography often enables a public to critically reflect on the values and protocols of its public sphere.

I make these arguments in order to further investigate the implications of the affective turn in public-sphere theory. Over the last decade a number of critics have challenged the traditional, classical model of the public sphere as founded on "rational-critical" debate.[1] Michael Warner, Lauren Berlant, Glenn Hendler, and others have suggested that we consider the affective dimension of the public sphere.[2] Much of this work has focused on the sentimental, and here I expand upon this scholarship by taking up some emotional structures that are usually considered rather more abject than the sentimental and therefore frequently granted little value, even as they are ubiquitous. But more significantly, I am interested in the ways affective response can be understood as a form of reflection and even something akin to critical thinking. This function of criticality is often assumed in public-sphere theory's turn to affect, but it is also in need of more explicit delineation.[3] This is by no means the standard way of conceptualizing criticality, but it is necessary because, without a clear understanding of the public sphere's sensory dimensions, Habermasian public-sphere theory is not particularly helpful in understanding the existing public sensorium of modernity. I hope this chapter takes a small step in that direction. Such a better understanding is essential if the public-sphere concept is to remain a tool for analysis and politics in our modern sensorium.

This set of arguments is developed by focusing on an important moment in the American history of the public sphere and pornography: the genre's unfolding as a popular, even mass-cultural, form in the thirty or so years before the Civil War. It was during these years that pornography became easily available to the public and became an issue of public concern that led to obscenity arrests and legislation. No one moment in the pornographic archive can be representative of the entire genre, but the antebellum period's "obscene reading" and "obscene literature"—to use the vocabulary of the news accounts and court documents of the era—offer a revealing view into the genre's emergence and development in relationship to the public sphere.[4] The archive reveals the way its texts attempted to construct a specific form of reading—that is, a specific relationship between text, reader, and public sphere. But before turning to these intricacies, a brief overview of the rise of obscene publication during the antebellum period is necessary, because these details are not well known outside of a handful of experts.

The Emergence of Obscene
Reading in the United States

In his exhaustive *History of Prostitution* (1858), William W. Sanger, a prominent New York physician working at Blackwell's (now Roosevelt) Island charity hospital, off Manhattan's eastern shoals, detailed the city's obscene book traffic:

> Recent legal proceedings have checked this nefarious trade, but it still exists. Boys and young men may be found loitering at all hours around hotels, steam-boat docks, rail-road depots, and other public places, ostensibly selling newspapers or pamphlets, but secretly offering vile, lecherous publications to those who are likely to be customers. (521)

Sanger was a respected reformer, and one who usually avoided puritanical panic. His meticulous *History* marshals an impressive array of charts and statistics, and he progressively advocates education and enlightenment as a salve for antebellum Manhattan's chronic prostitution problem. But even as Sanger avoids the graphic, gothic horrors that often characterized sexual reform tracts of the period, he calls for the strongest condemnation of the "nefarious trade." The danger, he writes, is close by and growing:

> Despite all precautions, there is every reason to believe that the manufacture of these obscene books is largely carried out in this city. It is needless to remind any resident of the large seizures made in New York during the last two years, or to particularize the stock condemned. More caution is observed now, and the post-office is made the vehicle for distribution. Circulars are issued which describe the publications and their prizes, modes of transmitting money are indicated, and the advertiser plainly says that he will not allow any personal interviews on account of the dangers which surround the traffic. (522)

Sanger provides one of the most detailed overviews of the antebellum circulation of obscene literature that we have today, and he is surely correct in guessing that much of his 1858 audience knew all too well of the trade's existence and workings, as the subject preoccupied the daily papers.

On September 29, 1857, the *New York Herald* reported on its front page that, at three o'clock the previous afternoon, an undercover Manhattan police officer had bought "for a small investment of forty five cents" a collection of "obscene literature" from a roving book peddler at Lovejoy's Hotel, at the corner of Beckman Street across from City Hall Park. The purchase included "some very scandalous looking prints" and a single longer work — "a book styled 'Fanny Greely.'" The officer followed the peddler back to his distributor at 12 Ann Street and confiscated, according to the *Herald*, a considerable amount of obscene material — "cart loads of both books and pamphlets." The publisher was arrested and held on bail, and his trial was closely observed by the papers. The pamphlets and books were incinerated under the careful scrutiny of municipal authorities so as to ensure that none of the obscene material leaked back into the public marketplace.

Similar events were common in the fall of 1857. The major dailies — the *Herald*, the *Tribune*, and *The New York Daily Times* — all ran stories on recent sting operations and raids by the city police, which exposed the most extensive obscene literature ring to date in the United States. "Great Seizure of Obscene Literature" the front-page headline read in the *Herald*; then two weeks later, "Another Alleged Obscene Publisher Arrested"; and a month later, "Another Seizure of Obscene Literature."[5] The *Herald* reported on September 23 that, in a bonfire on the previous day, one ton of obscenity had been set ablaze by New York police (5). The paper was especially concerned with the genre's wide distribution, condemning its expansive circulation in editorials and going so far as to publish the subscription list of one print shop. Obscene material was spreading not only to Boston and Philadelphia, but also further south and west, and was easily available at quasi-clandestine shops on Ann Street or from boys on the avenues and at city hotels, the *Herald* reported.[6] The *Tribune* repeated these charges, warning that urban spaces like hotels and steamboat landings were infested by "half grown boys"—one of the city's newest and most troubling demographics—with their arms full of "a large assortment of obscene books." Readers were informed that these boys were easy enough to collar, but that their suppliers often remained just out of the authorities' reach.[7] For the city's mainstream editors and reporters, obscene literature was a kind of mass-cultural social disease, of promiscuous circulation and uncertain, often anonymous origins. This period—a decade and half before Anthony Comstock's notorious rise to power in the early 1870s—represents the first real outburst of obscene publications in U.S. history.

What, precisely, went up in smoke in that 1857 bonfire? What were the material forms, content, author names, and titles of that obscene literature?[8] Newspaper arrest reports are a good place to begin to answer such questions, because they offer wide-angle views of the emergence and development of obscenity production. Between 1815 and 1877, there were at least 104 unique obscenity incidents reported in U.S. newspapers, involving hundreds of different authors, printers, importers, sellers, and buyers. (An appendix lists all of these arrests, with as many names and details as its limited space permits.) In reporting on the arrests, newspapers also described the confiscation and destruction of thousands of articles of obscenity. The graph in figure 1 shows very few arrests in the first quarter of the nineteenth century, then a fairly sharp escalation throughout the 1830s, with spikes in the 1840s and 1870s.[9]

Newspaper arrest reports indicate that this deluge of obscenity comprised several different material forms of print culture. Most prominent are "obscene prints," various newspapers known as "sporting" or "flash" papers, and "obscene books." It is extremely difficult to know what exactly constitutes an obscene print. Perhaps this refers to visual material or broadsides.[10] For the most part, the more ephemeral material has disappeared from the archive. But the two other predominant forms—sporting newspapers and cheap novelettes—have proven more durable.

FIGURE 1. U.S. obscenity arrests by decade, 1800–1870.

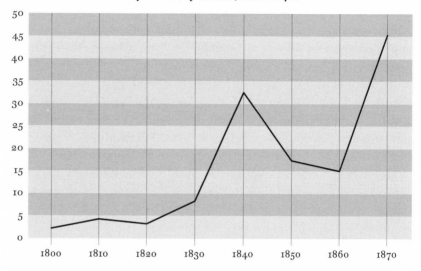

In 1842, New York newspapers indicated that there were twelve convictions in the city for "publishing obscene papers," while Philadelphia
papers reported eight convictions for the same. During the early 1840s,
sporting papers like the *Flash*, the *Libertine*, and the *Whip*—which reported on prostitution and recreations of other 'racy' sorts among a new
urban class of low-level clerks, apprentices, journeymen, and laborers
(known as "sporting men")—repeatedly found themselves in legal trouble. In the 1850s, the *Broadway Belle*, *Venus' Miscellany*, the *Phoenix*,
and the *New York Miscellany*—all newsprint publication—were deemed
obscene, both by the more mainstream papers and by legal authorities.
The obscene sporting genre included a number of other papers (see figure 2); many are extant and can serve as an archive for our investigation
of obscene reading.

These papers delighted in prostitution, celebrity, deformity, the crimi-
nal underworld, murder, and beautiful and battered bodies. For instance,
the front page of the *New York Arena* of May 24, 1842, featured stories
about an erotic ballet in Boston, the "Nigger Exhibitions" in New York,
a New York actress who might be "knocked up," and a cross-dressing
incident at a public lecture. *Ely's Hawk and Buzzard* catalogued the
prostitution houses and their locations.[11] Under the title "The Actual
State of Public Morals in New York, and the True Organization of its
Society," the *Arena* outlined the city's prostitution traffic, describing the

FIGURE 2. Years of publication for "flash" or "sporting" papers.

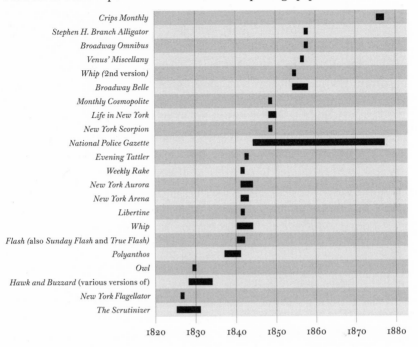

tiers of the trade down to specific streetwalkers, introducing the major prostitutes, and ushering readers through houses of prostitution.[12] The *Owl* published "A Peep at the Boudoir" and a poem about the pleasures of buying prostitutes.[13] The *Whip and Satirist of New-York and Brooklyn* provided a weekly report called "Diary of a Rake," the purpose of which was to chronicle "accustomed rambles among the various Houses of Pleasure" and "to report for the benefit of our readers and the morals of our city, the doings of certain classes of society — to show the pranks of the base and the deluded, to warn off the young and uninitiated."[14] A favorite topic was the duplicity of the elite ("of certain classes of society"), who were often discovered in compromising positions. The *Owl*'s "Moderation" wrote in from the streets of Brooklyn that he had seen a vomiting alderman: "He was seen near the Battery, straining as if he had swallowed a camel, whilst a stream issued from his mouth, which bore a remarkable similarity to the *Cataract of the Ganges*."[15] The papers often took up this moralistic pose — which was surely, in part, legally self-protective — but always seemed more interested in serving as a kind of *Baedeker's* of urban pleasures.

Nevertheless, the papers were much more than prostitution guides. The papers also saw themselves as mediums of critique and supervision of urban authorities. Some, such as the *Hawk and Buzzard*, were loosely connected to Jacksonian party politics in New York. In the pages of the *Arena*, readers argued over bankruptcy laws, national politics, appointments to local positions (customhouse inspector, for instance), and censorship.[16] The *Owl* printed letters about alms-house reform and school reform for mechanics.[17] The *Hawk and Buzzard* clearly stated this project of public oversight: "We were ever on the watch—faithful and fearless—with a full determination to ferret out the secret movements of our city authorities, that we might lay their proceedings before our readers on each Saturday. In doing this, our only aim was the *Public's good*" [italics in original].[18] In general, the papers are probably best described as anti-bourgeois and anti-authoritarian, rather than working class or underclass, as it would be naïve to think that readership was limited to a particular class.

Their arrest accounts suggest that, in the late 1840s and '50s, the business of obscene publication was changing. The focus of obscenity arrests shifted from the sporting papers to cheap, paper-covered novelettes about one hundred pages long. The more outrageous sporting papers had been regulated out of business, and their most industrious entrepreneurs, like George Wilkes, moved on to new ventures like the *National Police Gazette*—still sensational, but much blander than the *Whip*, his earlier project. As both the variety and lewdness of obscene sporting papers decreased, the production of obscene pulp novelettes increased (compare figures 2 and 3). In most reports, these novelettes are not named by title, but we occasionally receive glimpses of specific material: *The Curtain Drawn Up*; *Belshazzar's Feast*; *The Mysteries of Venus, or the Amatory Life and Adventures of Miss Kitty Pry*; *Fanny Greeley, or the Adventures of a Free Love Sister*; and *Our Maseppa*. One author, Charles Paul de Kock, is repeatedly mentioned, but the name seems to be a punning pseudonym that signaled obscene content rather than the actual French novelist. Almost all of the books and authors referenced in newspaper arrest reports appear in Marcus McCorison's recent bibliography "Risqué Literature Published in America before 1877," which is derived in large part from publishers' circulars and back-cover advertisements that indicate books long lost from the extant archive. McCorison lists 159 books, the vast majority appearing between the mid-1840s and the mid-1860s (see figure 3). In addition, he lists many of the sport-

FIGURE 3. Numbers of risqué books published in the United States before 1877.

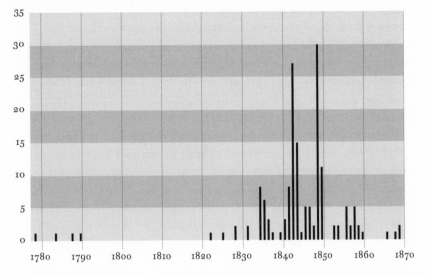

ing papers published in the United States. McCorison's bibliography conveys a sense of the significance of this collection of interrelated print culture, of works that were considered obscene or that just skirted the obscene. The books are described in publishers' advertisements as "risqué" or "racy" or "yellow-covered" novelettes, and sometimes, perhaps tellingly, as "peoples novelettes." Although they were clearly directed at an audience seeking a specific kind of material, it is unclear whether all of the listed books were considered obscene by the authorities or the public. From a comparison of figures 1 and 3, however, an increase in the publication of risqué novelettes appears to correspond with an increase in obscenity arrests and confiscations.

Most of these novelettes were published anonymously or pseudonymously. They often conformed to a certain formulaic design: about one hundred pages, with the plot rather quickly resolved on the final page. They are episodic, fantastically repetitive, and often hopelessly disjointed, as if their plots were thrown together on a factory floor.[19] The genre seems aimed at a wider, more general audience than their precursor, the sporting press. They forgo the insider pseudonyms and coded language of the sporting papers, which occupy the boundary between artisan and mass-market productions. These signs of mass-cultification—formulaic design, assembly-line production, and more general audience—mark some of the ways that obscene novelettes differ from the flash papers, but the two forms also share a great deal, as we shall see.

While adhering to specific conventions, obscene novelettes are also obsessed with the unconventional, particularly unconventional sex. They often serve as something like erotic guidebooks — sometimes wickedly imitating the gaslight tours of the comparatively conservative George Foster — ushering readers through the streets of New York or Boston, from one sexual excess to the next sensational perversion. They share some characteristics with George Lippard's urban gothicism, particularly his sensational violence, but lack Lippard's religious fervor and replace his preoccupation with darkened private spaces and ghostly mysteries with gritty reportage and street style. Like the sporting press, such novelettes are bent on making public those acts which had come to define privacy — especially sexual acts.[20] A short list of titles published in northeastern cities is suggestive: *Harriette Wilson, or Memoirs of a Woman of Pleasure* (written by herself, 1845, 1851, ca. 1870); *Amours of a Modest Man* (anonymous, 1864); *Red Staff, or the Mysterious Lover* (anonymous, 1864); *The Amours of a Quaker* (anonymous, 1856); *The Seducer's Fate: or, The Adventures of Zizina* (Kock, n.d.); *Six Mistresses of Pleasure* (Kock, 1844); *Amours of a Musical Student* (Kock, ca. 1853); *The Curtain Drawn Up; or the Education of Laura* (anonymous, early 1840s, 1870); *The Countess, or Memoirs of Women of Leisure* (Thompson, 1849); *Venus in Boston* (Thompson, 1849); *The Ladies' Garter* (Thompson, 1851); *The Gay-Girls of New York* (Thompson, 1853); *Anna Mowbray, or Tales of the Harem* (Thompson, 1856); and *The Delights of Love, or the Lady Libertine* (Thompson, n.d.).[21] The list of narrated sexual encounters begins to look like a sexology report from later in the century: incest is frequently toyed with; dinner parties erupt into orgies; black servants strip and whip white mistresses while proclaiming the injuries to their race; castrated men spy on young nymphs; lecherous grandfathers find themselves married to beautiful young women. There is group sex, cross-racial sex, cross-class sex, cross-generational sex, and same-sex sex.

Forms of Obscene Reading

THE SPORTING PRESS AND ITS STRUCTURES OF READING

How do these papers and books construct their readers' experience of reading?[22] It is helpful to begin by emphasizing two elements that are perhaps obvious. First, the sporting press is about current information. The papers address readers with a sense of now-ness; there is a simultaneity of information and readership (the papers are dated, the stories topical). The readers are constructed as news readers, even as that news is often of the most outlandish sort. Second, the papers tend to address readers as bodies. The current information about the vomiting alderman and "the secret movements of our city authorities" isn't offered for analysis, interpretation, or critical reflection as much as it's presented to elicit reactions we usually associate with the body: disgust, loathing, exhilaration, thrill, arousal. These reactions are linked to information about the city, and especially to information about power and class in the city. I emphasize that the papers do transmit important information, but they do so in embodied form, rather than rational-critical form. Even when they discuss topical and political issues, the "racy" papers make their claims in ways that do not necessarily invite the deliberation of ideas.

If the papers so obviously address their readers as bodies and as subsisting in the here-and-now of news transmission, they also attempt to shape other parts of the reader experience that, while not as immediately apparent, are nevertheless extremely important. The projected reader is encouraged to cultivate a self-consciousness about mediation, a sense of distance and detachment. It's important to note that the papers consist almost entirely of letters from readers (editorial content is kept to a minimum), and these letter-writers themselves understand the sporting press as a medium of public discussion and an instrument for their own circulation in the public sphere. The letters repeatedly begin, "Mr. Editor, Sir,—through the medium of your valuable paper"[23]; in contrast, contemporaneous mainstream papers like the *Herald* or the *Tribune* ran reported news stories and editorials but published comparatively few letters from readers. The sporting papers place a great deal of emphasis on the protocols and technicalities of the dissemination of readers' letters. This emphasis contributes to the self-consciousness about mediation, as well as the readers' sense of anonymity and generality. Letters could be dropped off in boxes at many of the same places where the papers were sold: at hotels, porter houses, boarding houses, clubs, meeting rooms, reading rooms, or hangouts near the theaters. Early versions of the papers were careful to give the exact addresses of the drop-off sites; the thoroughness of these directions indicates that reader (and potential letter writers) were not a small clique or cadre already in the know, but a more diffuse collection of strangers, both to each other and to the papers' editors.[24]

Indeed, the reader-writers seem to have understood themselves as strangers in communication with each other. For instance, they frequently portray themselves as incognito, as "spies" who roam the city streets, or as birds of prey (in the case of the *Hawk and Buzzard* and *Owl*) who can see everything and go everywhere in the city without notice. These correspondents allow readers to walk the city while remaining detached. In fact, the "spies" of the *Flash* "walk invisible and intangible," we are told, and they are careful to maintain their anonymity and distance: "You have sought them without finding them."[25] The participants in this interactive sporting community go by pseudonyms like "Invisible," "Observer," "A Reader," "Honorable," "Moral Reform and Co.," "Hawkeye," or "Argus,"[26] which emphasize their anonymity, generality, and Archimedean position of sharp-eyed objectivity. Their letters are not about private self-making. They are not personal correspondences plumbing psychological depths that the public eavesdrops upon, as in epistolary novels like *Clarissa* or *Les Liaisons Dangereuses*, but letters addressed by anonymous types (a "reader," an "observer") directly to an equally anonymous public. This sense of generality and anonymity is further underwritten by the assurance of reasoned, impartial debate among freely acting individuals, a demeanor of "politeness" where everyone is treated as equal. Thus, in the most polite and reasoned voice, and from a position of utter impartiality, a correspondent for the *Arena* pulls back the curtain on a city scene, saying, "Do we advocate this? Oh! by no means. We advocate nothing. We describe what is—We foretell what inevitably will be. Our remarks neither make things worse nor better. We describe things *as they are*."[27] Of course, what the reader finds behind the curtain isn't meant to be deliberated upon; it's meant to disgust or excite. In one sense this is an artificial pose, a parody of the polite impartiality often performed by correspondents and commentators, going back to the *Spectator* and the *Tatler*. But in another sense the parody suggests a different relationship between reader and what is read, one in which reading connects itself to the power associated with impartial debate but isn't necessarily a practice of reason. Paradoxically, this reader is both detached and embodied; he or she participates in a double movement.

In a moment I'll return to the meaning and significance of this idea of a double movement, but first it is worth recognizing just how different this picture of obscene reading is from the standard picture of such reading. Obscene literature has been frequently characterized, since the eighteenth century in Europe, as absorptive, addictive, idiocy-inducing, and generally enfeebling. As Thomas Laqueur has suggested, the problem with early print pornography wasn't simply its immorality or its anti-aristocratic politics (in France, at least), but the sense that it created the wrong kinds of subjects for modern social structures, subjects who were absorbed in their own imaginations and possessed little self-control. For instance, to be absorbed in a text or addicted to a text was not conducive to becoming a good capitalist worker (302–58) or, for that matter, a productive member of a rational-critical public sphere.[28] I'm suggesting, however, that we shouldn't take these accounts of absorptive obscene reading as very good or fair renderings of the structure of obscene reading, in that their emphasis on absorption doesn't capture obscene reading's complexity and double movement. The absorptive account has also played a significant role in late twentieth-century scholarly work on eighteenth- and nineteenth-century pornography by cultural historians like Steven Marcus and Jean Marie Goulemot. They tend to reverse the emphasis of the anti-masturbation tracts and see absorptive reading as producing an at least partially subversive fantasy space—a "pornotopia" (271), to use Marcus's wonderful term. Both of these accounts are extremely helpful and accurate as far as they go, but they leave unexplained the double-movement of early obscene reading. This double movement is also central to the reading of obscene novelettes.

OBSCENE NOVELETTES AND THEIR STRUCTURES OF READING

My general argument about the novelettes is that they construct their readers' relation with the text in ways similar to the sporting press. Reading is understood as a public act—a way of participating critically in the public sphere. That critical participation isn't carried out through rational-critical argument but through embodied reactions to issues. Because obscene novelettes are often about current issues and the news, they construct their readers as news readers. George Thompson, one of the most prolific authors of such books in the late 1840s and early '50s (he published dozens), always embedded his novelettes in contentious issues.[29] Thompson's *Fanny Greeley, or Confessions of a Free-love Sister Written by Herself*, was named in newspaper reports of the obscenity arrest at Lovejoy's hotel that I mentioned previously. We have only a fragment of this text, but it is clear that the work was topical and public sphere-oriented because the daily papers immediately understood it as a form of political pamphleteering. The *Herald* opined that *Fanny Greeley* and other obscene literature like it would lead readers into the clutches of the "black republican" party and "anti-slavery agitators," and toward "new fangled ideas, agrarian, socinias [sic], socialistic, and otherwise." Somehow it would expose readers to the "women's rights mania" as well as "the Women's Rights Conventions, the preachings and teaching of which have carried sorrow to many a hearth."[30] In a similar fashion, obscene books appearing under the name Charles Paul de Kock were linked by the *Herald* to the Know-Nothing Party (whose Northern members would soon join with the anti-slavery or "black" Republican party). Even Thompson's title (*Fanny Greeley*) and subject matter (free-love societies) were a wink to contemporary news readers, who would recognize the allusions to two New York personalities: Horace Greeley (editor of the *Tribune*, an outspoken backer of the city's working-class organizations, a progressive on race issues, and a Fourierist supporter) and his rumored associate Fanny Wright (a sensation in antebellum New York for advocating free love, free thinking, women's rights, and the establishment of socialistic, interracial communes among workers).[31]

Thompson's novelettes themselves never seem as politically engaged or as closely associated with various groups as the *Herald* makes *Fanny Greeley* out to be, although it is difficult to tell much about the politics of this specific book because we can read only a small piece. But the one extant excerpt, found in the annotated bibliography of Victorian collector Henry Spencer Ashbee, does offer a view of a structure of reading. It is presented slyly, with a great deal of self-consciousness about the context of obscene reading. In the excerpt we meet Nabal, who oversees the free-love society of the book's subtitle (*Confessions of a Free-love Sister*) as a kind of spiritual leader. Nabal isn't beautiful like the others of the society, but mysteriously "pale and sallow," "thin and attenuated" with an "attitude full of languor" (214); however, he occupies a privileged position that allows him to watch members of the society have sex. One character explains this arrangement to a new initiate (Fanny of the title), after they have had sex together under Nabal's watchful gaze:

> "Nabal . . . has one ruling passion, that of women. They are his adoration, the subject of his thoughts by day and night. But a mysterious and extraordinary accident he met with in his childhood, while sleeping in the woods of his native south, deprived him of his powers of manhood. He is doomed to perpetual virginity of person, though his imagination revels in all the wildest enjoyments of passions. When

the powers of his imagination have brought him to the highest intensity of desire, fruition can be obtained but by means of others. Thus,
whilst gratifying our own passions for each other, we satisfied the passion your surpassing beauty and his vicinity to your glowing charms
had excited in him." (216)

Rather frustratingly, the excerpt ends just after this revelation, but it
still suggests a great deal. To begin, we should note that it's not difficult to see Nabal as a manifestation of a reader and to see this scene as
a playful scene of reading. He watches as a kind of voyeur-reader from
a distance, "doomed to a perpetual virginity of person" but "reveling
in his imagination." In fact, he has all the physiological characteristics
of the masturbator-reader that are endlessly repeated in the dozens of
anti-onanism tracts published in the nineteenth-century United States.
They "are commonly pale and thin . . . they are feeble, cacochyic, chilly,
apathetic," and "[e]verything fatigues them; or rather they are always
fatigued" (Teste 102), just as Nabal is "pale and sallow," "thin and attenuated" and his "attitude full of languor." Indeed, Nabal's "accident"
sounds very much like one particular masturbator who has lost a testicle
on account of his onanist practice (Woodward 28). But if Nabal is a
kind of emblem for the masturbator-reader of the reform tracts, he is
also unlike this reader in that the above passage venerates the obscene
imagination as exhilarating and interconnecting. Rather than an anti-
onanist condemnation of absorptive, enervating, and isolating mastur-
batory reading, this scene seems, in the end, like a celebration. Nabal's
fantasy leads him outward, not inward: "fruition can be obtained but by
means of others."

Nabal offers a rather extreme example of the obscene reader's imagination as a form of engagement rather than private absorption, but the
novelettes do still present themselves as publicly engaged in less extreme and sensualized ways. In almost all of Thompson's novelettes,
he theorizes their link to public discourse in the first few paragraphs.
He does this by pledging their truthfulness and realism, and reiterates
how they should be distinguished from other novels, which are mere
romances, simple fictions. This kind of pledge is of course ubiquitous in
late eighteenth-century American novels; one of its central functions is
to suggest that what the reader is about to read isn't just fancy, but important to public life and civic society. Early republic–era novelists had
to repeatedly assure readers that suspicious-looking novels were actually

closely aligned with histories or newspapers, forms of writing which were above suspicion because they contributed to civic life and thus meshed well with republican ideology. Thompson's novelette *The Countess* does precisely this when it calls itself a "romance of the real" because "[t]o the sensible mind of man or woman, fact, uncontradictable and solid fact, is that food of which it loves to partake" (3). *The Countess* goes on to be interested in the sex lives of newsworthy figures like Madame Restell, the abortionist and author of early feminist tracts on contraception and sexuality (who would commit suicide two decades later rather than face Comstock's dragnet), and Richard P. Robinson, the accused in one of the most famous prostitute-murder trials of the antebellum period. *The Countess* also introduces the rakish Harry Rush—son of the famous Benjamin Rush—who meets his match when he attempts to seduce the novel's female protagonist. This scene is typical of the genre:

> [Harry Rush's] hands were soon in close communion with my breasts, and various and many were the compliments bestowed upon form and feature. His passions rose by degrees, and I saw the proud aristocrat changed to a slave. His eyes flashed fire, and his impetuous passion longed to burst the cord which bound it, and satisfy itself by attaining the wished for object. I yielded to him in all his embraces, and nearly all the liberties he chose to take were allowed, only occasionally refused him for the very sake of granting him pardon for the offense. From my breasts, he commenced an examination of my dress, and gradually did his hand descend, and in leaving the fabric, I felt it encircle my ankle. A single word, and it returned to the side of its owner. Another series of caresses, however, soon followed, and again the truant hand obeyed the instructions of its master's desires. After a time I allowed it, and what a sensation was mine, as I felt that hand slowly and easily rise to the knee, and then still higher. He undoubtedly felt that I was completely in his power so resigned and patient were appearances—but just as he was about to achieve his fancied final triumph over my resistless form, I broke from his embrace, and censured him for daring to attempt such liberties. (16)

The episode concludes when the corrupt Harry Rush loses all capacity for reason and attempts to stab the virtuous seductress in the heart; but, in his state of aroused passion, he faints just before the moment of triumph.

This scene is silly and absurd, like many in the antebellum obscene genre, but it is also full of keywords from the popular political vocabulary of the late eighteenth and early nineteenth centuries: reason, virtue, "aristocra[cy]," "slave[ry]," "liberties," and "power" are all under discussion, albeit not in the standard way. In one respect, the passage suggests a very old idea: that the concerns of governance and civil society are played out in the most intimate realms (this idea, taken to a parodic extreme here, is central to Benjamin Rush's own notion of "republican motherhood"). But what is of greater interest in this instance is the way that the reader is asked to engage with these ideas of political discourse, not at a critical distance but as an embodied experience. The text develops reciprocity with readers who are encouraged to project themselves—especially their bodies—into the text. In Thompson's passage, the hand becomes strangely disconnected from any physical body—first "his hand," then "that hand," and finally "the truant hand," and it is not hard to imagine the reader imagining it as his (or her) own on some level. Its movement over the surface of breasts, clothing, and body tries to transform the passage's concerns with reason, virtue, aristocracy, slavery, liberties, and power into sensual concerns, concerns of touch.

The collapsing of reading into sex—or perhaps it would be more accurate to say the collapsing of reading into masturbation—was a not uncommon joke in the obscene sheets like *Venus' Miscellany*. Books are like female genitals: "Why are the private organs of a wench like a book?" one wag asks in the paper. "Because it must be opened to read (red)." Another jokes, "Why is a lady's petticoat like a novel? Because it is taken up for a little innocent amusement."[32] One letter to the editor compliments the paper on its power to give him an erection.[33] It is hard to know exactly what produces an erection in any given text, but a strategy which some of the obscene literature returns to often might be called the intimate blason, where body parts are described as the eye moves across them. Indeed, the intimate blason directs the reader's eye here and then there and finally there. In such instances, the sensualized body in the text addresses the (male) reader's body about as directly as possible in a print text. The above encounter between Harry Rush's hand and the body parts in *The Countess* are an example of an intimate blason. The anonymously authored *The Amorous Intrigues and Adventures of Aaron Burr* (1861?)—a pornographic biography of the former vice president—offers intimate blason after blason. One example:

Burr put his arm around the waist of Angelina, and pressed her to his throbbing heart, applied his lips to those ivory globes which rounded up over her dress, almost to her nipples. . . .

He threw up her clothes, and revealed such charms as seldom have been exposed to the light of the sun. The smooth, round belly, the voluminous yet compact thighs, the robust calf, and small foot and ankle, the satin smoothness of the skin, and other graces not to be mentioned, but whose parting and moist freshness betokened a guarded virginity, which, however, longed for the pressure of manhood. (18)

Again, this description verges on the ridiculous, but its strategy is easily recognized. It produces an embodied object which then calls upon the reader's own body.

The Burr porno-bio and Thompson's *The Countess* share a common characteristic in their eroticization of the political. At this antebellum moment, however, there is of course another popular discourse of the body that attempts to transform questions of liberty and power, virtue and reason, into feeling. But the "sentimental" is very different from the obscene. Although sentimental and obscene reading are both built on imaginative projections into scenes and a reciprocity between text and reader, the sentimental has as its goal a moral response, which the obscene lacks or even attempts to destroy. Susan Sontag captures this difference in an essay on sensationalistic pornography, which she surprisingly and brilliantly compares to the silliness of slapstick. "In both," Sontag writes, "there is a deadening or neutralization or distancing of the audience's emotions, its ability to identify in a 'humane' way and to make moral judgments about situations of violence" (*Will* 55). The silly, absurd, and often violent quality of antebellum obscenity is indeed de-emotionalizing and anti-moralizing. The obscene attempts to turn emotion into what it might be in the first place — embodiment — before it is attached to moral codes. There are no emotions here in the standard sense because there are no humans to have emotions. The characters have no interiorities; there are only surfaces — clothing, skin, breast, ankle. What we commonly think of as emotion or feeling isn't the goal of the obscene. The reciprocity between text and reader is founded, we might say, on a de-emotionalizing embodiment.

The Uses of Obscene Reading

The previous section attempts to outline the structures of reading — that is, the relationship between text, reader, and public sphere — encouraged by obscene newspapers and novelettes. It is a fairly complex structure, and certainly much more complex than its panicky censors from the nineteenth century (or its celebratory critics from the twentieth) recognize. To review, the sporting papers and novelettes are very conscious of their readers' experiences, developing a kind of reciprocity between text and reader. In the two genres, the reading practice involved a specific sense of time and place (engaging with the here and now of news) and a sense of both distancing detachment and absorbed embodiment. In other words, the obscene texts ask readers to become intensely, even physically, absorbed at almost precisely the same time that readers are encouraged to be distanced and highly aware of topical reality, as well as conscious of the mediated aspect of their reading. Finally, the reciprocity and absorption do not operate using the same emotional material and logic as sentimentalism and other "moral" emotions, but rather exercise a de-emotionalizing embodiment. Now, with the intricacies of this obscene reading outlined, what sense can be made of its meaning and uses?

Michael Warner offers one of the most sophisticated accounts of the way public spheres work and, at least in part, obscene reading fits with his account. Warner posits that the modern public sphere is governed by an antinomy: it addresses infinite, anonymous, indeterminate strangers (this distinguishes the modern form of the public sphere from the form of the group, bounded audience, etc.), even as it attempts to concretize or embody this abstract field and these abstract addressees. In other words, participants in any modern public sphere find themselves addressed as both an abstraction and an embodiment (*Publics* 74). Being part of such a public sphere entails a constant double movement between abstraction and embodiment. The obscene literature reproduces this antinomy; its readers are repeatedly addressed as abstract and embodied.[34]

But to what end? Saying that obscene literature reflects (or allows readers to experience) an antinomy inherent to the modern public sphere still does not show how readers of the genre used the reflection or experience. Warner is again helpful up to a point. He notes that the abstraction/embodiment antinomy is always unstable and often produces an unsettling dissonance. For some people the movement between poles is fairly easy because there isn't much difference between their self-understanding as abstract addressees and embodied addressees. But for many (especially people of marginalized identities), moving between these poles is much more difficult and often triggers a deeply embodied dissonance, which Warner suggests might be experienced in any number of ways—as an "erotic-aggressive disturbance" (176), or a "double movement of identification and alienation" (182) or just "noise" (176). Such dissonance is a registering of the instability of the antinomy. It's a kind of marker of the unease with which, for many, abstraction and embodiment fit together. In Warner's view, the dissonance might be contained or it might be subversively dynamic. In his well-known essay, "The Mass Public and the Mass Subject," Warner suggests that various genres of mass culture—like disaster coverage and celebrity bashing—allow readers and viewers to momentarily inhabit embodiment and dissonance, but from a distance, so that the balance of the antinomy is never threatened. But Warner also suggests that under different conditions the instability of the antinomy might allow for a "fruitful perversity" that provides the "engine" for "social mutations" and "recharacterizations" that "g[o] well beyond any strategy of domination" and, indeed, provides the public sphere with "world-making" possibilities (*Publics* 113). The antinomy's instability and the embodied dissonance it produces provide the conditions of possibility for new public formations, new concretizations. Warner's key examples of such dynamic subversion are queer public spheres that have attempted to develop new forms of public interactivity—new counterpublics—out of the felt dissonance.

While Warner's two models suggest how important the antinomy is to the experience of modern public spheres, neither model fits very well with the antebellum obscene. Is the obscene best understood as participating in a "world-making" or "re-characterizing" project? The genre never seems that conative or purposeful. In many ways, I would certainly be partial to a counterpublic sphere with "world-making" aspirations—that is, say, as an attempt to value the body, rather than critical reason, as the foundation for public interactivity—but the obscene genre doesn't seem to lead to any kind of cohesive counterpublic that has much power to remake anything. It does associate itself with a new culture of young men and women in the antebellum city that was generally populist and anti-establishment, but it would be an incautious leap to suggest that the obscene public sphere had any effect on a dominant public sphere and its values. Like most cultural forms, this obscene literature didn't do or seek to do anything so grand. It's also easy to imagine that many readers participated enthusiastically in the obscene public sphere and any number of other more mainstream public spheres, thus making it difficult to understand the obscene public as a counterpublic. But, at the same time, it would be narrow-minded to understand the genre as simply mass-cultural mystification or a technology of interpellation into the dominant values of the public sphere. Perhaps we need a new way of understanding such cultural forms, one that places less focus on culture as either destabilizing or limiting. If we resist seeing the obscene genre as subversive or containing, purposeful or mystifying, how might it be understood as meaningful and useful?[35]

One of the virtues of the recent work on what is variously called affect, feeling, or emotion is that it begins to allow an avoidance of such dichotomies. Eve Sedgwick, Sianne Ngai, William Reddy, and Brian Massumi offer ways of thinking about affect/feeling/emotion as diagnostic, rather than subversive, containing, or purposeful. For instance, Ngai discusses what she refers to as "minor" emotions like "irritation" and "envy" which serve not to drive the subject to action but simply to notify (22, 27, and elsewhere). In Ngai's reading, such emotions typically identify or diagnose an impasse (1). Reddy, as discussed in the first chapter, focuses on the verbalization of emotion, arguing that such verbalizations—or emotives—are ways of testing or navigating a vast array of sensory inputs. The concept of the emotive is very helpful in understanding antebellum obscene reading and perhaps pornography more generally. First, what emotives are produced by obscene reading? As I argued above, obscene literature traffics in a de-emotionalizing embodiment that circumvents moral and purposeful emotions like sentimentalism. If any emotion or "emotive" can justly be attributed to antebellum pornography, it is an ambivalent combination of thrill and relief set in motion by stimulation, release, and repetition. The centrality of this cycle in the antebellum obscene is perhaps best indicated by the way that their episodic plots stimulate, release, then repeat. Susan Sontag notes just how "fatiguing" this repetitiveness can be in pornography (*Will* 62), and such fatigue does seem a particularly modern kind of experience, as many theorists of modernity have referenced it under the names boredom, ennui, or tedium. In this view, the experience of boredom or ennui is not the result of too little stimulation but too much. Georg Simmel for instance notes that "an immoderately sensuous life" results in what he calls the "blasé attitude"; such sensual activity "stimulates the nerves to their utmost reactivity until they can produce no reactions at all" (329).

Boredom in Simmel's view is paradoxical: the result of an intense experience that became monotonous. Walter Benjamin sees boredom in much the same way—as related to the stimulatingly repetitious experience of the urban gambler and flaneur (102). Nabal, the stand-in for the reader in Thompson's *Fanny Greeley*, is not unlike Benjamin's blasé gamblers and flaneurs; he is "full of languor" and outwardly bored from too much stimulation. (Just as the masturbator-reader described in anti-onanist tracts is enervated from too much stimulation.) However, Benjamin also sees a possibility in modern boredom or tedium that Simmel does not: as a protective emotion which allows for something else. Benjamin compares boredom to "a warm gray fabric lined on the inside with the most lustrous and colorful of silks" (105). It is a state of desire for something else: "In this fabric we wrap ourselves when we dream" (105). One scholar of Benjamin has suggested that Benjamin thinks of boredom as "a critically reflexive form of waiting" (Moran 179).

The work by Ngai, Reddy, and others on affect/emotion/feeling as diagnostic and navigatory helps outline the ways that the boredom/tedium generated by repetitious excitements might be "critically reflexive" in the antebellum obscene. In Reddy's model, a repeatedly articulated emotion like boredom is a way of testing a wide array of "materials" (as explained earlier, internal and external feeling, conscious and unconscious memories and narratives, and social schema). In this case, some of the most important material—the material shared by all readers—is the embodiment/abstraction antinomy central to both the obscene and any modern public sphere. It is this antinomy that is cycled through repeatedly so as to create the boredom of stimulation. The ritualistic boredom or ennui of the antebellum obscene, in other words, might well be understood as a way of navigating through or critically reflecting on the modern public sphere. It is a way of experimenting with one's relationship with the different poles of the antinomy. It is a way of testing one's ability to achieve the double movement required of a public sphere. This experience isn't immediately directed toward action or change; it isn't strategic or propulsive like the sentimental or another "major" emotion. Nevertheless, it provides important information about one's participation in a modern public sphere.

In suggesting that the experience of reading antebellum obscene literature can be understood as diagnostic or evaluative—and particularly diagnostic/evaluative of the public sphere itself—I am purposely resisting making the kinds of claims that are very common in contemporary literary and cultural studies. Specifically, I am trying to move beyond the limitations of interpreting these texts as either strategic or symptomatic. This isn't meant to suggest that they are not strategic and symptomatic in various ways, but that there are additional approaches to understanding the work they do. As we have seen, there is considerable evidence that obscene literature had a strategic function as a kind of rallying cry for a growing working class (and a burgeoning clerk class). The punctuated tedium so central to these texts perhaps suggests a particular audience of industrial and office workers whose rhythms of labor are reflected in and recognizable in the texts. The obscene's punkish railing against the "aristocracy" and other powers-that-be may have appealed to the same collection of readers. But I do want to resist turning this obscene literature into the foundation for a counterpublic, a subaltern public or what Lauren Berlant calls an "intimate public" (*Female* viii and *passim*). Such an approach would allow us to avoid seeing obscene literature as part of the everyday, mainstream, mass public sphere. It is the possibilities for agency in this mass public sphere, not a counterpublic sphere founded on a samizdat literature, that we still don't understand very well. How did readers use the emotions circulating in that sphere while not necessarily taking part in something that can be considered a counterpublic? It is after all this non-counterpublic experience that is so characteristic of modern life.

Antebellum obscene literature is surely symptomatic of a very complex political, ideological unconscious that shapes readers. This unconscious shapes them, as we have begun to see, in terms of gender, race, class, and belonging, to only begin a list of categories. But to interpret the genre as solely symptomatic of ideological formations that interpellate readers is to too easily avoid asking how the readers themselves used the genre. I have tried here to inquire into how readers utilized the particular affective characteristics of the antebellum obscene to navigate the public sphere. In this view, obscene texts allowed their readers—indeed, even taught their readers—to participate in a modern public sphere while simultaneously navigating its alienating demands for self-abstraction and their own desires for an intimacy associated with embodiment and affect. An approach that focuses on navigation and evaluation through emotion seems necessary to the development not only of a better understanding of obscene literature and the antebellum public sphere, but also of a better understanding of our modern public sensorium.

Chapter Four

Scandalous Reading

The Intrigues of the New Public Sensorium

The Public Sphere Gone Bad

The long history of the scandal press — from the Renaissance "intrigue" to the *chronique scandaleuse* and *bruit public* of eighteenth-century France, the *Literaturbriefe* of eighteenth-century Germany, the sporting press and spy papers of nineteenth-century America, and finally, to the twentieth century's yellow journalism, Hollywood tabloids, and their televisual equivalents — often looks like the Habermasian public sphere gone bad. In theory that public sphere practices a rational-critical discourse, produces intersubjectively formulated truths, and ultimately enables an agency in the form of supervision of institutions of power. Instead of truth and agency, the scandal sphere seems to offer little more than highly manipulated spectacle meant for easy consumption; it is often perceived as a product of the culture industry masquerading as news and information. One of the most frustrating aspects of scandal is that it perverts the theoretical goal — the utopian wish — for truth and agency at the heart of the public-sphere concept. Indeed, media-reported scandals seem to wickedly and willfully play off that wish — the public sphere will disclose the truth (the real person behind the politician's mask, the people actually running the system, the pathways of the money, the president's penis), and truth leads to agency. This wish is a central part of the pleasure of scandal, but that pleasure frequently turns melancholic: the knowledge that scandal brings is seldom accompanied by the wished-for agency. Instead, scandal consumption is often attended by the sense of finding oneself in an ever more complex system where the object of desire — effective knowledge — remains seemingly just out of reach. The structures of scandals are compulsively repeated, but little changes. We all know, but knowing changes nothing; knowledge leads nowhere.

In addition to being about the outré details of the rich and famous, and beyond being about the secrets of obscure and complex institutions, scandal is about dilemmas faced by all who live in the modern public sphere — problems of knowing, problems of acting on knowledge, problems of drawing a line of causation between knowledge and action. One of the central arguments made in this chapter is that representations of scandal often represent precisely these problems. But at its boldest the argument is something more: that the consumption of scandal is a way of navigating through these problems.

In light of both the modern ubiquity of scandal and its entanglement in these issues of the public sphere and agency, "[w]hat's odd," as Laura Kipnis notes in an overview of recent scholarship on scandal, "is how little inquisitiveness there's been about the social dynamics involved" ("School" 73).[1] What remains particularly under-investigated is the consumption of scandal. This chapter is in large part about that consumption — in the form of reading scandal — in the early and mid-nineteenth century. If the previous chapter focused on the ways people read about sex rather than on the representation of sex or the social construction of sex, this chapter focuses on the way people read about scandal.

This emphasis on reading scandal and its effects is no easy matter, because the experience of scandal reading is so conflicted and complex. Scandal reading is only partially an experience that can be understood as what might be called rational; instead, its consumption is in large part emotional, and those emotions are complicated. We habitually devour scandal stories, but self-loathingly. They are exciting, yet cloying. They produce a schadenfreude that quickly feels shameful. Scandals shock, but they also enervate; they bemuse even as they outrage. Kipnis has suggested understanding the emotional double movement of scandal in psychoanalytic terms: scandal allows both the individual and society at large to simultaneously desire and disavow certain wants and needs. In this sense, scandal is a "social purification ritual" where "the socially non-compliant [are] branded and expelled, allowing the system to assert itself and make its muscle" even as individuals get their enjoyments (*How to Become* 14). As consumers of scandal, we all participate in this not-unpleasant ritual of social management, regulation, and interpellation.

Kipnis's psychodynamic, subversion-containment model of consumption is compelling, but here I do want to investigate another dimension of scandal consumption in hopes of developing, in a somewhat different direction, what Kipnis calls "scandal theory" (*How to Become* 7). Her work focuses on the most dramatic emotions surrounding scandal—"Love, Madness, Enmity, Jealousy, Betrayal, Fatal Imprudence" (21)—written with emphatic capitals befitting the emotions' classical status. Certainly these are important. However, so are less spectacular responses like ennui, exasperation, laughter, knowingness, condescension, and doubt. In fact, such minor, de-dramatized emotions may be the most regular, everyday responses to scandal. Do they serve the same ritual of purification, the same logic of interpellation? If not, how are these minor responses used by readers? What sort of knowledge do they offer their consumers? If we were to see scandal as something different from subversion and containment, how would we see it?

This chapter attempts to make some progress in answering these questions by suggesting that scandal consumption is closely connected to evaluation—to trust and distrust—of large, complex systems and, especially, the complex system of the modern public sphere. To trust is to believe in and to be assured of effectiveness and ability. The experience of observing a scandal is often accompanied by a wish to trust and a corresponding promise of effectiveness and ability. The scandal will reveal something, and the knowledge that scandal brings will have some agency or, at the least, result in greater understanding, we hope (and trust).

Approaching scandal in this manner provides further support for a model of affect and the public sphere put forward in earlier chapters. As I've indicated, public-sphere theory has often been limited in its addressing of affect. This chapter instead suggests that affect can connect the citizen's practice of scandal reading to reflection, critique, and interaction with decision-makers. This is to see textually generated feeling and emotion not as ideological interpellation or a fissure in ideology (both common ways of understanding emotion) but as a kind of thinking essential to the democratic public sphere. Thinking about emotion and the public sphere in this way allows us to think anew about the work of scandal in the public sphere.

The Structural Transformation of Scandal
in the Early Nineteenth Century

There have always been scandals, from Cleopatra to Clinton. The word "scandal" has described a wide range of events, from revelation of political conspiracy to the uncovering of private foibles. Amid this temporal and categorical variety, social scientists like John B. Thompson and Ari Adut suggest that scandals do often hew to the same rough form, a form that can be generally summarized as a transgression of well-recognized social norms that incites some kind of public response. Scandal involves public rule breaking, where the rules are the extra-legal conventions of the community. But scandal entails rather more than transgression, in that it also requires the revelation of something hidden, the making visible of what has been obscured. Public righteousness masks private vice; a system of credit is built on thin air; virgins are anything but. Scandal in this view is often the result of the crisscrossing of structures normally thought to be clearly defined opposites—the public and private, the moral and immoral, what appears to be or ought to be and what actually is the case. The appearance-reality distinction is the anchor of scandal. Even the most complex scandals almost always rest upon such a dualistic construction.

These aspects of scandal have remained fairly constant across the *longue durée*, but the experience of consuming scandal in the United States changed in significant ways in the early nineteenth century. First, scandal began to reference something that was read about by an anonymous and extended audience—a public. Formerly, scandal had been thought of as a local, face-to-face event that did not involve reading or the press. Second, the press not only became the mechanism for reporting scandal but also constituted the scandal itself. Put in slightly different terms, scandal became understood as an event that the public sphere plays a role in creating.

These shifts can be observed by examining the way scandal was discussed in the newspapers and popular journals of the late eighteenth and early nineteenth centuries. It was a common topic of conversation, appearing as the subject matter of hundreds of articles, letters, and poems printed in U.S. papers. In the decades surrounding the turn of the century, it became important to discuss and even theorize scandal. Significantly, there was at the century's turn much more discussion about the nature of scandal than there was about specific scandals. The press's role was to meditate on the nature of scandal rather than to uncover scandal. The sudden foregrounding of scandal in public conversation in the 1790s—the subject appears relatively rarely before that time—is explainable in part by the slow dissolution of a politics based on honor and reputation. When the eighteenth-century genteel ideals of a behind-the-scenes personal politics came under increasing stress from the post-Revolution rise of the "middling sorts" (the eighteenth-century term for the middle class) and their progressively more active press, it seems to have become ever more important to discuss and outline the meaning of scandal. The Adams Administration's Sedition Act (1798) attempted to regulate this press, but to little avail. Several of these moments of scandal theorization can serve as starting points for better understanding the shifts in the conceptualization of scandal across this time period. The first is the quasi-poetic piece "On Scandal," which appeared dozens of times in the late eighteenth century and the first decades of the new century.[2] It adapts an eighteenth-century neoclassical tone and borders at times on poetry but is perhaps best described as a prose aphorism:

ON SCANDAL

Against Slander there is no defense. Hell cannot boast so foul a fiend; nor man deplore so fell a foe: It stabs with a word—with a nod—with a shrug—with a look—with a smile: It is the pestilence walking in darkness, spreading contagion far and wide, which the most wary traveler cannot avoid: It is the heart searching dagger of the dark assassin: It is the poisoned arrow, whose wound is incurable: It is the mortal sting of the deadly adder: murder is its employment; innocence is its prey—and ruin its sport.

The personification of scandal inevitably seems archaic and odd today. The twenty-first century is not beyond the use of personification—of commodities and certain concepts—but it is difficult today to understand scandal as a person. It is instead an event, one that is often beyond the power of any single individual. But in "On Scandal," scandal is figured as an assassin, a masculine sexual predator. There is almost no sense in this piece that scandal is associated with the media. It "stabs with a word," but that word seems to be spoken rather than written or printed. Scandal's other modes of expression are also of the face-to-face kind: a "nod," a "shrug," a "look," a "smile." Scandal here is conflated with "slander," which conventionally and legally has been associated with oral dissemination, not print.

Instead of as a modern media event, this text figures scandal as something akin to gossip or rumor, where gossip and rumor are understood as taking place among locally arrayed friends and neighbors instead of a larger, more general and abstract public. Members of a group gossip about other members of a group, but it is difficult to imagine the concept of gossip having much meaning among the general members of a public who don't know each other. Such a form of circulation among an anonymous generality would be something closer to modern scandal. It is the case in "On Scandal" that the circulation of information is hidden from view ("the pestilence walking in darkness, spreading contagion far and wide"), but this circulation is not yet associated with anonymity in the way it would be just a few years later. There is still the suggestion of an immoral actor, rather than an amoral media, behind this circulation. But perhaps this moment in "On Scandal" is registering a cultural shift toward an awareness of a more anonymous, mass public sphere.

This conceptualization of scandal as a localized and personalized phenomenon is often repeated in the late eighteenth and early nineteenth centuries. A magazine commentator in 1774 reminds his readers that scandals "proceed from those calumnies and reproaches which we spread abroad concerning one another,"[3] and another author—in this instance the novelist William Hill Brown—in 1789 complains that "[t]he editors of our periodical publications seem to be impressed with the idea, that all their readers are very much delighted with seeing the reputations of their neighbors stamped with some odious opprobrium."[4] Scandal is something that happens in a neighborhood and among a face-to-face group even, it seems, when it appears in papers. "Nothing more effectively destroys the blessing of [a] neighborhood, than scandal,"[5] the same author reiterates. Scandal, in other words, was a personal affair. It threatened personal reputation and operated within long-standing ideals of gentlemanly honor and republican virtue. This idea of scandal was deeply connected to a political culture and philosophy of the eighteenth century, where politics was understood as a personal rather than a party endeavor. Federalists and Republicans alike in the early republic often declared their disdain for parties (or "factions") and viewed governing as the work of individual men acting on their personal honor. Scandals and intrigues were thus a significant weapon in this politics of virtue (Freeman). As a personal affront, scandal is often understood in the late eighteenth century as a personal vice, a characterological shortcoming or flaw, one that is associated with crime. This early concept of scandal meant that it was linked with individual actors. The participants in scandal were individuals—the perpetrators, the spreaders, and the readers. The propagation of scandal—either by a repeater or a reader of it—was understood as a weakness in the individual's passions and even blood. One doctor warned "that scandal proceeds from the poorness of the blood," an ailment "promoted by tea visits, and watering places," perhaps because such consumption facilitates face-to-face interaction. Of course, the poor blood and the undisciplined passions of women and the working class were most susceptible but, as one paper puts it, "[t]here are very few who do not in some way or other sacrifice to this malevolent passion."[6]

The idea of scandal as community gossip or rumor that was attributable in large part to the moral and even physiological shortcomings of individuals was beginning to change even as these accounts were written. In 1789 one paper writes of "the NEWS-PAPER SCANDAL" (the direct article and capitalization emphasize that a new kind of event is being named) as a

> monster of a million tongues, which are forked, and perpetually darting venom. Its body is white, covered with small black scales, and is not very ugly to behold at first sight; but on a close examination, the scales become enormous, and you discover a venomous liquor to issue from them, the vapors of which will sometimes hurt the eye, and sometimes affect the understanding.[7]

It was not uncommon in the seventeenth and eighteenth centuries to depict the press as a monster, but this is one of the earliest depictions of scandal as linked to the monstrosity of the press. This million-tongued dragon also remains different from the modern investigative press; it is mainly a disseminator rather than an originator of information. It sits in its lair and people come and tell it rumors that it then circulates. The monster has only a single ear, apparently all that is required to spread rumor. Yet, even as this monster is deviously powerful and threatening, it still has an individual in control of it—"the operations of this animal depend entirely on the keeper." One can appeal to the keeper-editor simply by going to see him. Scandal has not yet slipped the reins of the local community.

From the perspective of our contemporary moment there is something quaint about this personalizing conceptualization of scandal. Slander and calumny are no longer in the foreground of scandals. Scandals are not generated by any one individual as much as produced by a complex amalgamation of the press. The shift from the old to modern notion of scandal is evident in the frequently reprinted "A New Mode of Scandal,"[8] which offers what is ostensibly a news account from Paris about a blind beggar who on "retiring in the dusk to his hovel after having spent the day in begging" is accosted by an unknown man who offers him charity. This unknown person tells the blind man that he is an author and, although he doesn't have any money to give the poor, he does have "parcels of tales and novels" that the street beggar can sell, then keep the proceeds. Elated by his stroke of good fortune, the blind beggar "sallies" out into the streets the next day to sell his new wares, hawking them "by the title of a new novel, as he had been directed." At first no one buys, but finally one book is purchased and "examined," and "the rest are met with the most rapid sale." Having exhausted his stock, the blind man returns to his hovel happy and satisfied, only to be quickly collared by the Paris police, for the book he has sold was not a popular new novel but "a most virulent and impudent satire against a person of rank." The blind man, the article reports, is compassionately freed by the police, "but he could give no information which could lead to the continuance of the very ingenious and new way of spreading abroad scandal with impunity."

"A New Mode of Scandal" describes just that. The new mechanisms of scandal are closely tied to print media and no longer look like what might be called gossip. This is a cautionary tale about the mediation of scandal and the problems raised by that mediation. Scandal of this sort cannot be easily traced back to its sources, and it spreads by a mechanism that is blind and cannot be morally to blame for its actions. In the previous examples, scandal is personalized and personified, even transformed into an evil monster; in this instance, it is commodified. In this transformation, the sense of the agent behind the scene changes — from an actual person to a system of exchanges beyond the control of any individual. That system of exchanges is the real subject matter of this (fictional?) news account. The underlying scandal is that there is no identifiable entity to blame. The hidden objects of scandal are no longer private, personal lives but the mechanisms of scandal itself. In other words, a scandal's circulation, its truth value, and the damage it might do become the central topics of the scandal.

The sociologist John B. Thompson calls this newer version of scandal the "modern phenomenon of mediated scandal"; in his view, it was "invented in the course of the later eighteenth and nineteenth centuries"

(*Political Scandal* 52). By "mediated scandal" he means not only a scandal reported by the media but also a scandal that is constituted in large
part by the media. There had long been scandals in print—indeed, the
novel genre in part owes its birth to the scandal of female seduction—
but the early novel recounted that scandal rather than produced it. In
the case of mediated scandal, disclosure through the media "was not a
retrospective commentary on a scandalous event, but rather, it was partly
constitutive of the event as scandal" ("New Visibility" 43). Thompson
provides several reasons for this historical shift, most prominently the
professionalization of journalism and the disconnection of the press from
political parties. Both developments led to a more investigative and scan-
dal-producing media. What is less clear than the causes of the shift are its
effects. How did mediated scandal change the consumption of scandal?

Celebrity Scandal

By the 1830s mediated scandal had become a common, everyday event in
American life.[9] Papers, pamphlets, and pulp novelettes were filled with
stories—ostensibly based on fact—that sought to outrage readers with
the exposure of the hidden transgressions of social standards. The 1828
election was one of the most scandal-ridden in American history. Jackson and Adams were both tarred with tales about their apparent sexual
indiscretions, and personality began to take precedent over policy. Stories of secret societies and secret religious activities were among the most
popular productions of 1830s print culture. That decade saw an explosion of quasi-news accounts of Free Masonry's nefarious deeds and the
diabolical activities of priests in Catholic convents. By the 1840s, scandal
had become a kind of popular entertainment, with P. T. Barnum appro-
priating many of its structures in the service of his American Museum.
A mysteries-of-the-city pulp genre was constructed around the exposure
of supposed wrongdoing behind the respectable facades of Boston, New
York, and Philadelphia. The raison d'être of spy papers and the sporting
press was scandal production.

During this time, scandal began to entwine with celebrity in ways that
will seem familiar because they remain common today. The Jacksonian
period saw the democratization of fame. Tennessee's Davy Crockett became a national celebrity in part through the publication of his autobiography and other myth-making accounts. The theater papers participated
in what they themselves began to call "the system of starring," through

which they manufactured stars in order to sell tickets.[10] The possibility of fame became available to a much larger and more diverse population—actors and frontiersmen, but also ministers, prostitutes, gamblers, and temperance advocates. Indeed, anyone might gain some measure of fame, especially through scandal. A genre of print culture began to develop that thematized such democratic celebrity, as well as its dangers. These pulpy novelettes told stories of how the ordinary became famous or infamous. They were both instruments of fame-making and commentaries on fame-making. Most of the stories are about young women who achieve some manner of notoriety—usually for their beauty and promiscuity—among a local urban population of semi-strangers (who see them in the street or brothel); such women then achieve much greater fame with their often violent and out-of-the-ordinary deaths. These narratives are about the machinations of celebrity, especially the movement from face-to-face fame to a much more expansive and highly mediated modern type of fame. Poe's "The Mystery of Marie Roget" (1842) is a well-known example. It uses the frame of a quasi-fictionalized story of Mary Rogers (renamed and transposed to Paris), who is locally famous even before her death, as the narrator is quick to remind us: "above all, her previous notoriety [due to her beauty and an earlier disappearance], conspired to produce intense excitement" (509). With her final disappearance, she becomes so famous that the fictionalization will be easily "recognized by all readers" (507), as the narrator says, from the story's coverage in the press and other true-crime pamphlets. In fact, Poe's famous detective, Auguste Dupin, attempts to solve the mystery not by investigating the facts but by investigating the way in which the story is represented in the press. Dupin is a master at uncovering the machinations involved in public representation, and the knowledge he gains is enough to solve this celebrity murder. The inner workings of public representation were a common topic for fiction in the Jacksonian and antebellum periods, although such narratives seldom present as complex an understanding of what is at stake as Poe's. The murdered prostitute Helen Jewett became a media-made celebrity—as did her accused murderer, Richard P. Robinson—through the public press and a series of novelettes. George Thompson's *The Countess* (1849), as discussed in chapter 3, barely masks the identity of its infamous characters—Madame Restell, Jewett, Robinson, and others. A later novelette, *The Eventful Lives of Helen and Charlotte Lenoxa* (1852), tells of the rise and fall of twin sisters through their manipulation of the public sphere. The arc of this tale will seem familiar: it's a precursor of the popular myth-making productions of the second half of the century—stories that elevated the likes of Buffalo Bill and others to stardom—and also a close relative of today's celebrity narratives.

Celebrity powerfully orients its consumers to the public sphere in various ways. It enables a vicarious circulation in which readers and viewers move through the public sphere in ways not otherwise available to them. As such, celebrity sometimes serves as a point of recognition and group identity. But celebrity also constantly runs the risk of commodity fetishism—indeed, it is perhaps the ultimate example of the fetishized commodity. If commodity fetishism erases the laboring body behind all commodities, then celebrity is doubly powerful in that it erases bodily labor even as it presents the celebrity's body. In addition, there is a disturbingly non- and even anti-democratic aspect to even the most democratic celebrity. Through celebrity, one circulates through the public sphere not by one's own ideas and actions but via another's, in a form of "representative publicness" associated by Habermas with kings and queens (*Structural* 5).

But none of these accounts of celebrity clearly explains the violence that is so often inflicted upon celebrities. We might ask why we like our celebrities so damaged. We seem to appreciate them most when they get bloated or emaciated or entangled in some sort of scandal that leaves them deflated or exposed. Almost all of the celebrity tales from the 1830s and '40s, like those of today, obsessively expose their celebrity subjects—expose their bodies, reveal their hidden desires, and make visible their ostensibly private lives. They are, in other words, scandalized. This obsession with the fallen star is why it is so important to think about celebrity and scandal together, to outline their connections. (There are, of course, different kinds of celebrity and different kinds of scandal, but the scandalous celebrity and the celebrity scandal are perhaps the most common.) How do theories of celebrity that emphasize salubrious identification or acts of fetishism explain the pervasiveness of (and the pleasure taken in) the violence inflicted upon celebrities? This question can be approached psychoanalytically. It may be that we project our most illicit desires upon celebrities, then love to see them beat up for having those desires. Using such an analytic lens, similar to that employed by Laura Kipnis to understand scandal more generally, it follows that wounded celebrity has a disciplinary function. The screens for these projections are quite frequently young, unattached, urban women—a population that was often, in the nineteenth century, a site for fantasy and discipline.

However, this analytic framework doesn't adequately address the role of the public sphere in these dramas. The projection of desires on celebrities cannot be understood as operating in the same way as such projections on family members, lovers, or teachers. In the case of scandalized celebrity, the projections are highly mediated through the structures of the public sphere. One might even say that the object of identification in celebrity worship isn't a particular person but the public sphere itself. One identifies with circulation in the public sphere. But what is the public sphere as it is represented in these texts?

The texts themselves are very revealing; they often thematize the public sphere. First, in rather conventional ways, they highlight the power of publicity to reveal corruption, conspiracy, and false appearances. The common trope is of publicity shining a light in dark corners; there is regulatory power in making something public that was previously considered private. The subtitle of George Thompson's *The Countess* makes the point with his customary drollery: *A Series of Intrigues with the Bloods, and a Faithful Delineation of the Private Frailties of Our Men, Respectfully Dedicated to the Lawyers, Merchants, and Divines of the Day*. From the start, this novelette announces its intention of deflating the power of public figures. It seeks to scandalize not only men, but also the powerful women who secretly rule New York (as members of the secret society "The Daughters of Venus"). The "delineation," as the subtitle phrases it, will be made through "fact, uncontradictable and solid fact," which is "that food of which [the reader] loves to partake" (3). There is a very old tradition of this sort of delineation, which sees publicity as an instrument that one can wield. In this sense, scandal is understood as a tool, a way of brandishing power. It is something that can be objectified and put to use. Hence, a genre like eighteenth-century France's *chronique scandaleuse* understood itself as exerting the power of the public sphere upon the hidden recesses (and especially the boudoir) of the aristocracy. In a similar vein, Thompson aims to disclose the obscure workings of power in the city. In *The Countess*, however, the public sphere isn't always figured as an objectifiable, useful instrument. The novelette's main character, Louisa, moves through the urban world in picaresque bildungsroman fashion, and frequently encounters dilemmas surrounding her own publicity. The public sphere in which she is enmeshed is an authority but also a blank. At one moment Louisa feels "the eye of public attention"

(41) upon her. To whom does this "eye" belong, and what does this "attention" do or mean? The attention is anonymous and unpredictable, and a very different kind of publicity than that often theorized by the novel itself as a form of agency. During a vignette told in her own voice, Louisa remarks: "while glancing over the columns of the 'Satirist,' I noticed some allusions made to my brother, in which he was called 'Count de Bang Wang'" (33). She is horrified to be associated with a scandal sheet like the *Satirist* and hopes that this mention doesn't "draw public attention the more towards [her]" (33). It is not simply her brother's reputation that is threatened but also her own; publicity can contaminate, and Louisa is no longer an autonomous individual within its field. But *The Countess* itself often deploys the tactics of the sporting press and spy papers. For instance, it slyly exposes people — one "companion" is identified as "connected with a magnificent establishment not a thousand miles from the park" (48) — and Thompson notes that "very many readers will recognize the portrait" (95) of one of his central characters. Thompson's narrative presents the public sphere as both an instrument and a mass that cannot be easily instrumentalized. *The Countess* both theorizes and participates in these two notions of the public sphere.

The anonymously penned *The Eventful Lives of Helen and Charlotte Lenoxa, the Twin Sisters of Philadelphia, with Elaborate and Minute Details of the Adventures, Intrigues, and Dark Crimes, of the Beautiful, but Sinful Women . . .* (1852) chronicles the two titular protagonists' encounter with the same kind of public sphere as the one to which Thompson's Louisa belongs, only with more murderous consequences. Although *The Countess*, like many of Thompson's novelettes, makes its way through sensational bloodshed to a sentimentalized end, *The Eventful Lives* concludes with the hanging of one sister and the suicide of the other, after they are convicted of murder. Their case "became the subject of much moment, comment, and small talk," and the "newspaper dwelt upon it with unctuous love of exaggeration" (27), the narrator reminds readers. The 41-page pamphlet novel is part true-crime potboiler and part old-fashioned confession narrative (albeit told in the third person), a genre that had been popular since the eighteenth century. The twins, Helen and Charlotte, are good girls from a good family, but their virtuous father — "an active, energetic, self-made man" (19) — slits his own throat when his firm is "embarrassed" in a "situation of trust" with another firm. The sisters learn a lesson from this episode, but not exactly the right lesson: they learn how public reputation and publicity can be manipulated, and they use this knowledge to their advantage. They feign an attitude and become successful gamblers largely on their falsified reputations. They know how to show off with money "in order to cause it to be noised abroad" (34), so that their lines of credit will remain open. The twins' rise to celebrity status dramatizes a public sphere that can be used like an instrument. But the instrument quickly turns on them. In one scene, an otherwise stilted and conventional novelette momentarily becomes terrifying. Among the "multitude" and "spectators" of the city park — an example of a modern public sphere — Helen is approached by a crazed stranger, methodically wielding a stick at her head. "He seemed to me," Helen later tells her sister, "to be trying an experiment of how near he could bring it to one's face, without absolutely striking you." The stranger then addresses her as someone else — an "old flame" — and takes her by the arm, saying "Come . . . it's of no use; we're old friends; what's the use of enacting scenes for the gaping multitude" (23–24). None of the multitude, however, moves to help Helen. She is finally saved from this frightening moment of stranger intimacy by yet another stranger — one she has seen a number of times before — who quickly becomes her lover. But the pleasure of the public sphere's stranger intimacy cannot quite offset its terrors. The moral of the story is that publicity is unpredictable and often uncontrollable. Or, more precisely, that the public sphere is an amoral multitude.

The most well-developed theoretical account of the experience of reading such work, which foregrounds our love for damaged celebrities, is offered by Mark Seltzer in a context that isn't precisely focused on the celebrity-scandal genre. In writing about serial-killer stories and other genres obsessed with violence, Seltzer outlines what he calls "the pathological public sphere" (*Serial* 5). This kind of public sphere is characterized by a double movement between the abstract system and the particularized body. We are drawn to the crime scene repeatedly because it makes available an experience that both joins us with the larger public-sphere complex (we witness the crime as an abstract mass rather than as an individual) and is intensely individualizing in its violence (bodies like our body are laid open and vulnerable).[11]

The parallels, then, between the pathological public sphere and the celebrity-scandal public sphere are fairly apparent: both rely on readers (or viewers) to participate in an abstract system in the most intimate ways. Celebrity allows readers to move vicariously through the amoral, abstract complexes of the public sphere; at the same time, the violence done to celebrities — and particularly their bodies — makes this abstract

mass or multitude very intimate. In addition to drawing out the operations of this structure, Seltzer makes another striking observation about
reader interaction with genres of violence that is also worth developing
in relationship to celebrity scandal. The pathological public sphere and,
especially, one of its central genres, the paradoxically named "true-crime
fiction," are often preoccupied with questions of knowing, with truth
and, ultimately, with belief. True-crime stories animate the issue of what
can be believed as truth. That truth cannot ever be known directly; it is
mediated in countless ways—through the materiality of media, through
the ideologies of media, through the structures of the pathological public
sphere. One of Seltzer's key examples is Poe's "The Mystery of Marie
Roget," because Dupin solves the case by analyzing not facts but the
mediation of facts (see *True Crime* 57–90). That all knowing is mediated
and constructed was becoming, in Poe's 1840s, a dimly recognizable reality of modern life; by the twentieth century, it becomes a commonplace.
Most people recognize that their knowledge of the world is constructed
and mediated. Seltzer argues not that the power of true crime is in its
revelation of this reality but rather that true crime "acclimatizes" its
readers to this reality of knowing, about the impossibility of knowing
beyond mediation. Such acclimatization is achieved because true crime
repeatedly performs this mediated knowing—for instance, scenes are re-
constructed, conversations are recreated, and actions are "witnessed" in
the form of reading or watching—even as this mediated knowledge is
made "real" through violence. The violence to the body serves as a kind
of reality effect for truth and knowledge known only from a remove.

Seltzer outlines how one of the central genres of the pathological public sphere—true-crime fiction—addresses the issue of truth. In doing so,
he both revises and extends Habermas's ideas about the truth-producing
powers of the public sphere. Affect plays a central role in Seltzer's pathological public sphere in ways that are only hinted at in Habermas's
rational-critical public sphere but, in both accounts, the public sphere
is an arena that produces knowledge and some form of truth. Celebrity
scandal, as is becoming clearer, is a genre not unlike true crime. Indeed,
scandal literature more generally is deeply connected to issues of knowing, truth, and belief in ways that will be examined more thoroughly by
turning to what might be called institutional scandal. I'll suggest that
such instances of scandal can function in ways that exceed "acclimatization" for readers. They can be useful for navigating modern institutional
systems and the public sphere itself.

Institutional Scandal

Central to the 1830s media landscape were accounts of nuns recently escaped from brothels, where they were imprisoned and made to bend to the sexual will of priests. The first nunnery scandal—*Six Months in a Convent; or, The Narrative of Rebecca Theresa Reed*—appeared in 1835. It was quickly followed in 1836 by the notorious *Awful Disclosures, by Maria Monk of the Hotel Dieu Nunnery of Montreal.* This book was one of the strongest sellers of the mid-nineteenth century, according to Frank Luther Mott, and was eclipsed in popularity only by the publication of *Uncle Tom's Cabin* (1851). *Awful Disclosures* was not simply a book but a print-culture event. Refutations, refutations of refutations, sequels, and copycat books sprang up almost immediately after it was published. Titles produced in a mere twelve months following the original include *Awful Exposure of the Atrocious Plot Formed by Certain Individuals against the Clergy and Nuns of Lower Canada, through the Intervention of Maria Monk* (1836), which drew the response *Confirmation of Maria Monk's Disclosures of the Hotel Dieu Nunnery of Montreal* (1836), which in turn led to the *Interview of Maria Monk with Her Opponents, the Authors to the Reply to her Awful Disclosures* (1836). These books and pamphlets were themselves part of an intergeneric public sphere that included newspapers and a lecture circuit, each arguing the case for or against the validity of Maria Monk's accusations. In the most straightforward sense, there was almost nothing valid about the story. Although a Maria Monk did exist—and appeared on occasion to debate her claims in public—the books bearing her name fabricate their accounts of the nunnery, and it is doubtful that Monk penned them herself, although she may have contributed to their authorship in various ways. The books seem to have been orchestrated and authored by William K. Hoyt, J. J. Slocum, and George Bourne—a collection of Protestant ministers and anti-Catholic agitators from New York. However counterfeit they were, *Awful Disclosures* and its offshoots did create a sensation, even as they were repeatedly rebutted by the Catholic establishment and press. Other nuns and priests who claimed association with the Hotel Dieu arrived in New York to authenticate the details, but eventually the Montreal nunnery was opened to a small team of Protestant newspaper investigators who, after touring the building and grounds, declared that Monk was a fraud, with considerable detail to support this assertion.

The *Awful Disclosures* event is in many ways a typical scandal. It follows the classical structure of scandal, in which interiors are turned inside out and pious appearances are revealed to hide corruption. The logic is intensely Manichaean: it is a story of class warfare between nuns and priests, a story of innocence and vice, old and young, a world inside the convent and a world outside. The Hotel Dieu is portrayed as a brothel for Montreal's priests, complete with secret passageways that allow the monsignors to come and go as they like. Nuns are bound and gagged; one is beaten and crushed as part of a sadistic punishment ritual. Maria Monk, the first-person narrator of *Awful Disclosures*, discovers in the convent's basement the cells used to punish wayward nuns and the lime pit where infants and aborted fetuses are dumped. Monk herself becomes pregnant by a priest and escapes the nunnery so as to avoid the murder of her child.

Awful Disclosures has long been understood as a nativist, anti-Catholic response to increasing levels of immigration. It is also surely a reaction to the rapid and unprecedented urbanization that was just beginning in the 1830s, and a way of registering and disciplining the freedoms newly available to women in the expanding city (in this reading, the recounting of the dangers of the city and of new freedoms have a disciplinary function). But these accounts of the nunnery tales—as helpful and accurate as they are—are in some respects limited. They don't address the ultimate obsession of the nunnery narratives: the public sphere itself.

The nunnery texts are highly aware that they are part of a larger public sphere of ongoing argument and discussion of current events. The construction of the books themselves thematizes the back-and-forth of the public sphere. A subsequent edition of *Awful Disclosures*—published later in 1836—includes not only the original narrative but also some responses that appeared in newspapers and official police documents, a few responses to those responses, a sequel to the original, additional details inserted in the original to offer further proof of veracity and, in case any doubt remained, a fold-out map of the grounds and interior of the convent. The final section of this edition consists of an essay by a supposedly unbiased observer summarizing all the facts and arguments in this complex portfolio of a book. The preface to the same edition amounts to a theorization of the power of publicity. Having failed to get a court hearing to levy charges against the priests and nunnery, Maria Monk declares that she will appeal, through publication, to what amounts to a higher power: she has become "determined to make my accusations through the press" and "appeal to the world" (5). The book's final page underscores this faith in the truth-telling capacity of the public:

> I have now concluded all that I deem it necessary at present to say. The public, in this volume, have in their hands, as it appears to me, everything necessary to enable them to form a decisive opinion concerning the degree of confidence which my statements deserve. They have before them every thing like testimony which has been produced against me, together with the means of satisfying themselves on various points on which curiosity has heretofore been excited. (376)

The determination of truth and power is, in other words, in the public's hands.

With respect to the nunnery tales' fixation with a public and its power, it is not incidental that the title emphasizes "disclosures" rather than the more commonly used "confessions"—as in "The Confessions of a Drunkard" (1821) or "The Confessions of a Gamester" (1824). "Confessions" was a key word in hundreds of titles in the eighteenth and early nineteenth centuries, while "disclosures" appeared rarely. The word choice indicates a shift from the realm of the religious to the civic. One confesses to a priest and one discloses to a civic or public institution, like a law court. The imagined target of address shifts from an individual, private reader (the auditor of a confession) to a more general collection of readers (a public) who might act as a kind of unbiased jury. The context for reception is modeled on the courtroom rather than the confessional. In addition, the content of a confession is considerably different from that of a disclosure. The former is a revelation about the private, secret self; the latter makes visible the otherwise obscured entwinement of individual investments in markets or associations in business or government. In other words, disclosures lay bare networks, systems, and institutions. Where scandal had been about the private lives of people, it was now about the private lives of institutions.

This shift was symptomatic of larger shifts in Americans' understanding of themselves in relationship to institutions and systems. Large, anonymous institutions—banks, temperance societies, insane asylums, almshouses, schools, penitentiaries—were becoming much more central in everyday life. The depression of 1819, caused by the collapse of a speculative bubble following the War of 1812, exposed Americans to the vagaries of the business cycle on a large scale. The panic of 1837 repeated the lesson, furthering the sense of inescapable connection with abstract economic structures that cared little about individuals and little about the old forms of credit like individual virtue. Gordon Wood has outlined the ways in which the understanding of causation changed dramatically. Long-held notions of cause, consequence, and agency as being associated with individuals were slowly being superseded by modern understandings of direct causes as being un-locatable because they were part of a complex system. Democracy itself was becoming understood as a kind of mass system of causation. Wood points out that, in Jacksonian political theory, an understanding of power as emanating from the republican individual began to be replaced by an understanding of power as located in "the 'natural order' or the 'aggregate result' of events formed out of the diverse and clashing motives of countless insignificant individuals" ("Conspiracy" 438–39). The Democratic Party's *United States Magazine and Democratic Review* described this "voluntary" or "democratic principle" as an attempt "to work out the best possible general result or order and happiness from the chaos of characters, ideas, motives and interests: human society."[12] This suggestion that democracy is a kind of truth-producing system parallels the idea of the modern public sphere as a space of truth-producing discussion. For those living both in the modern public sphere and under the modern "democratic principle," aggregate consequences could not be easily traced back to individual intentions. The process or system in general had to be trusted to produce the right consequences. The relationship between cause and effect, belief and action, became more opaque.

Christopher Castiglia has written compellingly about the psychodynamics of the ever more prevalent institutional and systems experience of antebellum America. His work shows how civic institutions were privately experienced, how they developed a restrictive and disciplining "institutional interiority" even as they offered the fantasy of a freer future. *Awful Disclosures* serves as a kind of proof text for his argument. Its narrative in his view "[p]laces the panoptical mechanism of modern institutionality at the core of the convent's apparatuses of control" (100). The nuns internalize the gaze of their superiors and, ultimately the institution so as to become experts at proper self-management. Most don't even think of trying to escape, and when Maria Monk does escape (for the first of two times) she eventually returns of her own volition. The thrill of possible future escape and other small subversions ironically tends to allow Maria and the other nuns to live with the institution's subjugations. Castiglia uses *Awful Disclosures* as a vivid example of how institutions present "obsessive self-management as the simulacrum of participation" in civic life (100). The nuns voluntarily discipline themselves in the name of the institution and the freedom and agency that the institution promises (the non-material freedom and agency of heaven). The cost of this freedom and agency, as Castiglia indicates, is "making self-management rather than sociability the principal duty of the well-disciplined citizen" (99). The present is endured in the name of the oasis on the horizon. "Readers of *Awful Disclosures*," Castiglia suggests, "may have found in its ambivalence (its dis/closures) a way to comprehend the paradoxical institutional sensations of restriction [self-discipline] and stimulation [future freedom] in their own lives" (100).

The central narrative of *Awful Disclosures* does encourage readers to participate in a highly disciplining form of modern institutionality (probably best described by Foucault), one that is developed through the drama of the nuns' situation. But the multigeneric and multifold *event* (as opposed to the single text) of *Awful Disclosures* — one created and recorded in part by the various kinds of texts (narrative, sequel, commentary, notes to readers, maps, commentary on maps, newspaper accounts, etc.) collected between the covers of the book — encouraged readers to participate in a different drama. It's a drama about the institution of the public sphere and the power of that institution. This drama is evidenced by *Awful Disclosures*'s obsession with evidence. Evidence is marshaled and marshaled, then marshaled again. The smallest details are debated:

> I will now give from memory, a general description of the interior of the Convent of Black nuns, except the few apartments which I never saw. I may be inaccurate in some things, as the apartment and passages of that spacious building are numerous and various; but I am willing to risk my credit for truth and sincerity of the general correspondence, between my description and things as they are. And this would, perhaps, be as good a case as any by which to test the truth of my statements. (62)

The recounting of the interior becomes very boring very quickly. The same is true of most of the plot of *Awful Disclosures* — a plot that barely exists. The text is almost entirely description: of the rituals of the nunnery, the punishments received by the nuns, the daily activities of the inhabitants, and the architecture of the convent. The characters remain indistinct, even Maria. For instance, the book is never clear on what motivates Maria's escape from and return to the nunnery; she never evolves as a character. Indeed, a certain distance is maintained even with respect to the most horrific of crimes. It is difficult to believe that readers lost themselves in such descriptions, because they were constantly being reminded that this was the reporting of news. This distancing may be partly a stylistic failure. The author here is not a great horror writer like Poe, although the book's popularity is usually thought attributable to the grip of its sensation. But perhaps its power lies more in the question of its veracity. The text is sprinkled with passages in which the narrator addresses the reader, providing more facts and reassurance of its truth, as if the reader might be on the verge of putting the book down, and what holds his or her interest is only the question of the narrative's truth. *Awful Disclosures* is a strange kind of gothic horror tale, in that it only rarely tries to transport the reader into some wholly imaginative space. As a text, it is anxious about fictionalization because that fictionalization undercuts its truth claims. It is valuable to note here that Thompson's *The Countess*, the anonymous *Eventful Lives*, and nearly all sensational fictions of the Jacksonian and antebellum periods are preoccupied with factuality and truth. For *The Countess* and *Eventful Lives*, this emphasis on fact-telling is not incidental but the main thrust of their roughly one-thousand-word prefaces. Both texts seek to "establish literature on a foundation of facts" (*Eventful Lives* 16). Part of the rationale for this claim is to provide the text with the cachet of reality, but the effect is to constantly rub at the line between truth and fiction, belief and doubt. Poe reversed this obsession by presenting an outright fictionalization (Marie Roget) of fact (Mary Rogers), but the relationship between fiction and fact remains central to that text as well. What might be called the drama of evidence is perhaps the most intensely affective experience of these works, intensified by the fact that such evidence is often the violated body. These scandal stories work not through sympathetic identification with characters, but through identification with questions of truth and evidence. How did readers use such an experience?

Trust

A preoccupation with truth and fiction is easily enough explained as a response to the increasing difficulty of telling one from the other in mid-nineteenth-century life. This was the age of confidence men and painted women, as a long line of cultural critics from Herman Melville to Karen Halttunen have noted. In an era of emerging mass culture and cities of "strangers," it was becoming more difficult to tell what was authentic and what was fake. Scandal typically irritates the line between the two. It both produces and frustrates a desire to know the difference.

Amplifying this experience of frustrated knowing is a sense of power not as an instrument but as an amoral mass of aggregate forces, ranging from something called "the economy" to "democracy" to "the public sphere." Several sociologists have recently emphasized that it is impossible to make one's way through such an environment purely rationally, and that most of us living under these conditions of modernity must necessarily resort to something else. Over the past couple of decades, the sociologists Niklas Luhmann, Anthony Giddens (79–111), Ulrich Beck (7–8), and others have suggested that central to the navigation of modernity's complexity is the constellation of emotions associated with trust and, more precisely, what Luhmann calls "system trust" (48). We modern subjects must emotionally invest in or "trust" what we cannot see or speak to; we must have trust in expertise, institutions, and strangers that remain abstract, opaque, and far too complex for any holistic understanding. In broad-brush terms, pre-modern trust was trust in kinship relations and local community, whereas modern trust is trust in distant systems and anonymous communities. Modernity requires trust in intangible corporate bodies—trust in trusts, so to speak. For these sociologists, trust is an important way of making sense of modernity and managing its risks; it allows subjects to act by evaluating systems that they cannot fully understand. This kind of system trust raises a number of questions that I will only note here. Does this trust have various forms? How should we understand its constitution—as affect or cognition or some mix of the two? To what extent is it constructed through (infant) socialization, and to what degree is trust pre-social, a kind of biological reflex necessary for human and animal survival? Trust has as many emotional cognates as there are relationships of interdependence. One who trusts is also one who relies upon and has confidence in another, counts on and takes heart in, commits to and hopes for. Trust usually entails a certain amount of desire and identification, as well as fear. It also tends to breed more trust; I trust in you so you'll trust in me so that I can trust you even more. Trust is frequently extremely fragile in both interpersonal and system relations, and it veers quickly into negative moods like mistrust, distrust, abandonment, and betrayal. There is a complex emotional language circulating around system trust that has yet to be fully explored. The central point to recognize here is that, under the conditions of modernity, trust becomes a salient psychoaffective dynamic for making sense of and communicating about information — information concerning relations between citizens and opaque and complex instruments of power and administration.

I want to suggest that the scandal media is a way of communicating about the risks of these complex systems, a way of discussing trust and mistrust within these systems. The scandal texts often thematize trust and distrust in their emphasis on revealing the hypocrisy of those who represent these systems — politicians, celebrities, reformers, newspaper editors — and who for most readers are both distant strangers and also familiar representatives of various systems. They dramatize trust and distrust in the texts' own calls for readers to trust the evidence they offer. From the perspective of the sociology of system trust, this ubiquitous discourse of scandal is at least as much about feeling one's way through the complex systems of modernity as it is about the questionable acts or morals of any single public figure or the veracity of any given text. The genre's work is best understood as communicating information in the form of disgust and outrage about these systems. Of course, this information might well be tainted itself; these texts might well be simply manipulating emotions of trust and mistrust, circulating the most highly commodified sentiments that are far from any kind of truth about these systems. But the point of this kind of modern system trust isn't to discover the truth. Instead, it is to establish what Luhmann describes as an "increasing functional awareness," "a perception of the foundations and functions of the creation of trust in society" (67). In other words, the function of scandal discourse and of other scenarios of trust and mistrust is not to discover the truth behind the scandal or, ultimately, to reveal whether trust is justified in a particular instance. Instead, the function in Luhmann's view is best understood as establishing the emotional dynamic of trust as a way of addressing complexity, of assessing risk and, eventually, of taking action when one cannot know whether trust, in truth, is justified. From Luhmann's perspective, it is impossible to determine whether trust is ever justified, because the system is just too complex. What is most important is learning to trust trust itself as a foundation for taking action within the complexities of the system. In this light, the scandal sphere might well be understood as a technology for communicating the ways trust and mistrust are central to the "foundations and functions" of modernity. What scandal communicates is not truth per se, but information about how the trust system works.

Such information is conveyed at the fundamental level of uptake practice — in this instance, reading practice. The content of the scandal novelettes and other productions is, of course, important (their interest in obscured systems, the news, and the media itself), but equally important is the relationship encouraged between content and reader. As we've seen, readers are encouraged to respond reflexively and affectively to the purported secrets of complex systems, but they are also encouraged to stand outside these systems, and even outside their own affective responses. Readers are constantly made conscious of their outside positioning through the voyeur trope and through reference to their own experience of mediation. The emotional reflexes of trust and mistrust are combined with distance with respect to these reflexes. Trust, mistrust, and their cognates come into consciousness as a ground for encountering modern, complex systems. In this way, readers are encouraged to develop "a perception of the foundations and functions of the creation of trust in society," in Luhmann's words.

Understanding the print culture of scandal as instilling in readers certain practices for reading trust offers a new way of thinking about emotion in the public sphere. The scandal public sphere, in this understanding, becomes a place for processing and communicating information about system trust. This isn't, of course, the kind of exchange of information that Habermas hoped the public sphere would provide. But Habermasian rational-critical debate and persuasion look unrealistic from the perspective of the sociologists of trust and of the scandal literature itself. Modernity's intricate and abstract social environment operates with such complexity that it makes the possibility of Habermasian dialogic debate, and the causal relationship between public criticism and decision-making, seem uncertain at best. If system trust isn't what Habermas imagined as central to the public sphere, neither is it what Michael Warner and other post-Habermasians imagined as being central to embodied counterpublicity. System trust isn't counter to anything. It doesn't operate as a subversive agent intervening in decision-making systems on behalf of citizens. But this doesn't mean it's without agency. It does provide a great deal of information, in a highly condensed and accessible emotional form, about how to relate to those systems. This situation isn't necessarily one to celebrate. It is simply a reality. In a society of complex decision-making processes, democracy is grounded, not on communicative reason, but on some of the most fundamental feelings of trust and mistrust that may be circulated through the media. It is Habermas who advises dismissing this sensorium sphere. The scandal literature of the antebellum period suggests instead that we take it as central to modern democracy.

Chapter Five

Prayerful Reading

Religious Affect and the Secular Public Sphere

Public Sphere Conversions

Susan Sontag observes, rather surprisingly at first blush, the similarity of religious and pornographic reading:

> In some respects, the use of sexual obsessions as a subject for literature resembles the use of a literary subject whose validity far fewer people would contest: religious obsession. . . . Pornography that is serious literature aims to "excite" in the same way that books which render an extreme form of religious experience aim to "convert." (*Styles* 47)

The parallels between the pornographic and the religious are perhaps only at first surprising; on further reflection, they are not particularly difficult to understand. A long and well-known tradition of religious reading, one partially outlined in chapter 2, seeks to short-circuit the distance from text to reader in ways similar to the pornographic. In such situations, the words on the page are meant to disappear, the consciousness of mediation to dissolve. To "excite," as Sontag puts it, is to "call forth" (from the Latin *ex-*, "out," and *ciēre*, "to set in motion") — to call the reader forth directly. To excite is to awaken or convert the reader from one state to another. Excitation and conversion are the same in the sense that to convert isn't simply to change one's way of thinking but to change one's way of being. Converting the self from one state to another — from sleeping to waking, from stasis to motion — extends far beyond changes in ideas.

The idea of conversion does not fit neatly with the usual idea of the public sphere. Where conversion customarily entails a converting from one identity to another, the public sphere, at least in theory, involves an ongoing questioning of positions, especially when they are tenaciously held as identities. Conversion is not usually understood as a process that is enabled by the public sphere, whereas persuasion, argument, and opining are. It is hard to imagine conversion reading, which often emphasizes transcendence, having much to do with public-sphere reading, which emphasizes the concerns of the here and now. Habermas himself thought of the public sphere as posed against the authority of the church. The philosopher Richard Rorty—in general supportive of Habermasian public conversation—called religion a "conversation stopper" and suggested its privatization (168). John Rawls called for the bracketing of religious commitments when participating in "public reason" (at for instance 458). In other words, the religious public sphere, in an important sense, seems like a contradiction in terms. It is not that a sphere of religious publication doesn't exist, but rather that the idea of a discussion and debate that will lead to a pragmatic kind of truth seems deeply at odds with such a sphere of publication.

Perhaps for these reasons public-sphere theory has not played a substantive role in the scholarship on the great public upswells of religion in American history.[1] For their part, public-sphere theorists have been little interested in religion. How, for instance, could reading that produced "weeping" and "awakening" during the Second Great Awakening (or, for that matter, sermon listening that generated yelling, shrieking, rolling in the aisles, crying and screaming)[2] possibly be understood as part of a critical public sphere? These are not unfamiliar modes of religious reading, but they are most often understood as outside of the public sphere, part of a very private relationship with a transcendent power. From the perspective of the public sphere, they are just examples of reading badly.

But what would happen if such reading—reading that was understood as conversion and awakening, as producing weeping and an opening to the spirit—was approached as participating in a critical public sphere rather than as diametrically opposed to or outside of such a public sphere? This chapter takes up this question by examining a specific public sphere that developed around religious print culture in the Pine Barrens of New Jersey during the 1840s. Ultimately, one of the central goals of this chapter is to break down the too-easy alignment of the public sphere, secularism, and critical reason on one side and private ritual, religion, and uncritical belief on the other. While familiar, this dichotomy is, I suggest, not historically accurate and more an ideological formation than an actual one. Several benefits that flow from breaking the dichotomy down will be explained at chapter's end. Part of its deconstruction involves the suggestion that the affective response to religious reading is not to be dismissed; rather, it is diagnostic and even critical.

Reading in the Pines:
An Evangelical Public Sphere

In 1841, the American Tract Society (ATS) implemented a colporteur system as a form of missionary work and, throughout the 1840s, young male students from Princeton Theological Seminary volunteered for the ATS as colporteurs in the Pine Barrens of southern and coastal New Jersey. "Colporteur" was a name used since the sixteenth century for a traveling bookseller, and colportage was important to the circulation of a wide range of print culture in colonial and early America. The most famous colporteur in American history was Mason Locke ("Parson") Weems, who wrote an immensely popular myth-making biography of George Washington (1800) and successfully sold an array of books, from the religious to the historical. The young, enthusiastic colporteurs who entered the Pine Barrens in the 1840s sold or gave away only Bibles and religious tracts. The New Jersey Pine Barrens were, in several respects, a wilderness for these young missionaries. Many living there were poor, unbelieving, and "ignorant"—one of the Princeton colporteurs' favorite terms for Pine Barren residents.[3] The best off were laborers in the small timber, coal, and glass-making outposts scattered throughout the Barrens; the worst off were like "Bedouins in the desert," as one colporteur put it (63), who moved from place to place in search of work. The booksellers kept meticulous notes on their encounters with those living in the Barrens, and these notes were then frequently included in their final reports, written for the ATS upon their return to civilized Princeton. The reports also offer considerable information about a number of other aspects of their experiences, ranging from the number of Bibles sold or given away, to the titles of tracts distributed, to the readers' various reactions to the material they read. The colporteurs usually begin their reports with a quantitative analysis of readership and book ownership in the specific region to which they were assigned. One account from 1841 begins:

In making our report to the Committee we would in the first place state that we visited near 500 families, consisting in all of 2571 souls, of whom 1336 can read, being a fraction more than half of the whole number; of the readers 798 were destitute of the Bible. Of the families visited 95 or 100 had no Bible in their houses. We disturbed [*sic*] 146 Bibles, and about 17800 pages of tracts. (4)

To such overviews are added details about the books sold and given away: the numbers received from the ATS, quality of books on arrival, original costs, and funds collected through sales. The reports also frequently provide a kind of qualitative analysis of the area, including anecdotes about local inhabitants. They tell of encounters with the drunk and the forsaken, as well as with the religiously awakened. They calculate what percentages of a population belong to which denominations, and offer guesses at the level of participation in church and Sabbath schools. In sum, the colporteur's reports offer a picture of a reading public and of a publishing industry that was attempting to reach that public on a mass scale. David Paul Nord's research on the ATS and other religious publishers of the Second Great Awakening suggests that this sphere of religious publication be understood as the first example of mass-cultural book publishing in the United States, in that its publishers used mass-distribution strategies like demographic research, differential pricing (where price points differ for different economic groups), and targeted distribution. The colporteur reports from the Pine Barrens bear out Nord's conclusion.

For our purposes, most salient are the reports' accounts about reading. Many residents, it seems, never read or rarely read the Bible. The colporteurs recount with frustration the numerous times they encounter families with Bibles that are covered in dust and stowed away on a top shelf, forgotten behind other articles. Some families are unsure if they even have a Bible; others want them just so they can write out family genealogies on the front and back covers. One woman mistakes a Greek lexicon she owns for a Bible. Another complains, on being pressed to buy the book, that he "can scarce buy rum much less a bible" (10). The view that reading is simply wasting time is not uncommon (46). These accounts might suggest a group of people for whom reading wasn't necessary to everyday life, but this doesn't seem to be the case. Indeed, the simple fact that only half of those who could read owned a Bible (according to the colporteurs' estimates) may well mean that they were reading something else. For every account of an unread Bible, the colporteurs offer an account that hints at a fairly robust reading culture, complete with novels, histories, and geographies, as well as libraries, Sunday schools, and reading circles. As we will soon see in great detail, the inhabitants of the Pine Barrens argue over the interpretation of the Bible and the value of other books. They recognize and question the status of the book as a commodity, and they comment on the relationship between church and state in the selling of Bibles. The people of the Pine Barrens seem "ignorant" only in that they are ignorant of reading and thinking in the ways that the colporteurs would like them to read and think.

When readers do read in the ways the colporteurs desire, the readers cry. They "burst into tears" (46), they "we[ep] freely" (19, 46), and they are left "in tears" (31 and elsewhere). The most intense moments of religious experience in the colporteur reports are not revelations brought about through the experience of nature, or the experience of the spoken word, but through the experience of reading. In this sense, the readers are responding in some of the most conventional ways to religious reading. Indeed, the crying is so conventional that it is difficult to make sense of, and one might wonder if such accounts are to be trusted at all. Perhaps they are manufactured — either purposefully or unconsciously — by the colporteurs, in order to fulfill their own desires and expectations as well as those of their mentors at the ATS and Princeton. There is a recognizable structure to the colporteur reports, which often build from statistical data to a climactic depiction of reading. This raises the possibility that the reader responses they describe owe more to the genre than reality. Or that readers may be following the conventions of religious reading and religious conversion that were well known to them through observation of others and through their own training in religious reading or even novel reading. These are certainly good reasons to be suspicious of the frequent incidence of crying, and scholars who have looked at the colporteur reports have shied away from discussing the seemingly ritualized emotional response. Nord observes the "cliché of the genre: reader reads, reader weeps, reader is saved" (145), but he does not linger over it. I doubt we will ever maneuver around all the dilemmas that are presented by these weeping readers; it is impossible to know exactly what was happening when readers cried or colporteurs reported crying. But as a cultural ritual or fantasy — one in which both readers and colporteurs partook — it can be interpreted.

How then should we understand the crying? It is surely what might be called an affective or emotional response to the text, but the meaning and uses of that response will become clearer only once it is embedded in a larger scheme of experience that is repeatedly included in the colporteur accounts. Crying was a small element of a much more complex dynamic. One should not think of this experience of tearful reading as outside of the public sphere, as happening in some utterly private, monkish realm of reading revelation. Even in the nineteenth-century Pine Barrens there exist the basic structural elements of the modern public sphere: the opportunity and protocols for anonymous argument, a consciousness of textual circulation, an impersonal market through which texts travel, and an understanding of reading that is based on critical distance from the text. A moment spent expanding on the public-sphere attributes of evangelical media circulation in the Pine Barrens will help develop an answer to the question, what role did weeping play in the public sphere?

There was a diverse market of print culture in the Pine Barrens; readers had access to much more than religious material. When the colporteur G. W. Newell arrived in May's Landing, New Jersey, in 1844, he was immediately asked for history and geology texts and criticized for selling only Bibles. "A *book-pedlar* should carry any thing he could sell" (74), Newell is told, the consumer evidently demanding that no strict dichotomy be made between religious texts and other kinds of texts. Another young colporteur, David William Eakins, discovers to his horror that a "rolling-mill" on the outskirts of Trenton has "a library for the use of the men employed in that establishment" that contains only novels (52). Novel reading—especially of the "flimsy 25 cent" sort (118)—is an ongoing problem for the missionary peddlers in the Barrens. However, a text even more dangerous than any novel is discovered by one team of colporteurs to be infecting a "destitute" outpost: "Tom Pains [*sic*] Age of Reason," "the worse plan for infidelity that we found while out" (101). The colporteurs are always conscious of their competition in the print marketplace; in 1846, Alexander Perry Silliman advises his ATS contact that the society should hurry to increase its presence in the market: "I have said that the field is perfectly accessible to the Colporteur. It should therefore be immediately occupied because it is equally accessible to the bearer of trash. . . . The truth is that some parts of the field is already preoccupied" (117–18). From the perspective of at least some readers in the Barrens, the market in print text should be free and open, with no monopoly or advantage given to religious material. One resident suspects that the state may be subsidizing the religious colporteurs. He will not buy because he believes "the public money of New Jersey was in some way appropriated, in part, to pay for these religious books" (40). Other inhabitants recognize even religious books as commodities; one accuses a colporteur of "speculating" (40) in religious books because he sells them to different people at different prices.

Within this marketplace of print culture, the colporteurs stumble (often unprepared) upon a culture of argument connected to print culture. As often as the colporteurs encounter crying in relation to a text, they also encounter debate. The denizens of the Barrens are a contentious bunch, and they pride themselves on argument (perhaps to be expected from readers of Tom Paine). One man emphasizes the importance of argument to his character, and the colporteur repeats the man's words verbatim in his report: he "would not *tack ship till convinced that he was wrong; then he would lie on the other lug awhile*" (72). Another emphasizes his freedom to choose his own reading and his own position on issues, saying, "This is a free country & all may think & say what they please" (46).

The debates that the colporteurs encounter occur face to face, but they always involve texts. The interpretation of religious text is often at issue, since lay ministers interpret the Bible in their own fashion. To a colporteur's dismay, one such preacher goes so far as to claim that St. Paul was mistaken on several points of doctrine (about who might be condemned and who saved). This leaves the colporteur wondering, "If these are the teachers what must the people be?" (18). These are readers, it seems, capable of making their own choices about how to interpret texts. Another preacher simply makes up quotations from the Bible. One woman tells of her husband's interpretation of the Bible as an opiate of the masses: "She stated that her husband who was killed by lightning a few years since considered it [the Bible] the work of man, of priests, got up to restrain men from the commission of open acts of immorality & crime, and that such was the opinion of her and some of her neighbors & sons" (101).

The missionaries continually find themselves in arguments about theology, especially over their dogmatic adherence to a doctrine of grace over a doctrine of works. The Presbyterian colporteurs argue with Methodists over the differences between Methodist books and Presbyterian books (54–56). They argue with Universalists over the value of free-thinking (46) and with Catholics over adherence to a "foreign power" (60–61). The colporteurs develop a relationship with these arguments—and with the different kinds of texts in Pine Barren marketplaces—that is aligned with the usual understanding of competing ideas within the modern public sphere. They do not try to censor arguments and texts that they find problematic, but instead suggest that their arguments will win out in a free exchange. One colporteur contends that if only the population had better access to religious reading, it would turn from novel reading: "while a great many of these [religious] books had never been perused by their community, and especially their workmen, it must be attributed to the fact that a great many of the people never had the opportunity of doing so, And this I believe to be the true state of the case" (52). In an unencumbered public sphere, these missionaries are confident that religious texts and, eventually, religious truth will be recognized.

The colporteur reports indicate that, even in the Pine Barrens, reading is structured within the context of the market, within the framework of argument over texts, and under circumstances where readers may freely choose between texts. It is also structured by an abstract or stranger relationality that is characteristic of the modern public sphere. That public sphere, as it is usually understood, is not a group or a collective circumscribed by space or direct contact; it is a mass, a collection of anonymous strangers who interact in highly mediated ways. The rise of denominationalism at the turn of the century had, as Michael Warner notes, thoroughly transformed religious experience into a public-sphere experience (*Publics*, 84–85). In other words, the faithful increasingly thought of themselves as members of an abstract community of, say, Presbyterians or Methodists, rather than as members of a specific congregation which, evidence suggests, was the case at least through the seventeenth century and into the eighteenth.

Almost all of the men and women encountered by the colporteurs think of themselves as members of abstract communities constituted by denominations. The colporteurs themselves underscore this sense of abstract relationality because they remind residents of the extent and anonymity of the public sphere in which they are participating. The colporteurs are strangers come from some other place, yet they are still part of this public (not unlike the itinerant preachers who also traveled through the Barrens). Sometimes the colporteurs recognize their position as strangers and even emphasize it. One asks his mentor at the ATS, "With what words shall I approach these people? How shall I state the object of my visit?" Should he identify himself in any way? Sometimes he wonders if it is not best to "act under cover & merely offer them [his wares] as cheap books?" (108). Is it not most beneficial to the missionary project to remain a stranger — a disinvested circulator of ideas — as much as possible? From the perspective of the inhabitants of the Barrens, to receive and read a book within such a public sphere framework is to understand oneself as participating in an activity with anonymous others who forever remain abstract.

Through this close examination of the colporteur reports, I am arguing that religious texts in the Pine Barrens in the 1840s were received in the context of a modern, critical public sphere that at least seems to aspire to Habermasian ideals. The ATS and the colporteurs thoroughly participated in the forms, protocols, and values of the public-sphere social imaginary. We might even go so far as to say that production, distribution, and consumption of religious texts played a significant role in constituting that modern social imaginary — simply because religious publication was so prevalent (the first mass culture, in Nord's view). This observation breaks down the conventional notion that a secular public sphere is separate from a religious public sphere. That argument is one of the results of the secularization thesis that dominated thinking about religion in the public sphere throughout the twentieth century. The secularization thesis has been generally discredited, not only because religion remains such a powerful force in modern life and not only because it is difficult to call so many Western nations secular. The secularization thesis has lost its explanatory power and the sense of confidence it instilled in rationality because it has become evident that there is no clear line between the secular and non-secular. Charles Taylor has even argued that secularity developed out of religious ideas in the eighteenth century (and before), not against religious ideas. Protestantism's emphases on choice and propositional faith, in Taylor's view, are essential to the development of the idea of secularity (221–69). He allows us to see that the idea of secularization in the eighteenth and nineteenth centuries was a backformation with many ideological roots, including liberalism's (and the public sphere's) ideal of a privatized faith that would allow free, unencumbered rational-critical discourse. If we understand the secular and religious as something other than opposites, we begin to see a more interesting and complex context for the reception of religious material in the Pine Barrens. Reading does not take place within a battle between the secular and the religious. This may have been the desire of ATS publishers, but it wasn't that of readers. Readers saw their use of religious texts as part of their use of all kinds of other texts and, indeed, as part of their interactions with a much broader secular public sphere. This insight will help explain the weeping.

"Little Winged Messengers": Tract Reading

In their reports, the colporteurs offer a detailed picture of the material they carried into the Pine Barrens, in packs on their backs and in boxes under their arms. Mostly they distributed tracts, or "little winged messengers" (49), as one colporteur called them. These tracts held more interest than Bibles for the colporteurs, the inhabitants of the Barrens and, it seems, others as well. The ATS annual reports, obsessed with numbers and evidence, declare the distribution of an extraordinary quantity of tracts and other print material. The 1839 report claims "5,000,000 of publications issued; 24,000,000 [more] of pages than during the previous year—in all 125,000,000 pages during the last twelve months" (11–12). These figures are not necessarily to be believed, but the quantity of ATS publications still extant in library archives suggests that the ATS published a considerable number of tracts and Bibles.

In 1848 the ATS published a listing of its tracts with descriptions and commentary in *Circulation and Character of the Volumes of the American Tract Society for the Society's Colporteurs*. The manual provides overviews of the society's publications so that bookselling missionaries might select the most appropriate tract for any particular situation or reader. It lists 168 tracts in English, and the genres and topics range widely—from narrative to polemic to dialogue, from stories of the poor to those of the rich, from temperance tales to accounts of natives brought to America from the South Seas. Predominant are narrative tracts: *The Dairyman's Daughter*, *The Young Cottager*, *The African Servant*, *The Spoiled Child*, *The Widow's Son*, *The Watchmaker and His Family*, and so on. The standard way of understanding the narrative impulse of such tracts is to see them as competing for authority with an emerging secular mass culture of novels and other forms of fiction. David S. Reynolds sees the tracts in this way, and there is a great deal of evidence to support this view. The following paragraph appears often in ATS documents and other religious magazines during the first half of the nineteenth century:

> [Religious publication] *should be entertaining*. A plain didactic essay on a religious subject may be read by a Christian with much pleasure; but the person for whom these Tracts are chiefly designed, will fall asleep over it. This will not do; it is throwing labour and money away. There must be something to allure the listless to read, and this can only be done by blending entertainment with instruction. Where *nar-*

rative can be made the medium of conveying truth, it is equally to be embraced, as it not only engages the attention, but it also assists the memory and makes a deeper impression on the heart. Dialogue is another way of rendering a Tract entertaining. The conversation draws the reader insensibly along . . . and the subject fixes itself stronger and deeply in the mind. (*Proceedings of the First Ten Years* 18)

This strategy, however, was a dangerous one: it could be difficult to draw the line between religious narratives and non-religious narratives. Even as the tract societies supported entertaining narratives, they railed against them. Novel reading was considered at best a waste of time and at worst pathological, as we saw in the colporteur reports and in the accounts of bad reading in the religious press and elsewhere (see chapter 2). Novels stole the reader's power to choose rationally; they were so immersive and addictive that they threatened the autonomy required for rational choice. Religious authorities certainly saw themselves as competing with the new mass print culture of novels and romances even as they took up the strategies of that mass culture. But understanding the novelistic tracts as in competition with mass culture doesn't capture what is happening here very well, in my view. It simply repeats the ATS's own view of their narrative, affective publications. Instead, the tracts may be better understood as bringing something beyond the secular into the secular frame. This perspective enables us to see how the religious and what is traditionally called the secular operated together.

This point can be made more fully by closely examining an exemplar text. One of the most popular and affecting narrative tracts, frequently associated with weeping conversions, is *The Dairyman's Daughter*. "One lady asked for the Dairyman's Daughter," comments a colporteur, "saying it was blessed to the conversion of her brother." The 1828 annual report of the ATS highlights *The Dairyman's Daughter* as one of the society's most powerful publications with the following story: "A Lady called at the Tract Depository to purchase some Tracts, and fixing her eyes upon the '*Dairyman's Daughter*,' observed, while the tears were flowing from her eyes, 'I owe all my hopes of heaven to the reading of that Tract'" (138). Another report (from the New York Tract Society, an auxiliary of the ATS) also describes the power of the book: "Many persons in this Ward," says one of the book's distributors, "expressed themselves as having been deeply affected in the perusal of '*The Dairyman's Daughter*.' . . . One lady [familiar with the tract], the moment I addressed her, burst into tears" (13). *The Dairyman's Daughter* was one of the most frequently republished tracts of other tract societies as well, with version after version appearing from about 1814 through the 1850s. The original was written by Legh Richmond, an evangelical minister who served as curate for several parishes on the Isle of Wight; he died in London in 1827. The abridged versions that I've examined were small enough to fit in a pocket — about six inches by four inches. The tract runs approximately 13,000 words in its abridged form.

With claims of authenticity, *The Dairyman's Daughter* tells the story of Richmond's ministrations to Elizabeth, about thirty years old and unmarried. Elizabeth does not require much ministerial care, however, because she is nearly perfect, in spiritual terms. She has already accepted God, after brief experience of prodigal life, involving a lust for fine clothes and other worldly possessions. She has returned to her family's poor dairy farm, where she patiently cares for her dying sister and elderly parents and seeks to convert them. The parents, like Elizabeth, are figured not as evil sinners but rather as poor and "ignorant" of the ways of a godly life. Elizabeth herself dies, slowly, of consumption. The story isn't about Elizabeth's conversion — she is already converted from her mildly profane younger days when we first meet her — but, through the narration of the good woman's death, it is a story meant to convert others. Her death is clearly meant to affect readers, and I will return to it in greater detail in a moment. Suffice it to say that we shouldn't underestimate *The Dairyman's Daughter* or think it naïve. It is highly sentimentalized, but it attempts to address fundamental concerns about death and human loss. There may be no ways of addressing such issues that are not highly emotional.

But before turning to the death scene, I need to emphasize the way the tract seeks to participate in a most secular scene of life and, more specifically, in the secular public sphere. The tract itself is not unlike the reports and manuals published by tract societies, in that it centers the reader's attention on the use of tracts. *The Dairyman's Daughter* lists other tracts that might be bought and read and, more importantly, its initial pages offer an account of its own circulation: "It may perhaps appear unnecessary to pronounce an opinion on productions which have been circulated by millions, and translated into twenty languages; and which, in a multitude of well-authenticated instances, have been, by the blessing of God, signally effective of good" (8). In prefacing itself in this way, the tract announces itself as something that is not exactly a sacred text; it is a text directed at a mass, a text upon which opinion may be pronounced. It is to be understood as a text in competition with other texts in a public sphere. It is going to make an argument, these prefatory remarks suggest, from "well-authenticated instances" that will be "effective of good." This sense of participation in a public sphere of argument is further underscored by an elaborate biography of the text's author, which describes Legh Richmond's various church positions, the places where he lived, and important dates in his life. In other words, it marks the narrative of Elizabeth, the dairyman's daughter, as a production of secular space and time. As the reader is told from the beginning, this tract does not occupy what Benedict Anderson (after Walter Benjamin) has called "Messianic time" (24)—as is customary in religious texts, where past, present, and future can be simultaneously present—but rather occupies a sense of time common to secular modernity, in which one moment leads to the next.

The Dairyman's Daughter also dramatizes the stranger relationality that is central to the experience of reading a text "circulated by the million." With the exception of Elizabeth's immediate family, none of the characters in book know each other at the beginning of the story. In the opening scene, the unnamed narrator—a minister like Legh Richmond—receives a letter from Elizabeth, who is a stranger to him. She asks that he come to attend to her dying sister and to her poor mother and father, who are also strangers to the narrator. The regular minister assigned to the family's parish cannot come, for unexplained reasons, but this situation is not anomalous in the story. Elizabeth's original conversion (which occurs five years before the present story takes place) is sparked by the chance hearing of a sermon by an itinerant "preacher" who is momentarily "detained by contrary winds" (43) and thus unable to board ship in Elizabeth's harbor town; she is never to see him again. At her conversion, she is in a sea of strangers—"a great crowd of people collected together" (44). Indeed, with the exception of the family members, no one seems to know anyone else in the narrative. When Elizabeth becomes ill for the final time, a young soldier previously unknown to the minister arrives at his door to beckon him to her home. The soldier himself has only known Elizabeth for "about a month" (53) but immediately recognized her piety. At the end of the narrative, "friends" gather around Elizabeth's deathbed, but many of these friends had only "become acquainted with her during the latter stage of her illness" (63). The word "stranger" and its plural appear eight times in the short narrative. The important point here is that the text highly values the abstract sociality it enacts. The religious society that *The Dairyman's Daughter* imagines is not a congregation or a particular church institution but, in large part, a web of strangers.

In such a society, religion is a matter of personal choice. One chooses to recognize God's grace. It comes neither through the regimes of an established church nor through a particular minister, but through "a course of private prayer, reading and meditation" (46). "Sir," Elizabeth tells the narrator, "what a Savior have I found!" (46). Of course, there are other choices that might be made in this marketplace and, for a brief period of her life, Elizabeth had chosen "foolish finery" (44). But this past mistake only underscores the high value that *The Dairyman's Daughter* places on personal choice; it is a key tenet of the tract's religious theory.

In these ways the tract fully participates in the modern public sphere, with that public sphere's elements of abstract relationality, mass circulation, secular space and time, arguments about texts, and emphasis on choice. However, against this backdrop is a cynosure of the most intense embodiment: a touch of the hand. Elizabeth lies on her deathbed and wishes all goodbye: "Dear Sir . . . Dear father, mother, friends, I am going . . . but all is well, well, well——" (59). After she has fallen silent for an hour, the narrator says, "I pressed her hand as I was taking leave . . . She gently returned the pressure." The narrator finds this moment seared in his imagination: "I never had witnessed a scene so impressive as this before. It completely filled my imagination" (59). It is impossible to say precisely how readers might have responded to this moment, or to know with certainty if this was a passage that provoked tears. However, in the context of all the abstractions that precede it in the story, the touching of hands does shock and perhaps even move. It suggests the thinness of abstract relations.

Something similar occurs two pages later with another affective cynosure: Elizabeth's corpse. The reader is addressed directly in this instance, and he or she is made to realize that secular time eventually comes to an end, that all arguments one day cease:

> It is not easy to describe the sensation which the mind experiences on the first sight of the dead countenance, which, when living, was loved and esteemed for the sake of that soul which used to give it animation. A deep and awful view of the separation that has taken place between the soul and body of the deceased since we last beheld them, occupies

the feelings; our friend seems to be both near and yet far off. The most interesting and valuable part is fled away; what remains is but the earthly perishing habitation no longer occupied by its tenant. Yet the features present the accustomed association of friendly intercourse. For one moment we would think them asleep; the next reminds us that the blood circulates no more—the eye has lost its power of seeing, the ear of hearing, the heart of throbbing, and the limbs of moving. Quickly a thought of glory breaks in upon the mind, and we imagine the dear departed soul to be arrived at its long-wished-for rest. It is surrounded by cherubim and seraphim, and sings the song of Moses and the Lamb on Mount Zion. Amid the solemn stillness of the chamber of death, imagination hears heavenly hymns chanted by the spirits of just men made perfect. In another moment the livid lips and sunken eye of the clay-cold corpse recall our thoughts to earth and to ourselves again. And while we think of mortality, sin, death, and the grave, we feel the prayer rise in our bosom, "O let me die the death of the righteous, and let my last end be like his!" (63–64)

The collective "we" asks readers to project themselves into this scene, to allow this corpse to remind them of their own losses and the eventual, inevitable loss of their own "powers." A few sentences later, the narrator suggests that this scene serve as a "meditation" (64) for readers. Two pages later, the narrator tells his readers that if they have not been changed by Elizabeth's narrative, they should "read this story once more, and then pray earnestly" (69).

What is the relationship between this pietistic practice of meditating on touches and corpses and the secular public sphere valued by other parts of the text?

"An Awareness of What's Missing"

Habermas begins a recent essay about religion and the public sphere with an account of the funeral of a friend, the Swiss playwright and novelist Max Frisch. Frisch was agnostic, but he directed in his will that his memorial service be held in St. Peter's Church in Zurich. Within this setting, the service was adamantly non-religious. Frisch's own directive was clear on this point: "We let our nearest speak, and without an 'amen'" (quoted in Habermas, *An Awareness*, 15). Habermas is moved by this juxtaposition of the religious setting and resolute secularity. In

Habermas's view, Frisch was leaving his friends and family with a final question or injunction: how might we think of religion and secularity together?

Habermas puts it this way: "the enlightened modern age has failed to find a suitable replacement for a religious way of coping with the final *rite de passage* which brings life to a close." This, he goes on to say, "tells us something about secular reason, namely that it is unsettled by the opaqueness of its merely apparently clarified relation to religion" (15–16). These are surprising words, in part because Habermas's most important philosophical works have confidently held to the secularization thesis; for instance, *The Theory of Communicative Action* rarely discusses religion and, when it does, sees it as slowly displaced by communicative reason: the goal is that "the authority of the holy is gradually replaced by the authority of an achieved consensus" (*Communicative Action*, vol. 2, 77; quoted in Reder and Schmidt 4). More recently, and especially since September 11, 2001, Habermas has shown considerable interest in re-thinking his confidence in secularization, but as yet his arguments in this area have remained far less developed than those that take for granted the value of secularization. Nevertheless, Habermas has begun to find the normative idea of a public sphere based solely in rational-critical debate to be too thin to serve as the foundation for solidarity and pur-posive action. In the short essay that recalls Frisch's memorial service, mentioned above, Habermas suggests that post-metaphysical philosophy might develop an "awareness of what is missing" in its encounter with religion (19).

I have been arguing here that such an encounter is central to our un-derstanding of *The Dairyman's Daughter*, as well as to the tract societies' use of the print public sphere more generally. Imagine the scene of recep-tion for a tract like *The Dairyman's Daughter*. You receive a book and a few words of conversation from a stranger, not a friend or family mem-ber. You have a choice to take his book, perhaps paying for it or perhaps accepting it for free. You recognize on some level that the tract is part and parcel of commerce, of an extended community of anonymous buy-ers. You have a choice to read it. The tract is from far away—New York or Boston or Philadelphia—and it has the potential to connect you to a world of reading and readers that extends far beyond your neighbors. The text itself—and perhaps even the stranger who gives it to you—suggest that there is power in this circulation, that so many pages in print must indicate some sort of truth. The narrative is a simple story about the connection between strangers. It takes place in the here and now, unlike the Bible. In this way, it addresses you in a manner more similar to the novels or geographies that also circulate through the local community. Indeed, you know that these tracts are in debate with those novels and other books. By taking this book and reading, you enter into that debate, one that involves arguments with your neighbors but also with strangers whom you will never know.

In this way, reception and consumption of religious texts in places like the Pine Barrens in the 1840s were determined by the protocols and ideals of the modern, critical public sphere. But on reading the tract from the stranger, you also realize that this book is about something that is not usually part of the protocols and ideals of that public sphere. It is about the finality of death and loss, and about feeling these limitations on a visceral level. About this death, and this feeling about death, you have no choice. The tract reminds you that there is much beyond the power of your personal choice. It also makes you ask if there is something beyond the here and now. It suggests that there is some value that is beyond argument among strangers. It asks you to consider mechanisms of determining value other than propositional logic and debate; it asks you to recognize touch and other forms of embodiment as having value. Reading and re-reading the book is about meditating on these facts; it is something like the practice of prayer.

In other words, a religious tract like *The Dairyman's Daughter* simultaneously suggests two very different things: the power of the public sphere and the wish for something more than that secular power. Moreover, such a tract provides readers with a way of experiencing the power of the public sphere at the same time that it makes them wish for something more than that power alone. It creates the awareness that something is missing. I have been arguing here that we should think about these two different experiences of tract reception in some relation other than opposition. It seems that both were available to readers and probably experienced concurrently. Freud described such a double experience — an ongoing awareness of what is missing — as at the heart of melancholia (being aware of something missing without being able to pinpoint what it is). The weeping, then, is a manifestation of this melancholia.

Can this weeping awareness be thought of as an emotive — as a diagnostic, navigating affect? Religious affect is often considered unthinking and without individual agency. But I have suggested that we see it here in a different light. The anthropologist Saba Mahmood has examined religious practices of the contemporary women's mosque movement in Egypt, and her ethnography offers an example of how such practices can be both critical and capable of agency. The all-female mosque movement in Cairo of the 1990s shares with the Pine Barren readers an emphasis on embodied practices of personal piety. Muslim women participating in the movement gather to teach each other, through reading of and commentary on religious texts, how to shape a genuinely pious Muslim self through everyday practices. From one perspective, the mosque movement is deeply conservative and explainable as a reaction against Egypt's entry into a secularize modernity. Mahmood is aware that the women of the movement risk aligning themselves with deeply patriarchal, anti-feminist strictures, but she also seeks to reveal the possibilities for critique and agency in the embodied forms of their practice. She suggests that Foucault's late work, which re-envisions the notions of critique, provides a model for re-interpreting certain religious rituals of this Egyptian women's sect that have seemed irrational and oppressive to Western observers. Foucault writes about critique as an "attitude" or sensibility rather than a cognitive process of judgment. Critique for him is something that one inhabits like a practiced feeling:

> By "attitude," I mean a mode of relating to contemporary reality; a voluntary choice made by certain people; in the end, a way of thinking and feeling; a way, too, of acting and behaving that at one and the same time marks a relation of belonging, and presents itself as a task. A bit, no doubt, like what the Greeks called an *ethos*. ("What is Enlightenment" 39)[4]

Foucault poses this "attitude" against an understanding of critique as putting forward "a theory, a doctrine, or even as a permanent body of knowledge that is accumulating" (50). Embodiment in the form of "feeling" and practice is central to this kind of critique. For Foucault this critique is not about judgment, or revealing what is behind representation, or a "hermeneutics of suspicion"; it is about living in a particular relationship with one's social environment. Saba Mahmood understands the women of the Egyptian mosque movement as participating in such a critical attitude or "way of acting and behaving," "thinking and feeling." Neither Foucault nor Mahmood think of the participants in such a practice of critique as utterly autonomous and volunteeristic; they participate within modalities of power, moral codes, precepts, and so on. But they do have the ability to form particular relationships with those norms. As Mahmood writes in her ethnography of the Egyptian women, "there are many different ways of forming a relationship with a moral code, each of which establishes a particular relationship between capacities of the self (will, reason, desire, action, and so on) and a particular norm" (29).

It is revealing to understand the tract narratives in much the same way that Mahmood understands the reading and other religious practices of the women of the Egyptian mosque movement: as embodied, everyday tasks or practices of critique in Foucault's sense. *The Dairyman's Daughter*, I've been arguing, presents itself as a kind of critical *practice*, the development of an *ethos*. "My reader," the final page pleads, if you have not been moved to conversion "read this story once more, and then pray earnestly for like precious faith." Reading affectively is a practice like prayer. I've been suggesting here that this practice of reading does not take place within a private space of religious self-cultivation but, instead, cannot be separated from the secular public sphere. This public sphere helps to establish the form of the reading even as the practice of reading helps to establish a practice of critique of that public sphere.

This chapter and the two preceding it are thematically joined, in that each suggests that a particular form of print culture (pornography, scandal chronicles, and religious tracts) presents what William Reddy calls an emotive that is in turn repeated as part of a cultural ritual or practice. This emotive practice might well be understood as similar to Foucault's idea of critique as an attitude or feeling. It is a feeling that attempts to provide some guidance or navigation through the world by testing norms and codes. In the case of the religious tracts, the emotive diagnoses an insufficiency in the public sphere. The public sphere's emphasis on the power of argument, abstract sociality, and communicative reason results in a thinness, even a tininess. Religious tracts like *The Dairyman's Daughter* call upon their readers to question the secularity that constrains the normative ideas of the public sphere and to develop an awareness of what is missing.

Epilogue

In late November 2005, Secretary of Defense Donald Rumsfeld boasted—with a staccato inarticulacy commonplace in the Bush Administration—about U.S. success in building a democratic Iraq:

> The country is—has a free media, and they can—it's a relief valve. They could have hundred-plus papers. There's 72 radio stations. There's 44 television stations. And they're debating things and talking and arguing and discussing.

The following day the *Los Angeles Times* reported that Rumsfeld wasn't exactly providing the whole picture.[1] He had failed to mention that the Pentagon had hired the Lincoln Group, a Washington, D.C., public-relations firm, to write U.S.-friendly stories about Iraq, which would then be translated into Arabic by U.S. intelligence and funneled through an organization established by the Pentagon called the Baghdad Press Club, which would then pay Iraqi reporters to place the pieces in Iraqi newspapers under the Iraqi reporters' bylines.

Beyond a duplicity which, by that moment in 2005, had long since ceased to surprise anyone, Rumsfeld's remarks reveal just how important the idea of a public sphere—a media arena where participants develop their political authority through open criticism, through "debating things and talking and arguing and discussing"—is to the idea of a functioning democracy. The Bush administration knew on some level that if you purport to have a democracy and you don't have a public sphere of argument and debate, you better fake one. Yet, even in faking it Rumsfeld reveals some of the central problematics of the classic idea of a public sphere. For one, he seems to believe that a public sphere is simply analogous to free media and freedom of argument, and that out of such freedoms will precipitate the critical discussion and action necessary for democracy. But one of the important contributions of public-sphere theorists—from Jürgen Habermas to Alexander Kluge to Michael Warner—has been to outline the complex assumptions and habits of thinking required for formation of such a public sphere. They extend far beyond the idea of a free media and freedom of argument. The coming-into-being of the kind of public sphere which enables critical discussion and debate (and perhaps gives rise to democracy) is interwoven with the way we understand ourselves as subjects, with our relations to capitalism and the state, with our practices of reading and criticism, with our understanding of the very meaning of public and private, and much more. Such deeply embedded habits of thinking and modes of self-understandings are not put in place overnight, and they are not easily exported to other cultures, which may already have in place very different habits and modes.

But perhaps most interesting in Rumsfeld's remarks is his characterization of the public sphere. He describes the "free media" of newspapers and TV and radio as "a relief valve." But what exactly is being relieved? Violence? Passions? Pain? Passions and pain that might lead to violence? It's hard to pin down, but clearly is something that is conceived as the opposite of argument and debating. The rhetoric of relief does not fit well with argument, which we don't speak of as being relieved. One can only be relieved from those things one *feels* in one way or another— anger, an ache, a weight. This lack of clarity aside, Rumsfeld's relief metaphor captures a central, if unsurprising, opposition which appears repeatedly in our understanding of the public sphere—an opposition between feeling and argument, between the emotional and the critical. Rumsfeld here is simply repeating the commonplace view of the public sphere: if it is to be in the service of democracy, it should be based in reason, not emotion. In this view, a well-functioning public sphere dissipates emotion as it boils things down to reason.

A similar set of concerns is apparent in a very different contemporary realm, one involving American adolescents more often than Iraqis. "Like so many other teenagers Nadia, 15, is addicted," the *New York Times* announces in the lede of a recent article.[2] Nadia suffers, we learn, from a "wreck[ed] attention span" and "hours spent prowling" about. She is, as my reader will already have guessed, "addicted to the internet" and, specifically, to reading online. Nadia is "obsessed" with hypertextual reading. She reads fantasy and fan zines on the web, participates in role-playing sites, and "spends most of her time on quizilla.com or fanfiction.net, reading and commenting on stories written by other users and based on books, television shows or movies." Nadia's story is told in a 2008 series of articles called "The Future of Reading," profiling her and other young readers apparently addled by hypertextuality.

Nadia's story, of course, isn't a new one. The Internet has spawned a small cottage industry of both scholarly and popular publications focused on how bad it is for us, our kids and, in general, futurity. It is also not a new story in another sense: for centuries, new forms of media (and the new genres created in league with those new forms of media) have ignited panics. On some level we have known this for a long time — scholars in particular have recognized it — but I believe we have still much to learn about what is behind these panics. The conventional answer is that panic is a response to the threat of freedom and power that comes with increasingly open access to media communications. But this strikes me as only the start to an adequate answer, mainly because the pathologizing is so intense. In a deeper sense, the fear expressed in such panics, I would suggest, is a fear of an array of elements encountered on a daily basis in modern life: for instance, a fear of highly mediated communities, an anxiety about culture-industry determinism, a sense that our most powerful desires might mean nothing in the public sphere, and a collection of doubts about the public sphere's ability to provide agency and a sense of reason and meaning to the world. The language and imagery of addiction, obsession, mental distraction, and emotional overinvestment that surrounded reading in the late eighteenth and early nineteenth centuries also registers these modern worries.

Fever Reading has tried to trace out some of these deeper reasons for such panic. It has also tried to think in new ways about these often pathologized forms of emotional reading. Rather than looking for "relief valves" or dismissing out of hand such pathological emotion in the public sphere, *Fever Reading* has attempted to take seriously a public sphere full of emotion, one full of thrills, turn-ons, disgust, shock, trust, distrust, and longing for something more. Here I have suggested that emotion circulating through the public sphere might serve as a form of reflection (and even critique) that contributes to democracy. The question I have posed, then, is, how to understand an affectual, rather than a rational and critical, public sphere? In a certain sense, I continue the classic Habermasian project of examining the workings of a critical public sphere, only I substitute his key phrase "rational-critical public sphere" with "affective-critical public sphere." Of course, this transforms the project considerably. I am certainly not the first scholar to suggest consideration of the affects of the public sphere, but the questions raised by previous work served as the research agenda for *Fever Reading*. How can the affective public sphere constitute critical interaction between citizens and decision-making institutions, which Habermas argues is one of the public sphere's essential functions? How would it provide participants with the means of critical reflection and the power to demand accountability with respect to the state and other entities of power? Habermas's account of the public sphere was in part an attempt to bring to light the norms necessary for the development of an authority and agency among citizens, yet can emotions ever serve as norms?

Such questions seem ever more significant as the West realizes that public spheres of non-Western locales practice a different set of protocols and hold a different set of values. In other words, people in all parts of the world do not read in the same way. They do not connect reading to the public sphere in the same way that Westerners do. Robert Darnton remarks that "reading has a history" ("Toward" 88) by which he means that its practices, forms, and meanings change across time. I suspect that he also would agree that reading has *histories* — that reading changes not only across time but also across cultures. Donald Rumsfeld ignored this point when describing the forced development of a public sphere in Iraq. But that fact became more difficult to ignore when violence broke out in many European and Middle Eastern cities in 2006 and 2007, on the publication of caricatures of Muhammad originally printed in a Danish newspaper. This crisis highlighted a very different relationship between one's reading and the public sphere than that commonly held in the West. The rioters were imagining a very different kind of public sphere.

I hope that this book will begin to denaturalize our seemingly commonsensical notions of a critical public sphere, that *Fever Reading* can begin to open up new possibilities for thinking about the public sphere and the way it enables reflection on authority. Although I doubt this study will prevent policy makers from future Rumsfeldian mistakes, I do hope it might have ramifications in our general, everyday experience. For academics like me, everyday experience often means teaching.

The subject matter in my undergraduate courses frequently alternates between works of high seriousness and kitsch: *The Tempest* and *King Kong*, Marx and Mick Jagger. The texts inform each other, but this approach is also effective because it complicates students' ideas about categories like "art" and "popular culture," and requires them to rethink the relationship of critical tools to the experience of everyday life. On their best days, the students behave like scholars-in-training when discussing Shakespeare or Marx. They read critically, against the grain; they argue with examples from the texts; they compare their opinions and predict how others might argue or respond; they circle texts from a critical distance; they think historically; and they underline, highlight, and produce marginalia. But when we turn to a popular novel or a slasher film, they respond rather differently. At this late date in the history of the analysis of popular culture, they are not necessarily surprised to find slasher films and the like in their college classrooms. But they tend to resist reading such texts in the ways I often encourage—that is, in the same "critical" modes they use to read Shakespeare or Marx. This is especially the case with younger students, who have not yet been socialized in the discipline's proper forms of critical reading; to them, such mass-cultural texts don't immediately seem like "texts" at all. Instead of reading against the grain, they revel in their absorption; rather than arguing discursively with the text, they catalog their feelings; in the place of a critical distance on characters and plot, they lose themselves in recognition, identification, and desire; instead of approaching the text as an object of analysis, they approach it as a screen for their self-projections. My customary response to such reading practices is to try to coax them into proper critical reading. The students usually comply, but not without some sense of frustration, and not without defending what feels to them like the more natural ways of consuming such texts. They find it peculiar that I cannot simply "enjoy" certain popular works but instead feel the need to perform analytic work on them. By demanding distance from the text, by questioning emotional response as ideological response, and by resisting the hailing address of texts, I am systematically eliminating what makes a text appealing, at least from my students' perspectives.

I am not about to stop teaching these modes of critical interpretation, but I also think that the students' responses are telling. Does their resistance suggest a narrowness in the kinds of reading or interpretation employed in English and cultural studies? Do these fields have fewer tools for understanding enjoyment, affect, and identification than they have for practicing critical reading? Although both English and cultural studies as fields have paid attention to readers' experiences — from various reader-response theories in English to the idea of "articulation" in cultural studies — we still know very little about the way emotion is used by readers and, especially, about the ways the ostensibly "private" experiences of emotions are used in our everyday, "public" lives. To gain further insight, we'll need to use the accounts of affect currently developing in a number of different fields, from the humanities to the experimental sciences, and pursue a better understanding of the past uses of emotion in the public sphere. This is some of what *Fever Reading* has attempted to do.

Such an attention to affective reading is important not just because our students already read in this way, but because, as I've said at several moments in this project, the kind of critical public sphere that Habermas hoped would be a democratic norm simply doesn't exist on a widespread scale and, in addition, doesn't seem to fit the non-Western world very well. If there is an existing public sphere that extends beyond pockets and enclaves to reach something like a majority, it is characterized by sensation and emotion, not critical reason. Hopefully, investigating this actual public sphere will allow us to think more clearly about modes of the critical discarded by both academic discussion and everyday talk about public discourse.

Appendix

Reports in U.S. Newspapers of Obscenity Arrests, 1800–1877

Year	Accused	Incident	City
1815	John Crosby	Arrested for showing obscene book in public	Westchester, PA
1815	Jesse Sharpless and others	On trial for exhibiting an obscene painting	Philadelphia
1817	William G. Lawrence	On trial for obscene libel	
1818	One person	Prosecuted for vending obscene books	Philadelphia
1820	Three men	Arrested for selling obscene books	Boston
1820	One person	Arrested for selling obscene books	Worcester
1834	Abner Kneeland	On trial for obscene libel	New York
1834	James G. Hart and Hiram Hart	Arrested for selling an obscene book	Boston
1834	"Panders of lewdness"	Arrested for selling obscene prints	Boston
1834	Eben N. Stratton	Arrested for selling obscene prints	Boston
1834	One person	Arrested for selling obscenity	New Bedford
1834	Four different stores	Selling obscene prints (one store had 1,100 prints)	Boston
1835	Cornhill bookstore	Selling obscene prints (French and American)	Boston
1842		Seizure of 140 volumes of obscene books	Boston
1842		Burning of large seizure of indecent prints	Philadelphia
1842	Cornelius Ryan (aka John Jones), Francis Kerrigan, Charles Heustis, William Bradley, Richard Hobbes, and Henry R. Robinson	Indicted for publishing and selling obscene books	Wall Street, New York
1842	Charles G. Scott, John Vanderwater, and George Colburn	Arrested for publishing *The Flash*	New York
1842	George B. Wooldridge	Arrested for publishing *The Libertine*	New York

Year	Accused	Incident	City
1842		Obscene pictures impounded on importation	New York
1842		Indecent prints confiscated	Boston
1842	S.G. Drake/dealer in Cornhill	Arrested for obscene prints	Commercial Street, Boston
1842	Twelve persons	Convicted for "publishing obscene papers"	New York
1842	Eight persons	Convicted for "publishing obscene papers"	Philadelphia
1843		Obscene prints seized	Baltimore
1843	George Wilkes	Arrested for publishing *The Whip*	New York
1846	William Haine	Arrested for *The Curtain Drawn Up* and *Belshazzar's Feast*	New York
1846	George Bowers	Arrested for selling obscene books	Boston
1846	Edward Thomas Scotfield	Arrested for offering obscene books in the vestibule of the Astor House	New York
1848	Moses Y. Beach, Moses S. Beach, and Henry D. Beach	Arrested for publishing obscene advertisements	Boston
1849	John S. Houghton (aka Dr. Weisselhoff)	Arrested for vending obscene books	Boston
1851	Willis, Little, and Co.	Prosecuted for publishing obscene literature	Keene, NH
1853	Albert Gazley	Arrested for obscene books and prints	New York
1855		Mayor Wood orders action against *The Broadway Belle*	New York
1855	John Atecheson	Arrested for selling obscene work, including *Mysteries of Venus; Or, the Amatory Life and Adventures of Miss Kitty Pry*	New York
1857	Dr. Hankinson	Arrested for obscene books	New York
1857	George Ackerman	Obscenity ring broken up, seizure of 15,000–20,000 copies of the *Venus' Miscellany*	New York
1857	Fredric Brady	Obscenity ring broken up	12 Ann Street, New York
1857	P. F. Harris	Re-arrested for publishing *The Broadway Belle*	New York
1858	James Cruise	Tried for publishing an obscene paper, *The Phoenix*	New York

Year	Accused	Incident	City
1858	Phillip Wolff	Arrested for selling obscene cards	San Francisco
1858	George W. Murray, Samuel Armheim, and James McGrath	Arrested for selling obscene prints	San Francisco
1858	Henry R. G. Bulkley, alias John Walker, alias C. J. Wilson; Fayette, Harper & Co.	Arrested for publishing obscene literature	Philadelphia (previously arrested in New York)
1858	H. P. Pearson	Arrested for selling *The New York Miscellany*	12 Ann Street, New York
1858	Arthur Crown	Charged with selling obscene books	New York
1858	two French men (de Bram and Moriale)	Arrested for publishing and selling obscene prints	New York
1859		Seizure of obscene prints	Stockton, CA
1859	H. H. Haight, Halsey, and Co.	On trial for selling obscene stereoscope views	New York
1860	H. S. Harris	Arrested for distributing obscene letters	New York
1860	Various persons	Arrested for selling obscene prints	Stockton, CA
1860	George and Edward Bonney	Arrested for selling obscene publications	San Francisco
1861	William Mack	Arrested for selling obscene books	Philadelphia
1862	James Murray	Arrested for selling obscene prints	19 Wall Street, New York
1864	George C. Powers	Arrested for obscene publications	San Francisco
1865	John Marlowe	Arrested for obscene prints	New York
1866	Theodore M. Hytton	Tried for publication of *Our Maseppa*	
1866	Le Grand Pierrepont	Arrested for selling obscene prints	16 Laight Street, New York
1866	David Friedborg and Arthur Whiting	Arrested for selling obscene literature	New York
1866	photographers	Arrested for "attaching the faces of respectable ladies to the bodies of abandoned females who make a business of posturing for indecent pictures"	San Francisco
1867	Charles E. Mackey	Arrested for obscene publication	Metuchen, NJ
1868	Dr. E. Z. Wickes	Arrested for publishing *Illustrated Medical Counselor*	New York

Year	Accused	Incident	City
1869	Thomas O'Connor (aka James S. Dexter)	Arrested for publishing the obscene	60 Warren Street, New York
1870	Calvin Willis	Arrested for selling obscene books	New York
1870	Simon M. Landis	Arrested and sentenced for *The Secrets of Generation*, an obscene weekly	Philadelphia
1870	J. S. Colgate	Arrested for mailing obscene photographs through the post office	New York
1870	Edward M. Grandin, (aka Garrett M. Evans of Evans publishing) and William DavisonArrested for publishing obscene literature	27 and 77 Nassau Street and 41 Liberty Street, New York	
1870	Richard Grist	Arrested for selling obscene books	Philadelphia
1870	Thomas M. Scroggy	Arrested for selling obscene book	Vine Street, Philadelphia
1871	George C. Bennett	Arrested for circulation of obscene printed matter	New York
1872	P. R. Randolph	Arrested for publishing obscene books	Washington Street, Boston
1872	William Simpson	Arrested for selling works of Paul de Kock	New York
1872	Woodhull, Clafflin, Blood	Arrested for obscene articles	New York
1872	John Meeker	Tried for vending obscene books	New York
1872	C Mackey (American Publishing Agency), E. M. Grandin (aka Garret M. Evans and Evans and Co.), Prof. Rogers and Silas Rogers and Co. (real name David Massey), and Henry Camp, alias Camer and Co.)	Arrested for publishing/selling obscene materials	New York
1872	Patrick J. Bannon, in connection with Michael Elmore (aka Daly)	Arrested for selling obscene books	14 and 16 Ann Street, New York
1872	James McDermott (Barnett and Co.)	Arrested for obscene publication	19 Ann Street, New York

Year	Accused	Incident	City
1872	Thomas Lyons, Charles and William Brooks	Arrested for obscene publication	New York
1872	Robert Hague, Solomon W. Rice, and Charles Manches	Arrested for obscene publication	New York
1872	John Makay (American Publishing Co.) [perhaps same as Mackey above]	Arrested for obscene publication	New York
1872	Henry Camp (Cameron and Co.)	Arrested for obscene publication	New York
1873	six men	Arrested for dealing obscene literature	New York
1873	Charles Mullen (aka Madame Mouche)	Arrested for circulating obscene literature	New York
1873	William Carpenter	Tried for mailing obscene publications	New York
1873	Carmello Bertolini	Arrested for mailing obscene literature	New York
1874	Charles Gillingham	Arrested for obscene pictures	New York
1874	William Simpson	On trial for obscene publication; in 1875 sentenced to 2 years and $5000 fine.	Philadelphia
1874	John H. Seaders and George Sharp	Arrested for selling obscene literature	San Francisco
1874	J. R. Mains	On trial for mailing obscene photographs	San Francisco
1875	Edward Murray (printer) and William Creighton	Arrested for obscene publication	New York
1875	Thomas Scroggy	Arrested for obscene prints	Vine Street, Philadelphia
1875	Hugh F. McDermott and Son	Arrested for obscene book selling (12,000 found on premises)	Jersey City, NJ
1875	George Wagner	Arrested for obscene prints	New York
1875	Joseph Hall, Horace Woods, and Henry Snellback	Arrested for obscene pictures	139 Fulton Street, New York
1875	John A. Lant	Arrested for mailing obscenity	New York
1875	Edward Murray (printer) and William Creighton (folder)	Charged with selling obscene literature	New York

Year	Accused	Incident	City
1876	George W. Conroy	Convicted for selling obscene literature	New York
1876	Victor Kauffmann	Indicted for sending an obscene postcard	New York
1876	George H. Gaulier	Convicted for peddling obscene pictures	New York
1876	Mathias (Albert) Zeigler	Pled guilty to two charges of vending and manufacturing obscene literature	New York
1876	Stephen Schall	Arrested for selling obscene literature	New York
1877	E. H. Heywood	Arrested for circulating obscene literature	New York
1877	John P. O'Brian	Arrested for mailing obscene material	New York
1877	E. B. Foot, Jr.	Convicted for circulating obscene material	New York

Notes

Introduction

1. All books, essays, and most other sources are cited parenthetically and listed in the works-cited list, but there are a number of newspapers and ephemera, which lead to very unwieldy parenthetical citation, and these are listed in the notes for the sake of readability. On mental dissipation: "The Young Men's Department," *The Michigan Farmer*, April 1, 1849, vol. 7, 110; on nausea: "Speculations of Scriblerus Secundus, Esq.," *The Album and Ladies' Weekly Gazette*; October 18, 1826, 1; on gonorrhea: Levi Aldrich, "Gonorrhea Dormientium," *The Boston Medical and Surgical Journal* 29.24 (1844): 480–87; on depravity of morals: "Novel Reading, A Cause of Female Depravity," *The New England Quarterly Magazine*, April–June, 1802, 2; on poison: "On Reading Novels," *The Churchman's Magazine*, May–June 1813, 1; on suicide and murder: "On Novel Reading," *The Guardian, or Youth's Religious Instructor*, February 1, 1820, 2; on alcohol and opium: Rev. Dr. Beasley, "Romance Reading," *The North American Magazine*, September, 1834, 4; on fevers, "a drunkard" and potential to "enslave": "Letter on Novel Reading," *Washington Theological Reparatory*, November 1, 1821, vol. 3, no. 4, 106; on fever: "Indiscriminate Novel-Reading," *The Happy House and Parlor Magazine*, July 1, 1856, 4, and "Thoughts upon Novel Reading," *The Yale Literary Magazine*, July 1840, 5.

1. The Senses of Reading

1. As an aside, it is worth mentioning that this obsession with penetration and fear of inundation is very male. Brown often addresses himself to women, and he frequently evokes that well-known trope of the bad female reader, one who reads too intensely, too emotionally, with too much attachment and not enough critical distance (like Charlotte Temple, Madame Bovary and, in a queer turn on the trope, Dorian Gray). This moralistic tradition is surely about (male) anxiety concerning the development of female community and agency newly available through a novel-reading culture and the expansion of print culture more generally. There is a considerable amount of scholarship on this subject of women readers (especially women novel readers), and the next chapter engages some of it. Also, albeit a smaller collection of texts, there is important scholarship on "feeling" readers. For instance, *Fever Reading* builds on the field-transforming work by Janice A. Radway, who has been particularly sensitive to the ways various subgenres—the romance novel and Book-of-the-Month Club selections—have "endowed us with an ample and refined vocabulary for articulating and achieving affective states" (*Feeling* 13). One of the goals of *Fever Reading* is to put this scholarship in dialogue with the history and

theory of the public sphere. Another goal is to augment the scholarship on "feeling" women readers by examining "feeling" male readers who were also thought to be threatened by certain kinds and practices of reading (as any number of anti-onanist tracts reveal). Let it suffice to say at this point that proper reading has a gender, however unconscious it may have remained for Brown and almost everyone else of his historical moment.

2. Brown here also sounds like his contemporary Immanuel Kant, as well as Habermas. In lines that Habermas quotes in *The Structural Transformation*, Kant speaks of the "public of the *reading world*" (italics in Kant's original; Habermas, 105; Kant, 59) as being a necessary element of reason. And Kant, like Habermas and Brown, famously called for a detached and distanced relationship with objects of art in his aesthetic theory in order to achieve objective reason and not suffer the perils of subjectivism. For Kant, Habermas, and Brown, an indefinite public of readers was essential for reason, judgment, evaluation, and reflection. These readers need to read in a distanced and critical fashion to achieve these desired ends.

3. Such an argument is made by Michael Schudson's "Was There Ever a Public Sphere?" That the public sphere was (and still is) exclusionary but might nevertheless be revisable and a tool for excluded groups is a central argument of many works of historical scholarship. See Mary Ryan's *Women in Public* and Elizabeth McHenry's *Forgotten Readers* for examples.

4. Habermas makes this point and others in relation to this critique in "Further Reflections on the Public Sphere" (especially 425–29).

5. Oskar Negt and Alexander Kluge make this argument throughout *The Public Sphere and Experience* (see especially 7–8). Fraser in "Rethinking the Public Sphere" has also suggested the difficulty of subaltern publics achieving intelligibility in a dominant public sphere (119), but she is more sanguine than some others about the possibility. Harold Mah argues, like Negt and Kluge, that the rational-critical public sphere that Habermas presents demands that certain characteristics of the subject be bracketed off in order to achieve entry. Russ Castronovo's *NecroCitizenship* and Elizabeth Maddock Dillon's *The Gender of Freedom* provide historical and (helpfully clear) theoretical accounts of how this exclusion operates in the United States in the eighteenth and nineteenth centuries. Warner's work on this issue, collected in *Public and Counterpublics*, is discussed more fully later in this chapter.

6. In its astute critique of recent public-sphere theory, Jennifer Greiman's *Democracy's Spectacle* notes the problem I am trying to articulate here: "[a]s scholars have refuted Habermas's presumption of public rationality, demonstrating the centrality of sentiment and affect in nineteenth-century public life and arguing that the U.S. public is indeed a space of intimacy, they have ultimately read into that intimacy signs of a passive and depoliticized public sphere" (5). This has certainly been the case with some critiques of the traditional public-sphere idea (if perhaps not all recent public-sphere scholarship; Greiman is I suspect thinking here of work like that of Lauren Berlant and Russ Castronovo, who describe the liberal public sphere as encouraging "dead citizenship" and "necro-citizenship," but work on counterpub-

lics suggests a form of the public sphere that is not depoliticized). With Greiman's critique in mind, how then do we maintain the important critical capacities of the Habermasian idea of the public sphere (after all, it was these critical capacities that made the public sphere so revolutionary an idea) but also focus on the emotion that dominates the public sphere?

7. The references given in the text are obviously not comprehensive, but meant to point readers to important scholarship. The discussion of emotion has complex technical aspects that will not be delved into here unless it is necessary for the specific argument about the public sphere and reading. This argument does not often require a distinction between emotion and all of its other near-synonyms or closely related phenomena: affect, feeling, moods, intensities, passions, investments, energy, and so on. Strict delineations are made in certain fields: psychoanalysis often distinguishes between emotion and affect, some neural scientists between emotion and feeling (Damasio), and some philosophers and theorists between affect and emotion (Massumi and Sedgwick). But, for the most part, these will not be essential demarcations in *Fever Reading*.

8. See, for instance, Joseph LeDoux's *The Emotional Brain*.

9. See, for example, Alice Isen and Gregory Diamond's "Affect and Automaticity."

10. Take, for instance, Eve Sedgwick's reading of anxiety and fear in homosocial texts of the last two and a half centuries in her *Between Men* and *Epistemology of the Closet*. But this mode of reading emotion is so prevalent that examples are hardly needed. Indeed, Sedgwick thinks of it as the dominant interpretive style across any number of approaches to literature ranging from psychoanalysis to ideology critique to New Historicism (see "Paranoid Reading and Reparative Reading"). In her view, professional readers of texts (like herself, she admits, in the two above works) are taught to peel back the veil of representation to find what is hidden beneath. As she points out, to single-mindedly deploy this approach and only this approach to texts is to risk descending into a kind of interpretive paranoia.

11. Shelley Streeby's *American Sensations* provides the example of both the former and the latter when speaking of George Lippard's sensationalism: "his emphasis on bodies and sensations responds to contemporaneous formulations of a disembodied soul and an abstract citizenship" (43), which in turn served as the affective foundation for a white, male, working-class community. Paula Bernat Bennett's *Poets in the Public Sphere* offers an instance of emotion deployed in both hegemonic battle and as ground for community when she understands nineteenth-century female sentimental poetry as unsettling liberal abstract personhood and contributing to the development of an alternative female reading public.

12. This perspective on emotion and ideological interpellation is central to much critical scholarship, including Allan Hepburn's *Intrigue*: "Novels habituate readers to social, psychological, and political fears" (29), and "[a]t the moment the reader is thrilled, he is interpellated. He becomes the subject of ideology" (47).

13. Work on emotion deriving from Aristotle and others of his tradition is considerable and well known; I will not try to list it here. Important recent theoretical

work on affect in the humanities includes Brian Massumi's definition of "affect" in *Parables for the Virtual* as "unassimilable" intensity, which owes a great deal to Deleuze (see, for instance, 32–34). Also, Eve Sedgwick's notion of "affect" (her solution to paranoid reading) relies on Tomkins (see her "Shame in the Cybernetic Fold"). The various traditions of thinking about emotion that follow from Aristotle (emotions influence judgment), Spinoza-James-Deleuze (emotions are a fundamental part of cognition), and Tomkins (emphasizing the biological basis for affect) — not to mention the psychoanalytic tradition of Freud — are very different from each other, but I will not attempt to mark out those differences here. In the following pages, I do attempt to develop a theory of affect founded in recent work in cognitive science, which holds some similarities and a number of differences with these various historical traditions.

14. Some readers will be more interested than others in these details, so in this note (and others following) I offer a more elaborate overview. It seems to me that the details are not necessarily essential to the argument I'm making here, but it is important in interdisciplinary scholarship to pay close attention to the complexities of the knowledge of the intersecting disciplines. This imperative seems particularly strong when working between the sciences and the humanities, because their languages and goals can be so different.

Like the cognitive scientists, Reddy understands that what is usually referred to as emotion is actually a complex process: "the term, *emotion*, in English usage, is frequently employed to refer to that which is activated but not yet in attention, to [thought] material that is available to, even calls for attention but has not got it" (89). This description will need some unpacking. Three of the key terms here — "thought material," "activation," and "attention" — have specific technical meanings. "Thought material" (87–89 *passim*) at first seems a misnomer because it suggests that ideas ("thoughts") rather than non-cognitive stimuli are the material, but Reddy's goal is to break down such distinctions. Thought material is thus several different kinds of stimulus — conventional sensory stimulus, proprioceptive sensation, interoceptive sensation — along with the consciousness of ideas, concepts, and frameworks that are usually associated with intellectualization, as well as the different kinds of memory ranging from that which allows specific movement and basic skills ("muscle memory" in lay parlance), to the kind of involuntary memory that enables, for instance, speech, to unconscious and more conscious memory of past experience. In short, "thought material" refers to a great deal of internal and external sensation, including the sensation of ideation.

At any moment, and especially in moments of strong stimulus, a considerable amount of thought material is brought to the fore; it is "activated." "Activation" (88–97 *passim*) is the state when thought material is made available for "attention" or, in other words, conscious processing. However, as the cognitive scientists have repeatedly shown, all of this activated thought material cannot be brought into attention. Much of it is not processed at all, and lingers in a state of activation without attention.

As I describe in the text, Reddy suggests thinking of the processes of thought material becoming activated and then being brought to attention as a form of "translation" (88–96 *passim*). This suggestion—that the cognitive scientist's term "processing" be replaced with the more nuanced and complex concept of "translation"—is one of his most exciting and important ideas. Reddy is particularly interested in translation across mediums, and not simply across languages. This is because what the cognitive scientists call "processing" is most accurately understood as conversion (or translation) across any number of mediums: say, from the senses to memory to expression. In an argument familiar to those working in the rhetorical sciences, Reddy makes the point that just as dance can be translated only partially and incompletely into prose, photography, or video, "processing" across emotional mediums leaves gaps and incompletions. "Emotion," as Reddy explains in his initial definition, is the word commonly used to reference all the thought material in the realm of activation that remains untranslated or incompletely translated into attention.

This is a very schematic definition of emotion. However, the schematism is one of the definition's virtues. It does not name emotions (love, anger, sadness) and then go looking for them. It opens up the possibility of understanding emotional experiences that don't have names.

15. A performative speech act doesn't describe something (as does a constative speech act like "the dog is brown") but rather does something in the world under certain conditions. The most famous performative is "I do," which under certain conditions (when said at the right time, before the right people, and under the right rules) marries two people, but under different conditions does something different, or nothing at all.

16. Again, for those readers interested in greater detail, Reddy writes, "Emotives are translations into words about, in 'descriptions' of, the ongoing translation tasks that currently occupy attention as well as the other tasks that remain in the queue, overflowing its current capacities" (105). He places quotation marks around "description" to indicate that the emotive is no simple description. The emotive doesn't exactly represent the thought material; it is a translation of that material, and is thus accompanied by all the gaps of any translation and the remainders that must be left behind in any translation.

Reddy's theoretical account of emotives' evaluative capabilities is grounded in experiments in cognitive psychology (as well as everyday, commonsensical experience), which suggests that emotional expression has the ability to test emotional states and even to lead to changes in emotional states. Cognitive scientists have often found that emotions feedback or rebound on themselves so as to confirm, disconfirm, intensify, or attenuate the original emotion. This point is supported by a great deal of work in psychology, which Margaret Clark summarizes: "There is . . . some clear evidence that choosing to express an emotion or to cognitively rehearse it may intensify or even create the actual experience of that emotion while choosing to suppress it or not think about it may have the opposite effect" (266, quoted in Reddy 104). To this end Reddy also turns to the work of Jerome Kegan (41, quoted in Reddy 104),

Phoebe Ellsworth (193, quoted in Reddy 104), and especially the research of Daniel M. Wegner. Wegner's work on the way emotions "rebound" (783, quoted in Reddy 27) and provide feedback on thought material is essential to Reddy's argument about the evaluative ability of emotives.

17. Paul Ekman's "Expression and the Nature of Emotion" discusses how smiles can produce physiological reactions associated with certain emotions.

18. In another important book about emotion, *Cato's Tears and the Making of Anglo-American Emotion*, Julie Ellison develops a position close to that of Berlant. Ellison criticizes the standard approach: "[b]y studying the 'ideological work' that sentiment is performing in any given text or cultural milieu, the scholar allies himself or herself with ideology as the analytical term" (6–7). Ellison doesn't want to ignore the ideological work of sentiment, but she also wants to remain open to how textually generated sentiment "exposes a complicated awareness of the human cost of national and imperial economies" and how it can be "the *admitted* connection between speculation, mood, and power" (7). For Ellison certain kinds of emotions can serve as "*knowledge* of ideology" (15). In this view, emotion is neither ideological nor strategic but knowledge producing. Ellison, like Berlant, doesn't turn to cognitive science, but the cognitive-science perspective does provide a theoretical structure for understanding emotion in this way.

19. For a summation of such a view see Clifford Geertz's *The Interpretation of Cultures*, 43–51. Making a similar call to break down the boundaries between subject, body, culture, and environment, the anthropologist Edwin Hutchins suggests, "Instead of conceiving the relation between person and environment in terms of moving coded information across a boundary, let us look for processes of entrainment, coordination, and resonance among the elements of a system that includes a person and the person's surroundings" (299; quoted in Elfenbein 490).

20. On the "implied reader," see Wolfgang Iser's "The Reading Process"; on the "informed reader," Stanley Fish's "Interpreting the 'Variorum'"; on "historical hermeneutics," James Machor's *Reading Fiction in Antebellum America*; on Roger Chartier's "appropriation and imposition," "Introduction" to *A History of Reading of in the West*; on cultural studies' concept of "articulation," see Jennifer Daryl Slack's "The Theory and Method of Articulation in Cultural Studies"; on how the concept might be applied to reading, Tony Bennett and Janet Woolacott's "Texts and Their Readers"; on the reader in the "information circuit," Robert Darnton's "The News in Paris"; on the "translation" of concepts from the field of the experimental psychology of reading (especially the helpful term "structures of coherence") to the field of the history of reading, see Andrew Elfenbein, "Cognitive Science and the History of Reading"; on reading and phenomenology, see Iser's "The Reading Process"; and on neophenomenology and reading, see Rita Felski's *Uses of Literature*. This list is not comprehensive and could be considerably expanded. It is meant to indicate key approaches from across many different fields and orientations.

21. The scholarship on female reading in eighteenth- and nineteenth-century America is voluminous; a good place to start is Nina Baym, *Novels, Readers, and*

Reviewers. Representative scholarship in other areas include, on race, Elizabeth McHenry, *Forgotten Readers*; on Native Americans, Hilary E. Wyss, *Writing Indians*; and on working-class men, Michael Denning, *Mechanic Accents*.

2. Good and Bad Reading in the Early United States

1. The comment, from 1954, is about comic book reading. See Fredric Wertham's *Seduction of the Innocent*, 87.

2. *New-England Courant*, February 18, 1723, no. 81, quoted in Shields, 268.

3. A. [William Livingston], "Of the Use, Abuse, and Liberty of the Press," *The Independent Reflector*, August 30, 1753.

4. This paragraph's discussion of the development of "public opinion" in the 1790s is derived in part from Gordon Wood, *Empire of Liberty*, 308–12, although he does not frame the discussion in Habermasian terms, as I have done here.

5. "Scraps, Literary, Miscellaneous, and Amusing," *The New England Quarterly Magazine*, July–September 1802, vol. 2, no. 2, 262; "The Ill Effects of Reading without Digesting," *The Port-Folio*, June 16, 1804, vol. 4, no. 24, 187.

6. "On Novel Reading," *The Panoplist*, October 1808, vol. 1, no. 5, 204; FZ, "The Importance of Missionary Reading," *The Panoplist, and Missionary Herald*, September 1819, vol. 15, no. 9, 399.

7. "Novel Reading," *New York Evangelist*, February 14, 1856, vol. 27, no. 7, 26.

8. "Hints on Reading," D, *The Ladies Magazine and Repository of Entertaining Knowledge*, March 1793.

9. "Advantages of Reading," *The American Moral & Sentimental Magazine*, November 6, 1797.

10. "The Method of Reading for Female Improvement," I. Schomberg, *The Ladies Magazine and Musical Repository*, March 1801.

11. "On the Means of Reading with Most Advantage," Juvenis, *Philadelphia Repository and Weekly Register*, May 2, 1801.

12. "On Reading," August 23, 1856, 11.

13. "Speculations of Scrilderus Secundus, Esq.," *The Album and Ladies' Weekly Gazette*, October 18, 1826.

14. "Observations on Novel Reading," *The Universal Asylum and Columbian Magazine*, October 1792, 262.

15. "On Reading History," Mrs. Chapman, *The Album and Ladies' Weekly Gazette*, August 2, 1826.

16. "On Reading History," Mrs. Chapman, *The Album and Ladies' Weekly Gazette*, August 9, 1826.

17. "Reading," Dorcas, *The Lowell Offering*, February 1843.

18. "French Reading Shops," *The Time Piece*, May 11, 1789.

19. "Novel Reading," Samuel Harris, *New York Observer and Chronicle*, September 15, 1853.

20. "Books, and the Reading Public," *Littell's Living Age*, April 3, 1847.

21. Melanethon, *Virginia Evangelical and Literary Magazine*, September 1818.

22. See, for instance, "Letter on Novel Reading," *Washington Theological Reparatory*, November 1, 1821, and "Romance Reading," Dr. Beasley, *The North American Magazine*, September 1834.

23. "The Method of Reading for Female Improvement," I. Schomberg, *The Ladies Magazine and Musical Repository*, March 1801. This article is a reprint from *The European Magazine and London Review*, December 1786.

24. "Advice to Readers," *The Massachusetts Magazine*, March 1789.

25. "The Method of Reading for Female Improvement," I. Schomberg, *The Ladies Magazine and Musical Repository*, March 1801.

26. "On Reading and Study," Crito, *The Guardian and Monitor*, November 1, 1826.

27. N. [Charles Brockden Brown], "Remarks on Reading," *The Literary Magazine, and American Register*, March 1806.

28. "Profitable Method of Reading Recommended," *The Rural Magazine*, December 22, 1798.

29. Crito, "On Reading and Study," *The Guardian and Monitor*, November 1, 1826, vol. 8, no. 11, 389.

30. Juvenis, "On the Means of Reading with Most Advantage," *Philadelphia Repository and Weekly Register*, May 2, 1801, vol. 1, no. 25, 196.

31. "On the Advantage of Miscellaneous Reading," *The Philadelphia Monthly Magazine*, July 1798, vol. 2, no. 7, 7.

32. "Scraps, Literary, Miscellaneous, and Amusing," *The New England Quarterly Magazine*, July–September 1802, vol. 2, no. 2, 262.

33. "Novel Reading, A Cause of Female Depravity," *The New England Quarterly Magazine*, April–June 1802, vol. 2, no. 1, 172.

34. "The Reading of Novels," *Weekly Visitor, or Ladies Miscellany*, July 21, 1804, vol. 2, no. 94, 332.

35. Brown's letter to Jefferson reads in part: "I am conscious, however, that this form of composition may be regarded by you with indifference or contempt, that social and intellectual theories, that the history of facts in the processes of nature and the operations of government may appear to you the only laudable pursuits, that fictitious narratives in their own nature or in the manner in which they have hitherto been conducted may be thought not to deserve notice, and that, consequently, whatever may be the merit of my book as a fiction, yet it is to be condemned because it is a fiction."

36. Jonathan Elmer, writing about sentimental deathbed scenes, explains the purportedly proper relation between the sentimental reader's emotion-infused body and the dying body represented in the scene: "the reading body and the represented body are out of synch or, we could say, syncopated: when the represented body undergoes erasure and dies, the reading body is opened up to tears and the affective: '*First* read it, *then* weep.' One is led toward a penetration by affect, and then back away from that toward a moralized understanding of the social meaning of that affect" (105).

37. One of Tompkins's important observations in this essay is that the reader-response criticism of the 1970s is no different from the New Criticism it attempts to displace in one specific way: both remain focused on the meaning of a text and not the way texts were used in the social world (although reader-response criticism and New Criticism are very different in terms of where they locate that meaning). Of course, the landscape of reader-oriented scholarship has changed tremendously since 1980, the date of Tompkins's essay. Scholarship originating in several different fields or subfields—the history of reading and cultural studies are perhaps most salient—have focused on the "uses of literacy" (to borrow the title of Richard Hoggert's foundational text in cultural studies) rather than the meaning of texts. In particular, Karin Littau's *Theories of Reading* updates Tomkins's argument with an emphasis on embodiment.

38. In the *Critique of the Power of Judgment* (1790), Kant's central ideas about aesthetic judgment rest on a presumption of disinterested contemplation that some-how escapes utility and desire. The New Critics acquired their Kantian aesthetics through Coleridge and Monroe Beardsley, a Kantian philosopher. I linger here for a moment over the New Critics because they represent a relationship between reading and emotion that was very powerful during the twentieth century and that was in-culcated in tens of thousands of American students. It is in part this relationship that I am trying to unsettle. I'm also suggesting here a different backhistory to the New Criticism—one that sees it as connected to the development of the public sphere and, in its need to objectify and contain emotion (in, say, the "objective correlative"), one that sees it as counter-intuitively connected to the Scottish Enlightenment and even the Romantic poets. In a moment I will suggest that such a modality of reading is at the forefront of the fictions of Hawthorne and Poe and that it is also closely aligned with the development of liberalism in the nineteenth century. Indeed, it is interest-ing to consider New Criticism as the aesthetic theory of Cold War liberalism with both formations' emphasis on disinterested proceduralism, formalism, and the strict delineation of public from private.

39. N. [Charles Brockden Brown], "Remarks on Reading," *The Literary Maga-zine, and American Register*, March 1806. This essay is identified as Brown's and reprinted in Myra Jehlen and Michael Warner, eds., *The English Literatures of America, 1500–1800*, 994–99.

40. The argument I make here about a shift from a republican style of public sphere reading to a liberal style of public sphere reading is influenced by Michael Warner's argument about such a shift in the understanding of the meaning of print, publication, and authorship at the end of the eighteenth century. See *The Letters of the Republic*, 131.

41. Hawthorne also thematizes reading at other moments in his work. For example, in "My Kinsman, Major Molineux," he presents—against the "shrewd" (70 and else-where), "rational" (78) Robin's "evening of ambiguity and weariness"—the memory of a scene of communal Bible reading, where family, neighbors, and even "wayfaring" strangers gather beneath a tree at the homestead while Robin's father reads aloud,

"holding the scriptures in the golden light that shown from western clouds" (80). In "My Kinsman" this kind of reading is associated with kinship community, lack of mediation (nature itself seems to read this text), and the piety of the heart (the experience promises to "keep his heart pure" [80]). But it is also a nostalgic and naïve form of reading in Hawthorne's narrative, one that can provide little help for Robin during his "evening of ambiguity." Robin needs to be a very different kind of reader, Hawthorne suggests — a hermeneutical reader rather than an exegetical reader.

3. Obscene Reading

1. See chapter 1 for a discussion of "rational-critical," and Jürgen Habermas, *The Structural Transformation of the Public Sphere*, 28.

2. For a more detailed discussion of this issue, see chapter 1, where Warner's work is carefully considered. In addition to Warner, Berlant, and Hendler, I am thankful for and indebted to the work of Bruce Burgett, *Sentimental Bodies*; Russ Castronovo, *Necro Citizenship*; and Paula Bernat Bennett, *Poets in the Public Sphere*. For a perspective on this issue from outside of nineteenth-century cultural studies, see Bruno Latour, "From Realpolitik to Dingpolitik."

3. The need for inquiry in this area is noted by Amanda Anderson regarding the uses of affect theory more generally, which she sees as productive in many respects but also a "problem" in that "it allows one to skirt the question of critical reflection." Without a clear conceptualization of affect's role in "critical reflection," Anderson argues, work on affect has a difficult time addressing "how practitioners might reflectively realize, promote, and ultimately even render habitual those postures that best encompass its intellectual and ethicopolitical values." In other words, from Anderson's perspective, even as affect serves as an important conceptual category for seeing into blind spots and new places, it remains unclear how affect might serve as a reflective, even normative foundation for ethical and political projects. I tend to agree with Anderson that more clarity in this area is needed, but I also think that those critics and theorists mentioned above as part of the affective turn in public-sphere theory have begun to provide this clarity. See Amanda Anderson, *The Way We Argue Now*, 9–10.

4. The various nineteenth-century U.S. newspaper databases indicate that the term "obscene literature" comes into usage in the mid-1850s (the earliest I've found is "Spread of Obscene Literature," *Weekly Herald*, January 28, 1854, 29). By the late 1860s the term had entered law in New York and other states (see, for example, "The Obscene Literature Bill," *Christian Advocate*, May 7, 1868, 19).

5. Because parenthetical citations of newspapers are often unwieldy due to length, I've cited newspapers in footnotes (otherwise I use internal citation). See "Great Seizure of Obscene Literature," *Herald*, September 16, 1857, 8; "The Seizure of Obscene Books and Prints," *Herald*, September 23, 1857, 5; "Another Alleged Obscene Publisher Arrested," *Herald*, September 29, 1857, 1; "Another Seizure of Obscene Literature," *Herald*, November 18, 1857, 1.

See also, "A Publishing Establishment Broken Up. Seizure of Improper Books," *The New York Tribune*, September 16, 1857, 5; "The Case of George Akarman," *Tribune*, September 22, 1857, 5; "Another Obscene Publisher Arrested," *Tribune*, September 29, 1857, 5; and "Another Haul of Yellow-Covered Literature – Arrest of the Dealer," *Tribune*, November 18, 1857, 7.

Furthermore, see "Injured Innocence!" *The New York Daily Times*, September 21, 1857, 4; "Burning Obscene Books," *Times*, September 22, 1857, 2; "Another Alleged Obscene Publisher Arrested – Cartloads of Books and Prints Found," *Times*, September 29, 1857, 1; "Another Descent Upon an Obscene Book Depot," *Times*, November 18, 1857, 3.

The spate of obscenity arrests in the fall of 1857 was particularly large, but similar arrests and seizures took place throughout the decade. See, for example, *Times*, September 6, 1853, 1; "Selling Obscene Books, Prints, &c.," *Times*, February 16, 1855, 3; "Selling Obscene Books," *Times*, January 26, 1858, 5; "Selling Vile Books," *Times*, April 12, 1858, 8; and "Selling Obscene Publications," *Times*, August 13, 1858, 8.

6. "Another Alleged Obscene Publisher Arrested," *Herald*, September 29, 1857, 1.

7. "Another Haul of Yellow-Covered Literature – Arrest of the Dealer," *Tribune*, November 18, 1857, 7.

8. These are questions that a handful of scholars of nineteenth-century U.S. history have taken up over the past few years and the brief overview in this section of "obscene literature" owes a tremendous amount to their historical sleuthing. See especially, Horowitz's and Dennis's books, and also Cohen, et al. Here I do offer a somewhat different historical perspective by tracing obscene literature through newspapers accounts of obscenity arrests. The arrest reports offer a general picture of the presence and development of the genre as well as a number of titles of obscene publications. The newspapers also offer a data set that has been fairly well preserved, unlike many of the legal records of these arrests and prosecutions. I also use the reports as a way of defining, in a sense, what is obscene – a category which is notoriously difficult to define. In other words, I allow the contemporary discourse and prohibitions to define the print material I call "obscene" (and sometimes "pornographic," although this terminology is of the twentieth century, not the nineteenth).

9. The emergence of this literature as a significant concern in the 1830s was the result of several well-known technological, social, institutional, and ideological transformations that bear mentioning. The rapid industrialization of the printing industry – including new technology like the steam press – meant more print, cheaper print, and easier access to print. Railroads and the fantastically rapid development of cities and urban culture did much the same. For an extraordinarily thorough overview of these transformations in print culture and their social effects, see Ronald J. Zboray and Mary Saracino Zboray's *Every Ideas: Socioliterary Experience among Antebellum New Englanders*. For sharp insights into how newly prominent urban institutions (like the New York Mercantile Library) in the burgeoning antebellum city shaped the modes of reading of a new population of young, socially and economically striving men, see Thomas Augst's *The Clerk's Tale* (especially 158–206). Both

of these works investigate the ways unprecedented changes in technology, institutions, and society more generally created new reading populations and new reasons to read; reform movements, in turn, attempted to control these new populations by controlling their reading. These influences conspired to create a flood of obscene texts and a panicky response to that flood.

10. It is clear from extant daguerreotypes that there was an active market in erotic photography in 1850s France and England, and U.S. newspaper and police reports do suggest that images also circulated in New York and other cities. However, I have been unable to find many of these images. It is interesting to note that one of the central tropes of 1850s European erotic photography was the young woman reading, and that these images are often stereoscopes, a fact which indicates that they were for public sale and consumption. For examples of such images, see Serge Nazarieff's *Early Erotic Photography* and Uwe Scheid's *1000 Nudes*. In addition, the Kinsey Institute Library and Special Collections owns a photographic reproduction of a stereoscopic image (dating from roughly 1880) that shows a woman masturbating while looking at a revealing picture book. The image on the cover of *Fever Reading*, similar to those appearing in the 1850s, is dated by its owner—the collector Mark Rotenberg—as approximately 1880. He also believes it is American in origin.

11. *Ely's Hawk & Buzzard*, September 6, 1834, 2.

12. *The New York Arena*, May 27, 1842, 2.

13. *The Owl*, September 25, 1830, 2.

14. *Whip and Satirist of New-York and Brooklyn*, April 2, 1842, 2.

15. *The Owl*, July 10, 1830, 2.

16. *The New York Arena*, May 24, 1842, 2.

17. *The Owl*, September 11, 1830, 1.

18. *Hawk and Buzzard*, September 21, 1833, 1.

19. One newspaper commentator in 1847 actually imagines a factory that produces novels. In his fantasy, individual novels are composed by a collection of authors who each have their own specialties—landscape description, characterization, etc. "Books, and the Reading Public," *Littell's Living Age*, April 3, 1847, 5.

20. Indeed, the novelettes and sporting press are part of a battle in the ongoing war of position over what counts as privacy and publicness. Here I have been focusing on historicizing publicness, but a differently oriented project might valuably outline the role nineteenth century obscenity played in establishing and resisting normative definitions of privacy. For the start of such a project, focused on nineteenth-century obscenity, see Burgett, *Sentimental Bodies*, 137–54.

21. Some of these texts are not extant (the titles are gathered from publishers' advertisements), but they are connected to a network of obscene publishers that was often in trouble with the law. In the mainstream dailies' accounts of obscenity arrests, Charles Paul de Kock appears more often than any other writer (although, as mentioned previously, the name was most likely a punning pseudonym used by an American pulp writer, or collection of writers, with no connection to the real French author). George Akarman, a chief publisher of Kock, was one of the central targets

of the 1857 vice raids discussed previously (see, for instance, "The Case," *Tribune*, September 22, 1857, 5). Akarman sometimes went by the name James Ramerio, who is listed as the publisher of books like *The Amours of a Quaker* and *Harriette Wilson* (the latter was evidence in an 1846 obscenity arrest, along with the books of Kock (see "Selling Obscene Books," *National Police Gazette*, December 12, 1846). The book *The Curtain Drawn Up* led to the conviction of William Haine in 1846 for selling obscenity (*National Police Gazette*, July 25, 1846, 12). Frederic Brady, another obscene entrepreneur arrested in 1857, was the publisher of the prolific George Thompson, who is discussed in greater detail later in this chapter. This publishing network calls out for closer analysis as a "communication circuit" ("What" 12) to use Robert Darnton's term, but that is beyond my focus here. Such a network has been best developed by Dennis.

22. In what follows I derive an account of reader experience in a number of ways—by examining modes of address, scenes of reading within texts, details about circulation and material form, and explicit statements about readers and "the public" within texts, to name a few strategies. However, I do not have reader reports or other sociological data. Such evidence simply doesn't exist for the nineteenth-century obscene, as far as I can tell. Although I would very much like to have such data, it still would not express the full story of readers' experience. After all, reader reports cannot be taken to transparently represent the experience of reading. I should quickly add that I am not simply trying to delineate the experience of what is sometimes called the "implied reader" or the "hypothetical reader." Actual readers can read in all sorts of different ways, of course, but their reading is shaped by modes of address, material form, etc. Mass-produced genres tend to repeat these forms when they are successful in creating a reading public. In this sense, it might be said that, at least to some degree, reception is built into a mass-cultural genre's form.

23. See, for example, *Ely's New York and Brooklyn Hawk and Buzzard*, March 15, 1834, 1; and Ely's *Hawk & Buzzard, or, Saturday Courier and Enquirer*, September 6, 1834, 4.

24. On the papers' circulation, see, for example, *Ely's Hawk & Buzzard*, September 6, 1834, 2; and *The Owl*, July 10, 1830, 2.

25. *The Flash*, October 31, 1841, 2.

26. See, for example, *Ely's Hawk and Buzzard*, vol. 3, no. 31, 1833, 1; *Whip and Satirist of New-York and Brooklyn*, April 2, 1842, 2; and *Sunday Flash*, October 17, 1841, 2.

27. *The New York Arena*, May 24, 1842, 2.

28. Laqueur's argument is not just about early print pornography but also about print culture more generally in the eighteenth century, when its power of absorption was often perceived as a threat. This argument is fairly well known by scholars with respect to the development of the novel in the eighteenth century. Laqueur's central contributions to the discussion are to show that the fear of novel reading was a more general fear of the power of mass print culture, and also to link eighteenth-century discussions of bad reading with discussion of bad sexual practices, namely

masturbation. It is also worth mentioning that although Laqueur focuses on Europe, the same kinds of arguments about absorption, obscene reading, print culture, and masturbation were made in the nineteenth-century United States. For instance, one American anti-onanist tract warns against reading in bed for there too easily the "mind becomes fascinated with the morbid gratification of exciting and libidinous reading and imaginings" (Bell 51). The *Boston Surgical and Medical Journal* in 1844 even went so far as to suggest obscene reading led to a pathology more serious than masturbation—gonorrhea, a disorder that was the result of "irritable state of the nervous system" that was "contracted by reading of books of an obscene character" (Aldrich 482).

29. For background on Thompson, see Reynolds, *Beneath the American Renaissance*, and Reynolds and Gladman, "Introduction." Also, Looby rightly cautions against seeing Thompson as subversive, and Stewart, in a tour-de-force essay, insists that we recognize the "bodiliness of reading" (251) in texts like Thompson's. I certainly agree with Stewart, but, as will become clear, think that this is only half the story. Reading texts like Thompson's involved a double movement between "bodiliness" and self-abstraction, as I explain.

30. On associations with the "black republicans," see "The Police Descent Upon the Obscene Literature," *Herald*, September 17, 1857, 4. On other connections, see "The Moral Conditions of the Country," *Herald*, September 18, 1857, 4. For the interesting association between Charles Paul de Kock and the Know-Nothing party, see "The Seizure of Obscene Books and Prints," *Herald*, September 23, 1857, 5.

31. On Frances Wright and her connection to Greeley and the antebellum labor movement (one group proclaiming itself "Fanny Wright mechanics," and the "Workingmen's Party" was nicknamed the "Fanny Wright Party"), see, among others, Sean Wilentz, 176–83 and 209–12, and Charles Sotheran, 96.

32. Both quotations are from *Venus' Miscellany*, May 16, 1857, 3.

33. *Venus' Miscellany*, June 6, 1857, 3.

34. In *Paper Money Men*, David Anthony, with great precision and obsessive research, has written revealingly about a similar double movement in much antebellum sensation (26–40 *passim*), although he does not use precisely this terminology. Anthony concentrates on how a double movement allows sensation readers both to experience the anxiety involved in new forms of finance capital (which characterized antebellum urban life) and to compensate for that anxiety with a utopian wish (which characterized much sensation fiction). This seems exactly right to me. Here, I am interested in a somewhat different issue, however: the way the double movement of abstraction and embodiment was essential to the dynamics of the public sphere.

35. Warner's work is most useful in seeing how counterpublics, by demanding that affect and embodiment be taken seriously, often challenge the very foundations of a dominant public sphere where disembodiment is the aspirational norm (especially in a public sphere governed by liberalism). But Warner is less useful in thinking about how affect and embodiment might be critically reflective. One might well want to escape from a public sphere founded on rational-critical debate to a public

sphere that values affect and embodiment, but it is doubtful that one would want to give up critical reflection, which is the power of the public sphere itself. This is, roughly, Amanda Anderson's critique of affect theory quoted above. But, Warner does ask the right question: "what if it isn't true, as we suppose, that critical reading is the only way to suture textual practice with reflection, reason, and a normative discipline of subjectivity" ("Uncritical" 16)? He just hasn't developed ways for thinking about how embodied, affective reading (rather than proper "critical reading") might make possible such suturing. That is one of the projects here.

4. Scandalous Reading

1. There are some exceptions to Kipnis's characterization of the field that bear mentioning—like the excellent work by the sociologists John B. Thompson and Ari Adut—but thus far the scholarly studies of scandal have been somewhat limited. What does exist has focused profitably on the structural patterns repeated in most scandals, on the social issues that are often animated in scandal, and to some degree on the historical and social conditions that make scandal so central to modern life.

2. The piece first appeared in *The Federal Gazette, and Philadelphia Evening Post*, June 4, 1789, 2. The final reprint of "On Scandal" that I've found is from 1824. It was the most popularly republished piece on scandal in the early national period. On the question of scandal and the Sedition Act, see Jeffrey L. Pasley, *"The Tyranny of Printers."*

3. "The Iniquity and Cure of Scandal and Detraction," *The Royal American Magazine* [Boston], August 1774, vol. 1, no. 8, 283. It is also worth noting that all the early examples (extending back to Shakespeare) of the use of the word "scandal" in the *Oxford English Dictionary* indicate that the word referenced an "injury to reputation" or a "disgraceful imputation."

4. "The Reformer, No. I: On Scandal and the Wickedness of Newspapers," *Massachusetts Magazine; or, Monthly Museum of Knowledge and Rational Entertainment*, February 1789, vol. 1, no. 2, 79. Brown was "The Reformer."

5. Ibid.

6. Fidelio, "On Scandal," *The New York Magazine, or Literary Repository*, September 1790, vol. 1, no. 9, 517.

7. "The News-paper Scandal," *The Federal Gazette, and Philadelphia Evening Post*, June 4, 1789, 2.

8. For one example of many instances see "A New Mode of Scandal," *The Literary Magazine, and American Register* [Philadelphia], January 1805, vol. 3, no. 16, 57.

9. This is not to say that there did not exist instances of highly mediated scandal before the 1830s: the panic over the Bavarian Illuminati and the politically motivated revelations about the relations between Thomas Jefferson and Sally Hemmings, as well as Alexander Hamilton and Maria Reynolds, were all facilitated and even generated by the press. But such scandals did not become a normal part of the public sphere until the 1830s.

10. The phrase "the system of starring" began to appear in 1827 (see "American Drama," *American Quarterly Review* [Philadelphia], June 1, 1827, vol. 1, no. 2, 331. In 1853 the system was compared to "humbuggery" (see "A Drop from the Drama," *Daily Picayune* [New Orleans], January 16, 1853, 1).

11. Seltzer finds the pathological public sphere to be a fact of life in mass-mediated modernity. One of its "pathological" aspects is its encouragement of what Seltzer calls "wound culture"—that is, a society where the sense of sociality and publicness, on the one hand, and physical and psychic trauma, on the other, feed on one another. This double movement explains the attraction not just to crime scenes in popular culture but also to identity politics (with its interplay of trauma and sociality) and an array of other contemporary phenomena.

12. "Introduction," *United States Magazine and Democratic Review*, October 1837, vol. 1; quoted in Wood, "Conspiracy," at 439.

5. Prayerful Reading

1. Important histories of the Great Awakening and the Second Great Awakening have investigated the centrality of print media to these movements, but the public sphere has not served as an important analytic frame. See Frank Labert, *Inventing the "Great Awakening"*; David Paul Nord, *Faith in Reading*; and Candy Gunther Brown, *The Word in the World*.

2. This account is provided by Perry Miller (155) with respect to a sermon by Jonathan Edwards, but Miller does not provide a citation.

3. The colporteur reports I've used are typescripts transcribed from original reports in 1940 by The New Jersey Historical Records Survey Project, a Division of Professional and Service Projects, Works Projects Administration. They are catalogued under the title *Transcriptions of Early Church Records of New Jersey: Colporteur Reports to the American Tract Society, 1841–1846*. The transcripts were made in Newark, New Jersey. For comments on the Pine Barrens inhabitants as "ignorant," see p. 4 and elsewhere. All the reports from colporteurs are found in this document, and I have cited pages parenthetically later in this chapter. A comprehensive account of the ATS and the colporteur reports is provided by David Paul Nord, *Faith in Reading*.

4. Critique also "has to be conceived as an attitude, an ethos, a philosophical life in which the critique of what we are is at one and the same time the historical analysis of the limits that are imposed on us and an experiment with the possibility of going beyond them" (50). I am thankful to Michael Warner, in his essay "Uncritical Reading," for pointing out the connections between Mahmood's work and reading practices.

Epilogue

1. Rumsfeld's quotation is included in Mark Mazzetti and Borzou Daragahi, "U.S. Covertly Pays to Run Stories in Iraq Press," *Los Angeles Times*, November 30, 2005.

2. Motoko Rich, "Literacy Debate: Online R U Really Reading," *New York Times*, July 27, 2008; available online at www.nytimes.com/2008/07/27/books/27reading.html.

Works Cited

To avoid many lengthy and disruptive internal citations of newspapers, magazines, and ephemera, I have provided full citation of such material in the notes. That bibliographical information is not repeated in this list.

Adut, Ari. *On Scandal: Moral Disturbances in Society, Politics, and Art.* Cambridge: Cambridge University Press, 2008.

Aldrich, Levi. "Gonorrhea Dormientium." *The Boston Medical and Surgical Journal* 29.24 (1844): 480–87.

Anderson, Amanda. *The Way We Argue Now: A Study in the Cultures of Theory.* Princeton, NJ: Princeton University Press, 2006.

Anderson, Benedict. *Imagined Communities: Reflections on the Origin and Spread of Nationalism.* New York: Verso, 1983.

Anonymous. *The Amorous Intrigues and Adventures of Aaron Burr.* New York: Published by the Proprietors, ca. 1861.

——. *Amours of a Modest Man.* New York: Cupid's Own Library, ca. 1864.

——. *The Amours of a Quaker.* New York: James Ramerio, c. 1870 [reprint from ca. 1856].

——. *The Curtain Drawn Up; or the Education of Laura.* New York: Grand Fancy Bijou Catalogue of the Sporting Man's Emporium for 1870, ca. 1870 [appears be a reprint from the early 1840s].

——. *The Eventful Lives of Helen and Charlotte Lenoxa: The Twin Sisters of Philadelphia . . .* Memphis: A. R. Orton, 1853.

——. *Harriette Wilson; or Memoirs of a Woman of Pleasure.* New York: Published and for sale by the bookseller, ca. 1845 [apparently reprinted in 1851 and by James Ramerio, ca. 1870].

——. *Red Staff, or the Mysterious Lover.* New York: Cupid's Own Library, ca. 1864.

Anthony, David. *Paper Money Men: Commerce, Manhood, and the Sensational Public Sphere in Antebellum America.* Columbus: The Ohio State University Press, 2009.

Aristotle. "from Rhetoric." *What Is an Emotion?* Ed. Robert C. Solomon. Trans. Jon. D. Solomon. Oxford: University Press, 2003.

Arnold, Matthew. *Culture and Anarchy.* Ed. Samuel Lipton. New Haven: Yale University Press, 1994.

Ashbee, Henry Spencer [Pisanus Fraxi]. *Catena Librorum Tacendorum: Being Notes Bio-biblio-icono-graphical and Critical, on Curious and Uncommon Books.* London: Private Printing, 1885. Reprint, London: Charles Skilton, 1960.

Augst, Thomas. *The Clerk's Tale: Young Men and Moral Life in Nineteenth-Century America*. Chicago: University of Chicago Press, 2003.

Austin, J. L. *How to Do Things with Words*. Second edition. Cambridge, MA: Harvard University Press, 1975.

Barnett, Douglas, and Hilary Horn Ratner. "Introduction: The Organization and Integration of Cognition and Emotion in Development." *Journal of Experimental Child Psychology* 67 (1997): 303–16.

Baym, Nina. *Novels, Readers, and Reviewers: Responses to Fiction in Antebellum America*. Ithaca: Cornell University Press, 1984.

Beck, Ulrich. *Risk Society: Towards a New Modernity*. Trans. Mark Ritter. London: Sage, 1992.

Bell, Luther Vose. *An Hour's Conference with Fathers and Sons, in Relation to a Common and Fatal Indulgence of Youth*. Boston: Whipple and Damrell, 1840.

Benjamin, Walter. *The Arcades Project*. Cambridge, MA: Belknap Press of Harvard University Press, 1999.

Bennett, Paula Bernat. *Poets in the Public Sphere: The Emancipatory Project of American Women's Poetry, 1800–1900*. Princeton, NJ: Princeton University Press, 2003.

Bennett, Tony, and Janet Woollacott. "Bond and Beyond." In Martin Barker and Anne Beezer, eds., *Reading into Cultural Studies*, 49–64. London: Routledge, 1992.

Berlant, Lauren. *The Female Complaint: The Unfinished Business of Sentimentality in American Culture*. Durham, NC: Duke University Press, 2008.

Brickhouse, Anna. *Transamerican Literary Relations and the Nineteenth-Century Public Sphere*. New York: Cambridge University Press, 2004.

Brokmeyer, Henry Conrad. *A Mechanic's Diary*. Washington, D.C.: E. C. Brokmeyer, 1910.

Brown, Candy Gunther. *The Word in the World: Evangelical Writing, Publishing and Reading in America, 1789–1880*. Chapel Hill: University of North Carolina Press, 2004.

Brown, Charles Brockden. "Letter to Thomas Jefferson." December 25, 1798. Available online at the Library of Congress Memory Project, Thomas Jefferson papers, http://memory.loc.gov/ammem/index.html.

Brown, Matthew P. *The Pilgrim and the Bee: Reading Rituals and Book Culture in Early New England*. Philadelphia: University of Pennsylvania Press, 2007.

Brown, William Hill. *The Power of Sympathy*. (With Hannah Foster's *The Coquette*.) New York: Penguin, 1996.

Burgett, Bruce. *Sentimental Bodies: Sex, Gender, and Citizenship in the Early Republic*. Princeton, NJ: Princeton University Press, 1998.

Calhoun, Cheshire, and Robert C. Solomon, eds. *What Is An Emotion? Classic Readings in Philosophical Psychology*. Oxford: Oxford University Press, 1984.

Carr, Nicholas. "Is Google Making Us Stupid?" *The Atlantic*. July/August 2008. 56–63.

Castiglia, Christopher. *Interior States: Institutional Consciousness and the Inner Life of Democracy in the Antebellum United States*. Durham, NC: Duke University Press, 2008.

Castronovo, Russ. *Necro Citizenship: Death, Eroticism, and the Public Sphere in the Nineteenth-Century United States*. Durham, NC: Duke University Press, 2001.

Chartier, Roger. *The Order of Books: Readers, Authors, and Libraries in Europe between the Fourteenth and Eighteenth Centuries*. Stanford, CA: Stanford University Press, 1994.

Clarke, Eric O. *Virtuous Vice: Homoeroticism and the Public Sphere*. Durham, NC: Duke University Press, 2000.

Cohen, Patricia Cline, Timothy J. Gilfoyle, and Helen Lefkowitz Horowitz. *The Flash Press: Sporting Male Weeklies in 1840s New York*. Chicago: University of Chicago Press, 2008.

Crawford, Michael. "The Spiritual Travels of Nathan Cole." *William and Mary Quarterly* 33 (1976): 89-126.

Connor, Steven. "CP: Or, a Few Don't by a Cultural Phenomenologist." *parallax* 5.2 (1999): 17–31.

Cressy, David. "Books as Totems in Seventeenth-Century England and New England." *The Journal of Library History* 21.1 (Winter 1986): 92–106.

Cugoano, Ottobah. *Thoughts and Sentiments on the Evil and Wicked Traffic of the Slavery and Commerce of the Human Species*. London, 1787.

Cutter, Calvin. *The Female Guide: Containing Facts and Information upon the Effects of Masturbation*. West Brookfield, MA: Charles A. Mirick, 1844.

Damasio, Antonio R. *Descartes' Error: Emotion, Reason and the Human Brain*. New York: G. P. Putnam, 1994.

Darnton, Robert. "An Early Information Society: News and Media in Eighteenth-Century Paris." In *George Washington's False Teeth: An Unconventional Guide to the Eighteenth Century*, 25–75. New York: W. W. Norton, 2003.

——. "Toward a History of Reading." *The Wilson Quarterly* 13.4 (1989): 86-102.

——. "What is the History of Books?" In David Finkelstein and Alistair McCleery, eds., *The Book History Reader*, 9–26. London: Routledge, 2002.

Davidson, Cathy N. *Revolution and the Word: The Rise of the Novel in America*. New York: Oxford University Press, 1986 [expanded edition 2004].

Deleuze, Gilles, and Felix Guattari. *What Is Philosophy?* Trans. Hugh Tomlinson and Graham Burchell. New York: Columbia University Press, 1994.

Denning, Michael. *Dime Novels and Working-Class Culture in America*. London: Verso, 1987.

Dennis, Donna. *Licentious Gotham: Erotic Publishing and Its Prosecution in Nineteenth-Century New York*. Cambridge, MA: Harvard University Press, 2009.

Derrida, Jacques. *Archive Fever: A Freudian Impression*. Chicago: University of Chicago Press, 1997.

Dillon, Elizabeth Maddock. *The Gender of Freedom: Fictions of Liberalism and the Literary Public Sphere*. Stanford, CA: Stanford University Press, 2004.

Douglass, Frederick. *Narrative of the Life of Frederick Douglass, An American Slave* [1945]. Ed. Houston A. Baker, Jr. New York: Penguin, 1986.

Eaton, Clement. "A Dangerous Pamphlet in the Old South." *Journal of Southern History* 2 (1936): 323–34.

Edwards, Jonathan. *A Jonathan Edwards Reader*. New Haven: Yale University Press, 1995.

——. *Edwards on Revivals*. New York: Dunning and Spalding, 1832.

Ekman, Paul. "Expression and the Nature of Emotion." In Klaus R. Scherer and Paul Ekman, eds., *Approaches to Emotion*, 319–44. Hillsdale, NJ: Erlbaum, 1984.

Elfenbein, Andrew. "Cognitive Science and the History of Reading." *PMLA: Publications of the Modern Language Association of America* 121.2 (March 2006): 484–502.

Eliot, T. S. *Selected Prose of T. S. Eliot*. Ed. Frank Kermode. London: Faber, 1965.

Ellison, Julie K. *Cato's Tears and the Making of Anglo-American Emotion*. Chicago: University of Chicago Press, 1999.

Elmer, Jonathan. *Reading at the Social Limit: Affect, Mass Culture, and Edgar Allan Poe*. Stanford, CA: Stanford University Press, 1995.

Equiano, Olaudah. *The Interesting Narrative and Other Writings* [1794]. Ed. Vincent Carretta. New York: Penguin Classics, 1995.

Fanuzzi, Robert. *Abolition's Public Sphere*. Minneapolis: University of Minnesota Press, 2003.

Felski, Rita. *Uses of Literature*. Malden, MA: Blackwell, 2008.

Fish, Stanley. "Interpreting the 'Variorum.'" *Critical Inquiry* 2.3 (Spring 1976): 465–85.

Foucault, Michel. *The History of Sexuality, Volume One*. Trans. Robert Hurley. New York: Pantheon Books, 1978.

——. "What is Enlightenment?" In Paul Rabinow, ed., *The Foucault Reader*, 32–50. New York: Pantheon Books, 1984.

Foster, George. *New York by Gas-Light and Other Urban Sketches* [1849–1854]. Ed. Stuart M. Blumin. Berkley: University of California Press, 1990.

Franklin, Benjamin. *Benjamin Franklin's Autobiography*. New York: W. W. Norton, 1986.

Fraser, Nancy. "Rethinking the Public Sphere: A Contribution to the Critique of Actually Existing Democracy." In Craig Calhoun, ed., *Habermas and the Public Sphere*, 109–42. Cambridge, MA: MIT Press, 1992.

Freeman, Joanne B. "Slander, Poison, Whispers, and Fame: Jefferson's 'Anas' and Political Gossip in the Early Republic." *Journal of the Early Republic* 15 (1995): 25–57.

Fried, Michael. *Theatricality and Absorption: Painting and Beholding in the Age of Diderot*. Chicago: University of Chicago Press, 1980.

Freud, Sigmund. "Mourning and Melancholia." *The Standard Edition of the Complete Psychological Works of Sigmund Freud, vol. 14 (1914–1916): On the*

History of the Psycho-Analytic Movement, Papers on Metapsychology and Other Works, 237–258. Trans. and ed. James Strachey. London: Hogarth Press, 1957–74.

Gates, Henry Louis. *The Signifying Monkey: A Theory of Afro-American Literary Criticism*. New York: Oxford University Press, 1988.

Geertz, Clifford. *The Interpretation of Cultures*. New York: Basic Books, 1973.

Giddens, Anthony. *The Consequences of Modernity*. Stanford, CA: Stanford University Press, 1990.

Gilmore, William J. *Reading Becomes a Necessity of Life: Material and Cultural Life in Rural New England, 1780–1835*. Knoxville: University of Tennessee Press, 1989.

Goulemot, Jean Marie. *Forbidden Texts: Erotic Literature and Its Readers in Eighteenth-Century France*. Trans. James Simpson. Cambridge: Polity Press, 1994.

Greiman, Jennifer. *Democracy's Spectacle: Sovereignty and Public Life in Antebellum American Writing*. New York: Fordham University Press, 2010.

Gronniosaw, James Albert Ukawsaw. *A Narrative of the Most Remarkable Particulars in the Life of James Albert Ukawsaw Gronniosaw, an African Prince, as Related by Himself*. Bath, England: Printed by W. Gye, 1770.

Habermas, Jürgen. *An Awareness of What Is Missing: Faith and Reason in a Post-Secular Age*. Trans. Ciaran Cronin. Malden, MA: Polity Press, 2010.

——. "Further Reflections on the Public Sphere." In Craig Calhoun, ed., *Habermas and the Public Sphere*, 421–61. Cambridge, MA: MIT Press, 1992.

——. *Justification and Application: Remarks on Discourse Ethics*. Cambridge, MA: MIT Press, 1993.

——. *The Structural Transformation of the Public Sphere: An Inquiry into a Category of Bourgeois Society*. Trans. Thomas Burger. Cambridge, MA: MIT Press, 1989 [German original, 1963].

Hall, David D. *Worlds of Wonder, Days of Judgment: Popular Religious Belief in Early New England*. Cambridge, MA: Harvard University Press, 1990.

——, and Elizabeth Carroll Reilly. "Eighteenth-Century Modalities of Reading." In Hugh Amory and David D. Hall, eds., *A History of the Book in America. Volume I: The Colonial Book in the Atlantic World*, 387–98. Chapel Hill: University of North Carolina Press, 2007.

Halttunen, Karen. *Confidence Men and Painted Women: A Study of Middle-Class Culture in America, 1830–1870*. New Haven: Yale University Press, 1982.

Hawthorne, Nathaniel. "My Kinsman, Major Molineux." In Roy Harvey Pearce, ed., *Tales and Sketches*, 68–87. New York: Library of America, 1996.

——. *The Scarlet Letter: An Authoritative Text, Essays in Criticism and Scholarship, Third Edition* [1851]. Ed. Seymour Gross, et al. New York: Norton Critical Edition, 1988.

Hendler, Glenn. *Public Sentiments: Structures of Feeling in Nineteenth-Century American Literature*. Chapel Hill: University of North Carolina Press, 2001.

Henkin, David M. *City Reading: Written Words and Public Space in Antebellum New York*. New York: Columbia University Press, 1998.

Hepburn, Allan. *Intrigue: Espionage and Culture*. New Haven: Yale University Press, 2005.

Hinks, Peter. *To Awaken My Afflicted Brethren: David Walker and the Problem of Antebellum Slave Resistance*. College Park: Pennsylvania State University Press, 1997.

Hoggart, Richard. *The Uses of Literacy: Aspects of Working-Class Life with Special References to Publications and Entertainments*. London: Chatto and Windus, 1957.

Horowitz, Helen Lefkowitz. *Rereading Sex: Battles over Sexual Knowledge and Suppression in Nineteenth-Century America*. New York: Alfred A. Knopf, 2002.

Howe, Daniel Walker. *What Hath God Wrought: The Transformation of America, 1815–1848*. New York: Oxford University Press, 2007.

Hutchins, Edwin. *Cognition in the Wild*. Cambridge, MA: MIT Press, 1995.

Isen, Alice M., and Gregory Andrade Diamond. "Affect and Automaticity." In J. S. Uleman and John A. Bargh, eds., *Unintended Thought: Limits of Awareness, Intention and Control*, 124–54. New York: Guilford Press. 1989.

Iser, Wolfgang. "The Reading Process: A Phenomenological Approach." *New Literary History* 3.2 (Winter 1972): 279–99.

James, William. "What Is an Emotion?" In Robert Richardson, ed., *The Heart of William James*, 1–19. Cambridge, MA: Belknap Press of Harvard University Press, 2010.

Jea, John. *The Life, History, and Unparalleled Suffering of John Jea, The African Preacher*. Portsea: Williams, printer, [ca. 1811?].

Jehlen, Myra, and Michael Warner, eds. *The English Literatures of America, 1500–1800*. New York: Routledge, 1997.

Jacobs, Harriet A. *Incidents in the Life of a Slave Girl, Written by Herself* [1861]. Ed. Jean Fagan Yellin. Cambridge, MA: Harvard University Press, 1987.

Jefferson, Thomas. Letter to Charles Brockden Brown, January 15, 1800. Available online at the Library of Congress Memory Project, Thomas Jefferson papers, http://memory.loc.gov/ammem/index.html.

——. Letter to Nathaniel Burwell, March 14, 1818. Available online at the Library of Congress Memory Project, Thomas Jefferson papers, http://memory.loc.gov/ammem/index.html.

——. *Thomas Jefferson: Writings*. Ed. Merrill D. Paterson. New York: Library of America, 1984.

Jones, J. [supposed author]. *Awful Exposure of the Atrocious Plot Formed by Certain Individuals Against the Clergy and Nuns of Lower Canada, Through the Intervention of Maria Monk*. New York: Printed for Jones and Co. of Montreal, 1936.

Kahneman, Daniel, and Amos Tversky. *Choices, Values, Frames*. Cambridge: Cambridge University Press, 2000.

Kant, Immanuel. *Critique of the Power of Judgment*. Ed. Paul Guyer. Trans. Paul
  Guyer and Eric Matthews. Cambridge: Cambridge University Press, 2000.
——. *Political Writings*. Cambridge: Cambridge University Press, 1991.
Kipnis, Laura. *How to Become a Scandal: Adventures in Bad Behavior*. New York:
  Henry Holt, 2010.
——. "School for Scandal: The Larger Meaning of a Sordid Little Tale," *Harper's
  Magazine* (March 2009): 73–77.
Kock, Charles Paul de. *Amours of a Musical Student*. New York: Charles S.
  Attwood, ca. 1850.
——. *The Seducer's Fate: or, The Adventures of Zizina*. Philadelphia: W. Meyers,
  n.d.
——. *Six Mistresses of Pleasure*. New York: Holland and Glover's Depot for Cheap
  Publication, 1844.
Lambert, Frank. *Inventing the "Great Awakening."* Princeton: Princeton University
  Press, 1999.
Laqueur, Thomas W. *Solitary Sex: A Cultural History of Masturbation*. New York:
  Zone Books, 2003.
Latour, Bruno. "From Realpolitik to Dingpolitik, or How to Make Things Public."
  In Bruno Latour and Peter Weibel, eds., *Making Things Public: Atmospheres of
  Democracy*, 14–41. Cambridge, MA: The MIT Press, 2005.
Lawson, Deodat. *A Brief and True Narrative*. Reprinted in *Narratives of the New
  England Witchcraft Cases, 1648–1706*, Ed. George Lincoln Burr. Toronto:
  Courier Dover Publications, 2002.
LeDoux, Joseph E. *The Emotional Brain: The Mysterious Underpinnings of
  Emotional Life*. New York: Simon & Schuster, 1996.
Lippard, George. *The Quaker City; or, The Monks of Monk Hall* [1845]. Ed. David
  S. Reynolds. Amherst: University of Massachusetts Press, 1995.
Littau, Karin. *Theories of Reading: Books, Bodies, and Bibliomania*. Malden, MA:
  Polity, 2006.
Looby, Christopher. "George Thompson's 'Romance of the Real': Transgression
  and Taboo in American Sensation Fiction." *American Literature* 65.4
  (December 1993): 651–72.
Luhmann, Niklas. *Trust and Power*. Trans. Howard Davis, John Raffan, and
  Kathryn Rooney. New York: John Wiley and Sons, 1979.
Machor, James L. *Reading Fiction in Antebellum America: Informed Responses and
  Reception Histories, 1820–1865*. Baltimore: Johns Hopkins University Press,
  2011.
Madison, James. *James Madison: Writings*. Ed. Jack N. Rakove. New York:
  Library of America, 1999.
Mah, Harold. "Phantasies of the Public Sphere: Rethinking the Habermas of
  Historians." *Journal of Modern History* 72 (March 2000): 153–82.
Mahmood, Saba. *The Politics of Piety: The Islamic Revival and the Feminist Subject*.
  Princeton: Princeton University Press, 2005.

Marcus, Steven. *The Other Victorians: A Study of Sexuality and Pornography in Mid-Nineteenth-Century England*. New York: Basic Books, 1966.

Marrant, John. *Narrative of the Lord's Wonderful Dealings with John Marrant, a Black*. London, 1785.

Massumi, Brian. *Parables for the Virtual: Movement, Affect, Sensation*. Durham, NC: Duke University Press, 2002.

McCorison, Marcus A. "Risqué Literature Published in America before 1877." Available online at The Bibliographical Society of America, www.bibsocamer .org/BibSite/McCorison/Risque.pdf (accessed December 17, 2006).

McGill, Meredith L. *American Literature and the Culture of Reprinting, 1834–1853*. Philadelphia: University of Pennsylvania Press, 2003.

McHenry, Elizabeth. *Forgotten Readers: Recovering the Lost History of African-American Literary Societies*. Durham, NC: Duke University Press, 2002.

Melville, Herman. *The Confidence-Man: His Masquerade* [second edition]. Eds. Hershel Parker and Mark Niemeyer. New York: Norton Critical Edition, 2006.

Miller, Perry. *Errand into the Wilderness*. Cambridge, MA: Harvard University Press, 1956; 1984.

Monk, Maria. *Awful Disclosures, by Maria Monk, of the Hotel Dieu Nunnery of Montreal, Revised with an Appendix*. New York: Published by Maria Monk, and sold by booksellers generally, 1836. [This is not the first edition.]

——, and J. J. Slocum. *Confirmation of Maria Monk's Disclosures Concerning the Hotel Dieu Nunnery of Montreal*, London: James S. Hodson, 1837.

——. *Interview of Maria Monk with her Opponents, the Authors of the Reply to Her "Awful Disclosures."* Published by Maria Monk, 1836.

Moran, George. "Walter Benjamin and Boredom." *Critical Quarterly* 45.1–2 (2003): 168–81.

Moretti, Franco. "Conjectures on World Literature." *New Left Review* 1 (2000): 54–68.

Nazarieff, Serge. *Early Erotic Photography*. Cologne: Benedikt Taschen, 1993.

Negt, Oskar, and Alexander Kluge. *Public Sphere and Experience: Toward an Analysis of the Bourgeois and Proletarian Public Sphere*. Trans. Peter Labanyi, Jamie Owen Daniel, and Assenka Oksiloff. Minneapolis: University of Minnesota Press, 1993.

The New-England Primer. Boston: Edward Draper [printer], 1777. Reprinted by WallBuilder Press, Aledo, TX, 1991.

Nietzsche, Friedrich. *On the Genealogy of Morals; and Ecce Homo*. Trans. and ed. Walter Kaufman. New York: Random House, 1969.

Ngai, Sianne. *Ugly Feelings*. Cambridge, MA: Harvard University Press, 2007.

Nord, David Paul. *Faith in Reading: Religious Publishing and the Birth of Mass Media in America*. New York: Oxford University Press, 2004.

Pasley, Jeffrey L. *"The Tyranny of Printers": Newspaper Politics in the Early American Republic*. Charlottesville: University Press of Virginia, 2001.

Poe, Edgar Allan. "The Fall of the House of Usher." In Patrick F. Quinn, ed., *Poetry and Tales*, 317–36. New York: Library of America, 1984.

———. "The Mystery of Marie Roget." In Patrick F. Quinn, ed., *Poetry and Tales*, 506–54. New York: Library of America, 1984.

Proceedings of the First Ten Years of the American Tract Society. New York: Flagg and Gould, 1824.

Radway, Janice A. *A Feeling for Books: The Book-of-the-Month Club, Literary Taste, and Middle-Class Desire*. Chapel Hill: University of North Carolina Press, 1997.

———. *Reading the Romance: Women, Patriarchy, and Popular Literature*. Chapel Hill: University of North Carolina Press, 1984.

Rawls, John. *Political Liberalism*. New York: Columbia University Press, 2005 [expanded edition].

Reddy, William M. *The Navigation of Feeling: A Framework for a History of Emotions*. Cambridge: Cambridge University Press, 2001.

Reder, Michael, and Josef Schmidt. "Habermas and Religion." In Jürgen Habermas, *An Awareness of What Is Missing*, 1–15. Malden, MA: Polity Press, 2010.

Reed, Rebecca Theresa. *Six Months in a Convent, or, The Narrative of Rebecca Theresa Reed . . .* Boston: Russell, Odiorne & Metcalf; New York: Leavitt, Lord and Co., 1835.

Reynolds, David S. *Beneath the American Renaissance: The Subversive Imagination in the Age of Emerson and Melville*. Cambridge, MA: Harvard University Press, 1988.

———, and Kimberly R. Gladman. "Introduction." In Reynolds and Gladman, eds., *Venus in Boston and other Tales of Nineteenth-Century City Life*, by George Thompson, ix–liv. Amherst: University of Massachusetts Press, 2002.

Richmond, Legh. *The Dairyman's Daughter, The Young Cottager; and The African Servant*. New York: American Tract Society, n.d.

Robinson, Jenefer. *Deeper Than Reason: Emotion and its Role in Literature, Music, and Art*. Oxford: Oxford University Press, 2005.

Rorty, Richard. *Philosophy and Social Hope*. New York: Penguin Books, 1999.

Rowlandson, Mary White. *A Narrative of the Captivity, Sufferings, and Removes of Mrs. Mary Rowlandson*. Boston: Massachusetts Sabbath School Society, 1856.

Rush, Benjamin. *Medical Inquiries and Observations upon the Diseases of the Mind*. Philadelphia: Kimber and Richardson, 1812.

Ryan, Mary P. *Civic Wars: Democracy and Public Life in the American City during the Nineteenth Century*. Berkeley: University of California Press, 1997.

Sanger, William W. *The History of Prostitution: Its Extent, Causes, and Effects throughout the World*. New York: Harper, 1858.

Scheid, Uwe. *1000 Nudes*. Cologne: Benedikt Taschen, 2002.

Schudson, Michael. "Was There Ever a Public Sphere? If So, When? Reflections on the American Case." In Craig Calhoun, ed., *Habermas and the Public Sphere*, 143–63. Cambridge, MA: MIT Press, 1992.

Sedgwick, Eve Kosofsky. *Between Men: English Literature and Male Homosocial Desire*. New York: Columbia University Press, 1985.

——. *Epistemology of the Closet*. Berkeley: University of California Press, 1990.

——. *Touching Feeling: Affect, Pedagogy, Performativity*. Durham, NC: Duke University Press, 2003.

Seltzer, Mark. *Serial Killers: Death and Life in America's Wound Culture*. New York: Routledge, 1998.

——. *True Crime: Observations on Violence and Modernity*. New York: Routledge, 2007.

Simmel, George. "The Metropolis and Modern Life" [1903]. In Donald N. Levine, ed., *George Simmel: On Individuality and Social Forms*, 324–39. Chicago: University of Chicago Press, 1971.

Shields, David S. *Civil Tongues & Polite Letters in British America*. Chapel Hill: University of North Carolina Press, 1997.

Slack, Jennifer Daryl. "The Theory and Method of Articulation in Cultural Studies." In David Morley and Kuan-Hsing Chen, eds., *Stuart Hall: Critical Dialogues in Cultural Studies*, 112–30. New York: Routledge, 1996.

Sontag, Susan. *Against Interpretation, and Other Essays*. New York: Anchor Books, 1990 [1966].

——. *Styles of Radical Will*. New York: Farrar, Straus and Giroux, 1969.

Sotheran, Charles. *Horace Greeley and Other Pioneers of American Socialism* [1892]. Westport, CT: Hyperion Press, 1975.

Spinoza, Benedictus. "On the Origin and Nature of Affects." In Edwin Curley, ed. and trans., *The Collected Works of Spinoza, Vol. I*, 491–543. Princeton: Princeton University Press, 1985.

Starr, Paul. *The Creation of the Media: Political Origins of Modern Communication*. New York: Basic Books, 2004.

Stewart, David M. "Consuming George Thompson." *American Literature* 80.2 (June 2008): 233–63.

Streeby, Shelley. *American Sensations: Class, Empire, and the Production of Popular Culture*. Berkeley: University of California Press, 2002.

Sztompka, Piotr. *Trust: A Sociological Theory*. Cambridge: Cambridge University Press, 1999.

Taylor, Charles. *A Secular Age*. Cambridge, MA: Harvard University Press, 2007.

Teste, Alph. *A Homeopathic Treatise on the Diseases of Children*. Trans. Emma H. Coté. Cincinnati: Moore, Wilstach, and Baldwin, 1854.

Thompson, George [Greenhorn]. *Anna Mowbray; or, Tales of the Harem New York*. New York: H.R.J. Barkley, 1856.

——. *The Countess, or Memoirs of Women of Leisure*. Boston: Berry & Wright, n.d.

——. *The Delights of Love, or the Lady Libertine*. New York: Farrell, n.d.

——. *Fanny Greeley; or Confessions of a Free-love Sister*. New York: HenryS. G. Smith, n.d.

——. *The Gay Girls of New York : or, Life on Broadway*. New York, 1853.

——. *The Ladies' Garter.* New York: Henry S. G. Smith & Co., 1851.

——. *Venus in Boston: A Romance of City Life.* New York: Printed for the Publisher, 1849.

Thompson, John B. "The New Visibility." *Theory, Culture, and Society* 22.6 (2005): 31–51.

——. *Political Scandal: Power and Visibility in the Media Age.* Malden, MA: Blackwell, 2000.

Tompkins, Jane P. "The Reader in History: The Changing Shape of Literary Response." In Jane Tomkins, ed., *Reader-Response Criticism*, 201–32. Baltimore: Johns Hopkins University Press, 1980.

Transcriptions of Early Church Records of New Jersey: Colporteur Reports to the American Tract Society, 1841–1846. Newark: The New Jersey Historical Records Survey Project, 1940.

Trilling, Lionel. *The Liberal Imagination: Essays on Literature and Society.* New York: Harcourt, Brace, and Jovanovich, 1950.

Turner, Nat. *The Confessions of Nat Turner* [1831]. Richmond, VA: Thomas R. Gray, 1832.

Walker, David. *Walker's Appeal, in Four Articles* [1829]. Boston, 1830.

Warner, Michael. *The Letters of the Republic.* Cambridge, MA: Harvard University Press, 1990.

——. *Publics and Counterpublics.* New York: Zone Books, 2002.

——. "Uncritical Reading." In Jane Gallup, ed., *Polemic: Critical or Uncritical*, 13–38. New York: Routledge, 2004.

Wertham, Fredric. *Seduction of the Innocent.* New York: Rinehart, 1954.

Wilentz, Sean. *Chants Democratic: New York City & the Rise of the American Working Class, 1788–1850.* New York: Oxford University Press, 1984.

Wood, Gordon S. "Conspiracy and the Paranoid Style: Causality and Deceit in the Eighteenth Century." *The William and Mary Quarterly* 39.3 (July 1982): 401–41.

——. *Empire of Liberty: A History of the Early Republic, 1789–1815.* New York: Oxford University Press, 2009.

Woodward, Samuel B. *Hints for the Young in Relation to the Health of Body and Mind.* Boston: G. W. Light, 1856.

Wortman, Tunis. *Treatise Concerning Political Enquiry and the Liberty of the Press.* New York: De Capo Press, 1970.

Wyss, Hilary E. *Writing Indians: Literacy, Christianity, and Native Community in Early America.* Amherst: University of Massachusetts Press, 2000.

Zboray, Ronald J., and Mary Saracino Zboray. *Everyday Ideas: Socioliterary Experience among Antebellum New Englanders.* Knoxville: University of Tennessee Press, 2006.

Index

politics: and democracy as truth-producing discussion, 113, 115; democratization of fame, 103–4; dissolution of honor/reputation-based, 99; eroticization of the political in obscene novelettes, 87–88; introduction of personal scandal to, 103; personal vs. party, 100; public sphere in, 53

pornography. *See* obscene reading

power: 18th-century public sphere, 40–42; scandal's role in challenging, 106, 116–17

The Power of Sympathy (Brown), xix, 3–6, 56, 58

prayerful reading: colonial-era ideology of, 31–33, 34–38; vs. depravity of novel reading, 50; evangelism and, 123–29; heart-piety reading, 32–34, 36–38, 54, 56; lack of modern alternative to, 135–39; public sphere conversions, 121–23; sacred internalization of text, 35–36; as spiritual direct-access experience, 31–33, 34–37; targeted marketing by publishers, 66–67; tract reading, 130–35

press, 98–99, 102–3, 141–42, 143. *See also* newspapers

print culture, 38, 66, 68, 165–66n28

private reading experience and emotives, 20–21. *See also* private vs. public spheres

private vs. public spheres: and loss of knowledge for public sphere, 4, 5, 6; and obscene reading, 71, 80, 81–84, 86–87; scandal's exposure of private to public, 98, 104, 106, 112. *See also* double movement in reading

public, transformation of concept, 8

publicity and celebrity scandal, 106–8

public opinion, 18th-century views of civic role, 41

public representation, scandal's exposure of, 104

public sensorium: vs. abstract public sphere, 7–13, 19; historical continuum of, xvi; importance of understanding, xix, 6; modern role in public sphere, 72–73, 93, 119; research issues, xvii; theoretical perspective, 7–13. *See also* obscene reading; prayerful reading; scandalous reading

public sphere: colonial-era social structures for, 31–42; 18th–19th-century transformation of, 7–8, 10, 25, 38–53, 66; emotive understandings, 19; epilogue/summary, 141–46; exclusion of groups from dominant, 10–11, 61–66, 154nn3, 5; introduction, 29–31; liberalism and hermeneutics of reading, 53–68; obscene reading and, 71–72, 85, 89–93; prayerful reading role of, 121–23, 126, 127–29, 131–39; rational-critical vs. affectual, xvi–xvii, 11–12; reading and, 5–6, 7–13; reading badly's effect on, xiii, xiv–xv; republican ideal, 41–42, 53, 68, 85–86, 100; sacred internalization of text, effect of, 35–36; scandal's role in, 95–97, 104, 105, 106–8, 110–19; sensationalism and pathology in, 108, 143, 168n11; social trust issue, 97, 106, 115–19; theoretical perspective, 7–13; truth-producing discussion role of, 109, 113, 115. *See also* affective-critical public sphere; conversation, reading as; private vs. public spheres; social anxiety over reading

public-sphere theory, xix, xx–xxi, 7–13, 40, 72–73, 118–19

publishing industry, early 19th-century transformation of, 66–67. *See also* mass-cultural book industry

sentimentalism, xvii, 12, 20, 72, 88

sexuality. *See* obscene reading

Shepard, Thomas, 32

Shields, David S., 38

Silliman, Alexander Perry, 126

Simmel, Georg, 91–92

Six Months in a Convent . . ., 110

slavery, social anxiety over reading by slaves, 63–64

Smith-Lovin, Lynn, 14

sociability vs. self-management as citizen duty, 114

social anxiety over reading: and addictiveness of affective reading, 46, 59–60; in Brown's *The Power of Sympathy*, 3–6; in early U.S., 29–31, 42–53; information overload issue, 49; male focus on women's reading, xiv, 35, 153–54n1; and the novel, xiv, 46, 49–53, 126; obscene reading, 75, 165–66n28; and slave insurrection threat, 63–64; synopsis, xiv–xv; women's reading, xiv, 35, 153–54n1

sociality of reading, early U.S., 43–47

social norms: basing on emotion, 144; novel as transgressor of, 50–51, 126; scandal as transgression of, 98, 103. *See also* social anxiety over reading

social trust issue, 97, 106, 115–19

Sontag, Susan, xxi, 88, 91, 121

spiritual autobiography, 36–37, 45

sporting (spy) newspapers, 75, 76–78, 77, 80–83, 103

Starr, Paul, 66

stranger relationality and mass-culture publications, 128–29, 133–34, 136–37

strategic framework for emotion, 15, 19–20

The Structural Transformation of the Public Sphere (Habermas), 7–9, 12

stuplimity, 21

symptomatic framework for emotion, 15

Talking Book, 61–62

Taylor, Charles, 129

theoretical perspectives: affective-critical public sphere, 72–73, 144, 162n3; affective reading, xiii–xiv, xix, xx–xxi; canonical aesthetics theory, 56; canonical reception theory, 54; cognitive role of emotions, 13–20; public-sphere theory, xix, xx–xxi, 7–13, 40, 72–73, 118–19; reading of reading, 20–24

The Theory of Communicative Action (Habermas), 136

Thompson, George, 83–85, 86, 92, 104, 106–7

Thompson, John B., 98, 102–3

Tissot, Samuel-Auguste, 46

Tompkins, Jane, 53–56, 161n37

tract reading, 130–39

translation, emotion as, 17

true-crime fiction genre, 109

trust, social, 97, 106, 115–19

truth and scandal reading, 109, 111–12, 113, 115

Turner, Nat, 63–64

verbalized emotions, 16–19

Vesey, Denmark, 63

Walker, David, 63

Warner, Michael, 11–13, 34, 36, 40, 50, 89–90, 128, 166–67n35

Weems, Mason Locke, 123

Western vs. non-Western modes of reading, 144, 146

Wieland (Brown), 50–51

Wilkes, George, 78

Winthrop, John, 35

women: books as conversation sources for, 44–45; men's anxiety over affective reading by, xiv, 35, 153–54n1

Wood, Gordon, 113

Wordsworth, William, 55

Wright, Fanny, 84